J. W Cooper

Games Fowls, Their Origin and History

With a description of the breeds, strains, and crosses. The American and English modes of feeding, training, and heeling; how to breed and cross, improving quality and preserving feather

J. W Cooper

Games Fowls, Their Origin and History
With a description of the breeds, strains, and crosses. The American and English modes of feeding, training, and heeling; how to breed and cross, improving quality and preserving feather

ISBN/EAN: 9783337256494

Printed in Europe, USA, Canada, Australia, Japan

Cover: Foto ©ninafisch / pixelio.de

More available books at **www.hansebooks.com**

GAME FOWLS,

THEIR ORIGIN AND HISTORY,

WITH A

DESCRIPTION OF THE BREEDS, STRAINS, AND CROSSES.

THE AMERICAN AND ENGLISH

MODES OF FEEDING, TRAINING, AND HEELING;

HOW TO BREED AND CROSS,

IMPROVING QUALITY AND PRESERVING FEATHER,

TOGETHER WITH A

DESCRIPTION AND TREATMENT

OF ALL

DISEASES INCIDENT TO GAME FOWLS.

BY J. W. COOPER, M. D.

STANDARD EDITION.

PUBLISHED AND SOLD BY THE AUTHOR—PRICE $5.00.
ADDRESS BY MAIL DR. J. W. COOPER, WEST CHESTER, PA.

HCT

Entered according to an Act of Congress in the year 1869,
BY J. W. COOPER, M. D.,
In the Clerk's Office of the United States, for the Eastern District of Pennsylvania.

PREFACE.

Ten years ago the writer of this work issued a small pocket edition for the use of Game Fanciers and Cockers. That work is now out of print, the limited number printed having been all disposed of in a year or two after the first issue. It was never the intention to re-issue it in that form, for though of some value, it was incomplete in nearly all respects—in not treating at proper length the important subjects of breeding and crossing, breeding in-and-in, breeding to a feather;—in describing but a limited number of breeds, strains and crosses;—in omitting, entirely, any theory upon the origin of Games, and any detailed facts connected with their history;—in omitting the foreign modes of breeding and feeding; and in giving less attention to a description and the mode of treating the many diseases incident to fowls. These wants are all at least measurably filled in this, the enlarged and standard edition. In the labor of writing and compiling the work we have been aided by some of the leading Fanciers and Cockers of the land, and wherever permitted we have credited their contributions, some, however, are anonymous, but all have manifested an interest for which we are thankful.

We believe that the work will answer all the needs of the lover of the sport derived from keeping or fighting games; and the amateur raiser and fancier. We have endeavored to make it answer every need of both classes of game admirers, and to meet all their present and future purposes. The question of our success or failure is now with them.

TABLE OF CONTENTS.

ILLUSTRATIONS, } Tartar Cock in Full Feather.
} Strychnine Cock Ready for Battle.

Origin and History of Game Fowls, ... Page 9
" " " " by WHEBLER, . . 15
" " " " from REES' ENCYCLOPÆDIA, . 21
Cocks and Cocking in England, ... 26
" " " Rules of the Royal Cock-Pit, . . 27
" " " English Ideas of Perfection, . 29
" " " English Modes of Breeding, . . 32
Cocks and Cocking in Ireland, ... 41
Peculiarities of Games, ... 46
" " Doctrine of Clucking Eggs, . . 48
" " Doctrine of Afternoon Eggs, . . 49
" " In Fighting, ... 52
" " Shufflers, ... 53
" " Wheelers, ... 53
" " In Stature and Shape, . . 54
Rules of the Pit.
" " Boston Union Club Rules, . 57
" " New York Rules, . . . 58
" " Southern, or "Old Red Lion" Rules, . 61
Directions for Keeping Cocks—The Author's Method, . 64
" " " EDINBURG ENCYCLOPÆDIA, . 71
Breeds and Strains.
" " Counterfeits, . . . 74
" " Sergeants, . . . 75
" " Virginia Grays, . . . 77
" " Clippers, . . . 79
" " Tartars, . . . 85
" " Thompson Whites, . . . 93
" " Claibornes or Mobile, . . . 95
" " Old Nicks, . . . 98
" " Prince Charles, . . . 100
" " Baltimore Top-Knots, . . . 102
" " Rattlers, . . . 104
" " Earl Derbys, . . . 106
" " Irish, . . . 110
" " Pittsburg Dominics, . . . 111
" " White Hackles, . . . 113
" " Warriors, . . . 114
" " Mexican Hen Cocks, . . . 115
" " Lord Seftons, . . . 117
" " English Games generally, . . . 119
" " Bob Mace English, . . . 122
" " Bob Mace Shufflers, . . . 123
" " Camerons, . . . 125
" " Billy Beards, . . . 127
" " Shields, . . . 129
" " Bailey, . . . 131
" " Eslin Stock, . . . 134
" " Jack McClellan Stock, . . . 138
" " Baker Piles, . . . 140

INDEX.

"	"	Delaware Dominics,	141
"	"	Red Strychnines,	142
"	"	Gee Dominics of Georgia,	143
"	"	Hen-Feather Cocks,	145
"	"	Black Reds (willow legs,)	147
"	"	Susquehanna Reds,	148
"	"	Black-Eyed Black Reds,	149
"	"	Black Brass Backs,	151
"	"	The Black Birds,	151
"	"	Ned Hall Stock,	152
"	"	Tilthammers,	152
"	"	Muffs,	153
"	"	Jersey Nub-Combs,	154
"	"	Irish Piles,	154
"	"	Irish Steel Grays,	155
"	"	Irish Reds,	155
"	"	Baker White Legs,	156
"	"	Irish Black-breasted Reds,	157
"	"	Bowman Stock,	158
"	"	Irish Blue Grays,	158
"	"	Cook Blue Reds,	159
"	"	Wild Irish,	160
"	"	Cook Grays,	160
"	"	Marksman,	161
"	"	Gad Muffs,	161
"	"	Cook Black Grays,	162
"	"	Cook Spangles,	162
"	"	Cook Whites,	163
"	"	Rigdon Black Reds,	163
"	"	Marshall Whites,	164

Dr. Stowey's Strains, . . . 164
The Barker Games, . . 167
The Peter Drum Games, . 169
The Kentucky Games, . . . 172
The LaRue Games, . . 173
      Shields' Silver Grays, 176
The John Bard Games, . . . 177
The Fred Bard Games, . . . 178
      Bowman White Legs, 180
      Kessinger Top-Knots, 181
The Welsh Stock, ... 182
The Goss Stock, . . . 186
The Conkey Stock, . 186
The Gwinn Stock, . 187
The Dr. Butler Stock, . 191
Crossing Game Fowls, . 192
Crossing for Pit Purposes, . . 193
Crossing to a Feather, . . 194
Approved Crosses,

"	"	Clipper and Tartar,	196
"	"	Clippers and Prince Charles,	197
"	"	Clippers and Baltimore Top-Knots,	198
"	"	Clippers and Strychnines,	198
"	"	Clippers and Rattlers,	199
"	"	Tartars and Derbys,	199
"	"	Duck-Wing Derby Grays and Strychnines,	200
"	"	Tartars and Prince Charles,	201
"	"	Rattlers and Tartars,	201

"	"	Tartar and White-Leg Derbys,	202
"	"	Derbys and Baltimore Top-Knots,	203
"	"	Tartar and American,	203
"	"	Conkey and Baker,	204
"	"	Brenimau Dark Reds,	204
"	"	Conkey and Bob Mace,	204
"	"	Conkey and McClellau,	205
"	"	Conkey and Eslin,	205
"	"	Tartar and Conkey,	205
"	"	Blood Reds,	206
"	"	Green-Leg Blue Reds,	206
"	"	Brown Red Red-Eyes,	207
"	"	Black Breasted Reds (yellow legs),	207
"	"	Blue-Legged Blue Reds,	208
"	"	Rattling Top-Knots,	209
"	"	Welsh and Eslin Grays,	209
"	"	Brown Reds,	210
"	"	Dusty Miller Grays,	210
"	"	Black Grays,	210
"	"	Green Leg Piles,	211
"	"	Yellow Leg Piles,	211
"	"	Blue Leg Piles,	211
"	"	Red McClellan's,	212

Remarks on Breeding and Crossing, . . . 213
Breeding In-and-In, . . . 221
The Pleasure in Raising Games, . . . 227
Dubbing Game Fowls, . . . 233
Rules for Gafting, . . . 235
Breeding Cocks, . . . 237
Breeding Hens, . . . 238
Hatching, . . . 239
Feed for Chicks, . . . 240
Feathering Chicks, . . . 240
Selecting Eggs for Setting, . . . 241
How to Preserve Eggs, . . . 242
Poultry Houses, . . . 243
Feeding in general, . . . 252
Laying, . . . 253
Breeding for Breeders, . . . 255
Packing Eggs, . . . 255
Worthless Games, . . . 256
Chicken Talk, . . . 261
Diseases,—Roup, . . . 267
" Cholera, . . . 268
" Pip or Gapes, . . . 269
" Rheumatism or Lifts, . . . 271
" Gout . . . 271
" Club Foot, . . . 271
" Inflammation of the Eye, . . . 272
" Indigestion, . . . 273
" Costiveness, . . . 273
" Diarrhœa or Scouring, . . . 273
" Obstructions of the Nostril, . . . 274
" Asthma, . . . 274
" Melancholy or Moping, . . . 274
" Fever, . . . 275
" Consumption, . . . 275
" Limed Legs, . . . 276

"	Chicken Pox,	276
"	Moulting,	277
"	Loss of Feather,	277
"	By S. M. SAUNDERS, Massachusetts Poultry Society,	278
"	By DR. J. C. BENNETT,	281

The Author's First Doings in Cock-Fighting, . . . 301

ORIGIN AND HISTORY.

The question of the origin of game fowls has always been a perplexing subject alike to the naturalist, historian or game fancier. There is yet great doubt as to the origin of fowls that have ever excited the admiration of man. Books disagree. One proclaims that they had their *sole* origin in the jungles of India; another, that they were known to exist in South America long before the Spaniards settled there—that cock-fighting was a favorite pastime of the Astecs of ancient Mexico; and still another, that they were known to the Island of Britian long before Cæsar conquered it, and in confirmation quotes Cæsar's own words, "that fowls were there in abundance, but only used for the purpose of amusement and past-time." All these stories seem well corroborated, but they point to a solution which all writers heretofore have *wished* to reach, viz :—"*that game fowls are necessarily the result of a cross between a wild pheasant and an ordinary fowl.*"

None will accuse the thorough game of being an hermaphrodite. The males perform their offices better than any other species known; the hens lay prolifically, hatch and guard and raise their young.

Amid all these conflicting opinions, some broached by known and very able authors, it is hard to judge. We find that the origin of Games is claimed in Eastern Asia, the jungles of India, in Great Britain, North America and South America.— That we are indebted for their sole origin to any one of these countries, we do not believe. Pride of country may have induced some to claim an honor that was not justly their due, until the claim has been handed down by tradition and the people now accept it as fully settled, and a not-to-be disputed fact. Or, mayhap, the origin *has not been confined to one country*—that, if not simultaneous, it sprang from lands remote, yet nevertheless truly had its beginning in more places than one.— But stay, before concluding that at last we have found the true reason, one that may uproot the prejudices of ages, and contradict old and long established book theories—let us examine more closely into the causes of origin.

First, to the claims of the wild Pheasant Cock.

To say that the opinion was not very prevalent that the game is but the result of a cross between the wild pheasant cock and a common dunghill hen, would be telling an untruth, and of which many would be prepared to convict us. We know that the idea is extensively entertained, that some persons reap additional pride from the fact that they think ther games half pheasant. We know also that fancy poultry raisers have a long list of so-called games, with the name of "*Pheasant*" following Sumatra, Java, Malacca, &c.; yet we are equally aware of the policy that induced the adoption of such names. We take it for granted that poultry raisers are as shrewd, generally, as other men who wish to reap a profit from the product of their stock, and that any name, which suits the tastes and prejudices of the people, will be given fowls to serve as their passport to public esteem. Hence the dubbing of fowls "pheasant games." The color, marks, size, and in part the characteristics in some measure sustain them in dubbing their fowls "pheasant," but we candidly believe that their claims to the "game" part are about on an equal footing with the common Bantams. Still the deceit is plausible, and many have been its dupes, and are still so.— Yet, for the reason that an error is prevalent, that a large proportion of our most respectable fanciers of fowl are votaries to it, does this constitute a fair reason that the error should not be exposed? We think not, and though in the attempt to prove our position we hazard the ill-will of many, and jar the sensibilities of still more, we prefer examining the matter, on plain principles of reason, sustained by known results.

Whatever may be the native quality of a pheasant, or even whether it be fact that they will and have been mixed with dunghills, our "credulity is not so magnaminous" to accept the fact as established, that games are necessarily half pheasant and half dung-hill. Now to the proof:

In countries where the pheasant is wholly unknown, in others where their plumage is radically different from ours, pheasant games have been in use hundreds of years before the christian era, and the inhabitants of such countries lay as strong claims to their origin as any other, and pretty well sustain the point by the traditions handed down to them from generation to generation, until the present day. But we do not rely upon this. We have one or two all-convincing facts, acquired by fair tests, and putting to its use a little common sense. Nothing is truer than that *half or three-quarter* game will not stand the steel;— that, while they may exhibit good pluck with their own heels and upon their own ground, when the deadly gaft (that severe arbiter of their courage) is upon their adversaries, their bravery fails them, at a time, too, when there is the greatest motive for its exhibition. We hold that this is true of all fowls not purely game, and those who have had most experience in the matter, and are impartial in their decisions, will bear us out. We are sure of the support of those whose purses have been emptied, by a false confidence, induced by the belief that pheasant games are infallible. Such, after their bitter experience, are now willing to conclude with us, that this class of fowls do not manifest the

>——" Spirit than can dare,
>The deadliest form that death can take,
>And dare it for the daring's sake."

Suppose that we have a good game cock, none better, and cross him with a hen half game;—the progeny will be three-quarters, but will they stand all the tests that good games should stand? We unhesitatingly say, after complete trials of the experiment, that they will not. Now extend the inquiry, and assume that we have a fine, wild, gamey looking, and savage pheasant cock. We cross him with a dung-hill hen. Will the progeny be pure game? We esteem the argument wholly applicable. It at once proves the error of the theory that games are part pheasant, or that such was their origin. Why should the progeny of that which is *half* prove superior to that which is three quarters? Taking as a basis that games are really half pheasant, it may be urged that the first—that which was the result of a cross between the game cock and half game hen, is, consequently, not fully half game, nor as much so as that which is the result of the cross of the pheasant. This has been anticipated, and had we not practical tests to prove the contrary, might serve as an urgent reason to demolish our reasoning.— But from long observation, and by the steel, as well as their own natural weapons, we have been forced to conclude that of the two, the cross between the game cock and half game hen are far superior, and exhibit more of the real qualities than the half pheasant. This also, not only goes to prove the foregoing fact, but serves as an additional prop to our theory.

Again, it cannot be urged that games are *in any part pheasant* —that they have any pheasant blood in their veins. We now speak solely of *pure games*, knowing very well that there are many breeds of *fowls* half or even three-quarter pheasant. The first crossing between a pheasant cock and common hen, breeds half pheasants. Now, take this progeny, half pheasant as it is, still keep a pure pheasant cock with them to breed, and the result must be three-quarters. Then take the three-quarters pheasant, again breeding these with the pure pheasant cock, and you have them returned to actual pheasants, with little alteration, except that they have become somewhat domesticated. So it will readily be seen, that if experiments with pheasant cocks are carried thus far, there would be danger of having them real pheasant, after three or four years breeding in this manner. As well might we catch wild pheasants, hens and all, endeavor to domesticate them, and then, with exultation proclaim to the world that pure pheasant games were in actual existence—that the opinions of long past ages were partly denied and greatly confirmed (if so great a contradiction is allowable)—that while games are not quite half dung-hill and pheasant, they are full pheasant, and consequently full game! 'Twere almost superfluous to expose the fallacy of such a theory, and yet we have endeavored to do it because of its great prevalency, not that there is any foundation for it.

With regard to other opinions entertained, we have not so much to say. It would be tedious, difficult and perhaps impossible for us to attempt to prove satisfactorily that the game is not partly indebted for its origin to the Java, Jungle, &c. Nor shall we attempt to do this; but we will affirm our belief that it had its origin from no one of them. We believe that game fowls had their origin in more countries than one, mayhap in Great Britain, as some of its inhabitants claim; Java, Persia, South America, or all and more of them combined.

That we have different varieties of game fowls no one pretends to deny; that these varieties are not all the result of crosses, seems very reasonable. We find the original Jungle cock gray, varied with white and red; the chest reddish; the neck and wing-coverts yellowish and ashy brown, and the tail glossy green, with neither wattles nor comb. On the contrary the Malay, (to which also the origin of the game is ascribed) has a double comb and wattles, beside other marks differing materially from the Java.

Those in England, Russia, and South America, Africa, Australia, &c., were radically different from the above, and from each other; and when we take into consideration the fact that these countries are so distant from each other, and that cock-fighting was common in all of them as far as we can trace their history, the presumption is reasonable that games were not originated in any single country, and that there were different original breeds of games. Cock fighting was known in England, when Cæsar invaded it. More than five hundred years before the christian era it was a favorite diversion with the Greeks, who it is said became attached to it from the example of the Persians. In China, Java, and the entire East Indies it has extended back to a "time wherein the memory of men knoweth nothing to the contrary." Wild Game Fowls have been discovered in South America, and cock-fights were common both there and in Mexico long before the Spaniards entered.

That the fowl tribes were domesticated and extensively spread at a very romote period, there is abundant evidence. Holy Writ, in enunciating the provisions for the use of Solomon and his household, makes particular mention of the "fatted fowl."

The fowl was among the domestic animals of Palestine, after the Babylonlish captivity; for Nehemiah, in the year 445 before Christ, says, in rebuking the Jews, (chapter V, verse 18,) "Now there were at my table, prepared for me daily, one ox and six choice sheep, also fowls." Of the kind of fowl fattened for Solomon or eaten by Nehemiah, we are not informed, and have quite as much reason for believing that it was a game as as a Shanghaie. But even before this period we have testimony indicative of the fact that *games* were in active use. Thus. Peisthetairus (Aristophanes) says, in his quaint and ambiguous way: "No lack is there of proofs to show the truth of our opinion, that birds, not gods, o'er men and kingdoms reigned, the Kings and sovereigns were of yore. And *first* I instance, in the cock, *how he the sceptre bore;* (the italics are our own,) how, long before their monarchs the Persians him obeyed, or ere Darius or Megabyzus swayed. And so, he's named the Persian Bird. And still he struts, no other bird there is that wears. the turban cock'd, but he." (The king among the Persians only wore the turban erect; and the knowledge of this fact makes still plainer Aristophanes' illustration, that the cock, [we believe the *game*] won more admiration and attention of the people than the King himself.) Now this quotation, to our view, seems to apply better to game fowls than any other. The Persians were passionately fond of cock-fighting and their fowls. were greatly noted for their courage, which trait elicited the admiration of the natives, and doubtless caused the rebuke of their king, who seemed jealous that the turban was worn more gracefully by the cock than himself.

Amid all these proofs, why should we believe that the origin of game fowls was not as early as others—and that there were different breeds the same as the Bantam and Shanghaie? As well might we contend that all fowls, all birds, and all beasts had a common and *single* orgin—that the Shanghaie was the origin, and the nicety of breeding has brought it down to the tiny Seabright; that the Ostrich is the absolute father of all birds, and the canary merely a dwarfed child; or going from great to small: that the mouse is the parent of animals, and climate alone has contributed to the size of the elephant!

To us the accounts of the origin of games, though meagre and not as fully satisfactory as they might be, are conclusive evidence that they are indebted for their origin to no other fowl; that they are and were distinct original varieties, the same as animals, wholly different from eath other—that in short, like *Topsy*, and many others in like situations, known to all countries and sections, they *just growed*, and that too in Europe, Asia, Africa and the American continents.

It will by many be perceived that the above views have never been promulgated in a poultry book of any kind, but we only ask that the *reason* of the reader should be brought to bear upon them, keeping in mind the facts quoted, when we are assured that our opinion will not be inconsiderately criticised.

These views are confirmed in the following article furnished for this publication by Marshall Wheeler, Esq., of Honesdale, Penn'a:

"Having among other things, requested my views on "The Origin of Games," I fear that you will have to submit to a somewhat lengthly epistle this time, (for the field is an extensive one), but you will have no one to blame but yourself, and it will only teach you to be more careful with your requirements in the future.

"Notwithstanding the fact, that man is quite a "knowing animal," yet when he attempts to give the origin, and the whys and wherefores of everything, he is apt to get into what our mutual authority—"Nick Whiffles"—calls, "condemned diffikelties." In his strife after the unattainable, he often pitches headlong into dark chasms of the wildest theories, simply because his feet have strayed beyond those bounds where the lamp of reason could no longer illumine his way, and he has been guided only by the delusive and often dangerous *ignis fatuus* of visionary speculations upon points of which he could possibly know nothing.

"This has been particularly the case with those foreign authors of works upon fowls, who in their (in other respects) laudable ambitions to gratify the curiosity or satisfy the cravings of their readers, have attempted to localize the particular spot upon this whole earth where game fowls first came into existence,—a habit in which they have been followed by nearly all American authors, who, to their shame be it said, have rested content by playing Poll Parrot in merely repeating what those authors have said, without apparently exercising a moment's reflection upon a subject demanding the most thought. Now, *if it be true*, that there is one spot only, where games were first brought into existence,—that spot from the very nature of the case, could only be known to the author of Being. For to begin at the beginning, by turning to Holy Writ we find, that the "fowl *that* may fly above the earth in the open firmament of heaven," was created the day before man, somewhere, and that after man had been placed in Eden, the fowl was brought there, or rather the fowls. Without express revelation, man can not tell of events which happened before his creation, and this happened to be the case in regard to game fowls—they were created before man, according to Holy Writ. We cannot even point to Eden as the ground where games were first created. The most that authors have ever been enabled to assert, with any show of accuracy is, that the *oldest accounts* we have, speak of games as existing at certain times at certain places,—a very vague and unsatisfactory solution of the question at best. For if we take *all* of the "oldest accounts," (if the contradictory expression may be allowed), we will find that games have existed from time immemorial, in nearly every known country of any considerable extent, on the face of the Globe. I have now come down to a point which, the while it agrees with my preconceived notions, is also suggested by the present state of the argument, and which may possibly enable us to give a *reasonable guess* as to the truth of the matter: and this is, that when the Creator created game fowls, it is not likely, judging from what we know of his attributes, that he set one section of the earth aristocratically above another, by blessing it alone with a fowl constituted, as it is; fit to exist and thrive in any and all climates, from torrid to frigid. I do not know but I am venturing in thus arguing, upon dangerous ground—upon ground fatal to many ideas which are now considered standard, aye, sacred. For if I may argue that because game fowls are fit to exist in any country, they were therefore created in all countries in the beginning, then the principle may not rest there, but be also applied to man with equal truth,—provided revelation is set aside. However, as I have not started out to give you a theological discussion, but only a little talk upon the origin of game fowls. I will stick to my text like a Continental shin-plaster to a Revolutionary hero, and leave you to find your own theological stilts to travel further, or else stay upon the original ground with me—as your inclinations or sense of duty shall dictate. In view of the above train of reasoning or argument, I must come to the result or conclusion, that game fowls are originally of all countries, and natives of all soils. That the Eastern hemisphere has its numberless varieties of games, created on the soil, and the western hemisphere its games, also created on the soil: and that no one country can in pride or vanity say to another "you are indebted to *us* for your games,—nature never granted them to *you*.

"But allowing the foregoing argument to be worthless, there is still another view to be taken of the question, which may still sustain, though perhaps to a more limited extent, the doctrine that those countries possessing games at all, possess games which have originated upon, and are natives of the soil. Suppose that I import from England a pair of Clipper Games, and that I obtain eggs from those games, and hatch those eggs here. Would not the chicks be as truly natives of this country, as though the parent Clippers had always existed here? Did not the chicks originate, or come into existence here? If you say not, please inform me where *else* they originated. Let us see :—is there such a person existing upon this continent as a full blooded, white American? And pray where did our forefathers come from? From England,—true,—they were Englishmen,—but are *we*? If not, how long a time—how many generations must pass, before we may consider ourselves Americans? Suppose again, in accordance with Holy Writ, Adam to have been the first man. Are we not, then Adamites—the whole world? If so, by what authority and upon what principle, do we style ourselves Americans, Englishmen, Frenchmen, Russians, Africans, and what not?— I will answer this question plainly, because this principle lies at the foundation of the whole matter. An Englishman claims to be an Englishman, *not* because Parliament has decreed that under certain circumstances he should be,—*not* because his mother resided there when he was born, but *because it was in England that the Creator breathed the breath of life into him.* By that act he was *created*, and he was created *there*, in *England*, therefore he is an Englishman. To go still farther back with the question : I cannot see that it makes any difference about the origin of games as to what *means* were used in creating them. Undoubtedly the first game fowl, (if a first ever existed), was created by different means from those succeeding. For if there was a time when game fowls did not exist, then, upon the creation of the *first* one, other means *must* have been used to create him than those known to us. But whether he was made out of the dust of one particular place of the earth, peculiarly constituted to make games, (I am not making "game" of you, Doctor, though I must confess it is slightly tinged with the ridiculous), or out of the common air of the heavens, or by other means, cannot of course, be known to us. That the origin of games is decided by the peculiar *means* of their creation,—that the original fowl must have been created by different means from those now known, in order to establish the *origin*, is simply nonsensical and unworthy of further attention. For aught that you or I know, game fowls may be as old as the earth's creations,—they as old as the earth, and the earth as old as eternity, though it is difficult to conceive of that which had no beginning.

"There is still another view to be taken of the question, whereby proof may be adduced to a great extent, that games have originated in all countries : and this is by referring to the species themselves. For we find upon the most casual as well as the most critical observation and examination, that the species is composed of a great variety and number of distinct breeds, each having its own peculiar characteristics, and differing almost as much from one another as the species does from dung-hills. Now, if they had all originated in one country they would inevitably long ere this late day, have been irretrievably mixed up by crosses, so that no distinguishing marks would have been left to know one breed from another. As an instance of this, look at what are called the Irish Games,—you see every conceivable breed mixed and crossed with each other to such an extent that you can tell nothing about them, save that they are a *hodge podge* of all breeds,—good, bad and indifferent,—of every color and of every size—no size, and almost shape. As you are well aware the Irish are "death" on Games, and if they find a good cock anywhere they are sure to take him home and breed crosses from him, in ninety-nine cases out of a hundred, without the least reference to fitness, and without following it up to a state of purity. In view of these facts we must still come to the one conclusion, that the different varieties of games which compose the species, had a separate and not a single origin in the beginning, and that too, in different countries.

"Thus far in my talk, I have gone upon the assumed ground that games are a distinct species of fowl, "not hybrids, or half-pheasant and fowl." With a few brief remarks upon this subject, I will close this, to you at least, tedious communication.

"We find upon looking through the order of nature, that everything is arranged upon a principle which may be expressed by the terms positive and negative—parts and counter parts; and that it extends down through the whole of her creations, animate or inanimate. We see it made manifest everywhere; in the solid and the fluid, in the mountain and the valley; in the prairie and the desert; in the hard-wood-tree and the soft; in the sour apple and the sweet; in the Arab horse and the "leather-flapper;" in the blood-hound and the cur; in the lion and the fox; in the hawk and the pigeon, and so on indefinitely. Now, would it not be a strange exception in the general order of nature, if the same distinctive principle did not apply to fowls? Is it not highly reasonable to suppose that there is no such exception?—that the acid-game has it's alkali—dung-hill?—that there is as much difference between a gamester and a dung-hill, as between a hard-maple and a soft—a beech and bass-wood—a horse and an ass—an ass and a zebra—a zebra and a gazelle? Among men, a Caucasian is not an African:—among fowls, a game is not a dung-hill, and the one thing is as plainly to be seen as the other. There is a dumpyness of carriage in the dung-hill not perceivable in the game. The game has a brilliancy of plumage and closeness and fineness of feather which the dung-hill cannot show; the game has a rising of the shoulders; a hooking of the beak; a hawkishness of the eye, an uprightness of form, and a certain familiar boldness when in the company of men, which the dung-hill is a stranger to and does not possess. What the Caucasian race is among men, the game species is among fowls —the first and best. In his veins courses a more noble blood than any other breed or breeds can boast. His proud crest never bows to dishonorable defeat, and when fighting to the death his last expiring act is an effort to retrieve the fallen fortunes of the day. But how about the dung-hill? Faugh! a clip or two—a squawk—a pair of cowardly legs in accelerated motion—a skulk in a convenient hole, and the ignoble strut has vanished! Wring his neck!

"Some authors ascribe the origin of games to a cross between a pheasant and a dung-hill. Unfortunately for this theory, that experiment has been tried effectually, and it has been shown that the cross is as unable to breed as is a mule or a hinny,—in other words the cross is barren. "Thus far shalt thou go, and no farther," Nature says in this matter, and plants her foot where the waves of man's progression and attempted creations dare not —cannot pass. She will maintain the purity of her creations where monsters are attempted, and even when the attempt falls short of that epithet, nature does not favor it. I recollect of seeing some years ago, a book, (which had been published by an appropriation made by the Legislature of this State, if I am not mistaken), upon the human hair. It showed among other things, that where there was a cross between two foreign races, one hair would have the peculiar form and shape peculiar to one race, and its neighbor in the same head, the form and shape peculiar to the other race; and that no one hair took a medium form between the two; and the book argued that a like division probably ran all the way through the body, blood and system generally, of the cross. The tendency of this discovery goes to show two things,—that of the plurality of origin of the human race, and that the races cannot be *mixed*, according to the common understanding of that word. Now, do we not find this equally true of crosses between games and dunghills? In the plumage of the dung-hill flock we find an improved appearance; but the opposite is the effect on a flock of games. So also, when we come to those other qualities which so strongly mark the difference between the two races,—qualities which are too well known to need repetition. I cannot but conclude that the game is of a pure race—an original creation, and is destined to remain so. That such is, and may continue to be, the fact, is the sincere desire of

Your friend, and well wisher,
M. W.

The fame and valor of the game cock is as old as the written history, and in modern days he is regarded as "the blooded horse of the feathered creation. He was in ancient and is yet used as the emblem of physical courage. The story is told of a brave Grecian general of old, pointing to the valor and gameness of two cocks fighting, as an incentive to the courage of his fagging and doubtful warriors—how they profitted by and imitated the example. It is related that during the war of 1812, the British on Lake Champlain were attacked by the American fleet under Commodore McDonough. The fleet of McDonough, much inferior to that of the English, suffered terribly in the first part of the battle. At the moment when it was raging fiercest—the heaviest fire of the enemy directed against the flag ship of McDonough—his men driven from their guns by the fierce canonade; when dismay sat upon every countenance, and the storm of iron hail, which seemed to threaten destruction not only to the ship but every living soul therein, was at its height, a cannonball struck a chicken coop and knocked it to pieces, killing all it contained but a moment before save only a game rooster, whose battered comb bore the marks of many a death-fight. Flying upon the bulwarks of McDonough's flag-ship, the noble bird, undaunted by the noise and confusion and carnage about him, with clarion voice rang out his notes of defiance and victory.

Sailors are ever superstitious, and when, in the pause of the thunder of the enemy's cannon, they heard the shrill "cock-a-doodle-doo" of the undaunted bird, they gathered new courage, and repairing again to their guns, returned the fire of the enemy, until the battle ended, and McDonough on Lake Champlain was victorious over the enemies of his country. The chronicler of this incident was one Chapman, a former editor in Indiana, who declares "that every naval historian makes mention of the fact, and history says that the bravery shown on that occasion by the rooster was the cause of victory, by the renewed courage it gave to the sailors in McDonough's fleet."

A similar incident is related in connection with a naval fight between the Gauls and Saxons. However extravagant the story may appear to some, there are admirers of the game who would think it no test to their credulity to affix a fitting final to the McDonough story by adding "that had the vessel sunk, the gallant cock would have kept his head up to the last, leaped from yard to yard until the tip of the mast was at the water's edge, and his graceful head was about to disappear forever, when he would have given one more cool glance at his enemies, flapped the water with his strong wings, and crowed a last, eternal defiance to his own and his country's enemies." The faith abiding in true admiration would have given the game a courageous and tragic ending, but it is not needed, either to preserve his fame or win for him any additional marks of admiration. Men have in all ages admired this quality of courage, and many have sought to emulate it. It is as old as chivalry, and so closely interwoven that the history of one is incomplete without the other.

The game cock was in the early ages found on the continent of India, and the islands of St. Iago, Pulcondore, Timor, Phillippine and Molucca, as well as on Sumatra, Java, New Guinea, Tonian and the isles of the South Seas. At Sumatra and Java [we learn from Rees's English Encyclopaedia] they were noticed as being particularly large. Latham has observed that they breed most freely in warmer situations; in very cold regions, though they live and thrive, they cease to multiply. We know that in Canada, the United States, Mexico and the West Indies they not only thrive but multiply quite as rapidly as any fowl.

According to Mr. Pegge in the "Archælogia" vol. 3, No. 19, the art of cock fighting is referred to the Greeks. Jacobus Palmirius, a writer cited by Mr. Pegge, says that the traces of this diversion may be discovered among the barbarians of Asia, as early as the reign of Crœsus, King of Lydia, A. M. 3426, and 558 years before Christ. The Dardanii, a people of Troas, had on their coins the representation of two cocks fighting; but as these coins are not of a very early date, the antiquity of game cock fighting cannot be inferred from them. Mr. Pegge suggests that, perhaps, it might have been introduced among them, and also at Pergamus, from Athens, where an annual festival was instituted by Themistocles after the conclusion of the Persian war. When this famous general was heading the Athenian army against the Persians, he saw some cocks fighting, and took occasion from this circumstance to animate his troops by observing to them : " These animals fight not for the Gods of their country, nor for the monuments of their ancestors, nor for glory, nor for freedom, nor for their children, but for the sake of victory, and that one may not yield to the other," and from the topic he inspirited the Athenians (vid Ælian, var. Hist. 2ch. 28.) Rees says, " If we may excuse the barbarity of this institution it may be considered in some degree as commendable, because it was an act of perpetual gratitude to the benevolent duty that presented him with an occasion of haranguing his soldiers with such effect as to induce them successfully to engage their enemies in battle, or at least, as a permanent encouragement to his nation. As to the barbarity of the institution, Ælian remarks that cruelty and every kind of debauchery were so generally interwoven with the religious observances and ceremonies of these polite Athenians, that they would be but little shocked and offended by it on this account, or, however, not more so than the more ignorant barbarians of the opposite coast of Asia, the Pergamenians or Dardanians.

We may further observe, says Rees, that the cock, on account of his vigilance, was sacred to Apollo, Mercury, and Æsculapius ; and for the same quality, in conjunction with his magnanimous and daring spirit, he was appropriated likewise to Mars. This was extremely apposite to the purpose and intention of the " Spectaculum," or public show, exhibited by Themistocles ; as these creatures called by Columella " rixosa aves," were supposed to be more addicted to fighting than any others. The scene of engagement, however, or in modern phrase, the " pit" was the theatre ; and the sport lasted one day. But others as well as Themistocles, have taken advantage of the sight of cock-fighting, and deduced from this circumstance an argument for incitement and encouragement of military valor. Socrates endeavoured in the same way to inspire Iphicrates, with courage (Diog. Laort. 2 § 30.) Cheqsippus also in his book " De Justitia" says, " our valour is raised by the example of cocks." Lucian likewise (de Gymnas 2. p 295) introduces Solon the great Athenean legislator, as addressing Ancharsis to the same purpose. Musonius also, cited by Stobaus (Serm. 29), deduced the same kind of instruction from the battling of quails and cocks ; and we are informed that the young men were obliged to attend the exhibitions of the theatre, in order to avail themselves of this instruction. It further appears that the other Greeks, as well as the Athenians held a good fighting breed of cocks in high estimation, and often amused themselves with this diversion. We learn from Pliny (ubi supra), and Colmella (8. c. 2) that the islanders of Delos were great lovers of this sport ; and Tanagra a city of Boetia, the isle of Rhodes, Chalcis in Eubœa, and the country of *Media* were famous for their generous and magnanimous race of chickens.

The kingdom of Persia was probably included in the last, from whence this kind of poultry was first brought into Greece ; and if a judgment may be formed of the rest from the fowls of Rhodes and Media the excellence of the broods at the time consisted in their weight and bulk (as the fowls of that country were heavy and large) and such as our sportsmen call "shakebags" or "turn-pokes."

At Alexandia, in Egypt, they had a breed of hens, called *Moyoogot*, which produced the best fighting-cocks. Upon the whole it would seem, that at first cock-fighting was partly a religious and partly a political institution at Athens ; and was there continued for the purpose of cherishing valor in the minds of their youth ; but it was afterwards perverted, both here and in other parts of Greete, to a common pastime, without any moral, political, or religious intention ; as is now practised among us.

The Romans, who were prone to imitate the Greeks, followed their example in this kind of diversion, without any good or laudable motives. Signior Haym (cited by Mr. Pegge) thinks, that the Romans borrowed the pastime from Dardanus, in Asia ; but it is needless to trace their derivation of it to such a distance, more especially as it was generally followed in Greece and was not introduced among the Romans at a very early period. From a passage that occurs in Columella (ubi supra) it appears probable that the Romans did not use the sport of cock-fighing in his time ; and he moreover speaks of it in terms of ignominy, as an expensive amusement, unbecoming the frugal householder and as often attended with the ruin of the persons that pursued it.

The Romans seem to have been more acquainted with quails

as fighting birds than with cocks. At length however, they paired cocks, as well as quails for fighting. A writer says:

"The first cause of contention between the two brothers, Bassianus and Geta, the sons of the emperor Septimus Severus, happened according to Herodian (3. § 33) in their youth, about the fighting of their quails and cocks; and as they had often accompanied their father into Greece, they had probably seen and learned this pastime there.

"It might naturally have been expected that after the introduction of christianity into the Roman empire, when the bloody scenes of the amphitheatre were discarded this barbarous and inhuman deversion, which had a tendency towards cherishing ferocity and implacability in the minds of men, would have been restrained and gradually aninhilated. Besides this pastime has been the bane and ruin of thousands here as well as of those "lanistæ arium," cock feeders mentioned by Columella, whose patrimonial fortunes were entirely dissipated and consumed by it.

"The cock is not only very useful, but so stately in his figure, and magnificent in his plumage, that Pliny speaks in high terms of his government among his own kind, and Aristophanes compares him to the King of Persia. Such also is his tenderness to his brood, that he will scratch and provide for them with an assiduity almost equal to that of the hen; and such is his generosity, that on finding a hoard of meat, he will chuckle the hens together and without touching a morsel himself, will relinquish the whole to them. The Cock was called the bird, by many of the ancients; he has highly esteemed in some countres, and in others, was even held sacred; insomuch that one cannot forbear regretting, that a creature so noble and so useful, sould be so cruelly treated. It affords however some satisfaction that the massacre of Shrove Tuesday, is now declining, and this circumstance encourages the hope that in a few years, it will be totally disused; but the cock-pit still continues a reproach to the humanity of Englishmen and to the benign religion which they profess."

This species of pastime was probably brought into England by the Romans, but the precise period of its introduction has not been ascertained. The bird was here before Cæsar's arrival ; but Mr. Pegge in his researches has found no notice of his fighting before the time of William Fitz-Stephen who wrote the life of Archbishop Becket, some time in the reign of Henry 2nd. William describes the cocking as a sport of school-boys on Shrove Tuesday called "Camilvaria." The theatre was the school, and the master was the director of the sport. From this time, the diversion, however abused and barbarous, has continued amongst us ; it was followed though disappproved, and prohibited, 39 Edw. 3rd ; also in the reign of Henry 8th and A. D. 1569.

COCKS AND COCKING IN ENGLAND.

The reader will have noticed that we have already quoted liberally from Rees's English Encyclopædia. We have done so because its information is valuable, and because we believe the work to be now out of print, or at least inacessible to American game-fanciers. For the following discription of "Cocks and Cocking in England" we are indebted to the same work:—

"By some, cock-fighting has been called "a royal diversion;" and much encouraged both by Henry 8th and James 1st; but it was forbidden by one of the acts of Oliver Cromwell, March 31st, 1654.

There are no documents that we are acquainted with to inform us in what state the act of fighting cocks existed prior to the reign of Henry 8th, who it is supposed founded the celebrated Cock Pit at Westminter afterward, renewed and encouraged by Charles 2nd, whose pile cock, the introduction of this monarch, are in high estimation among breeders at this day. From that period annual mains have been fought at the royal cock-pit in Westminster to the present time.

The institutors of this establishment enacted certain laws for the better regulation of these sports, and the leading features of which as belonging to this act, we shall here briefly describe.

There are three kinds of mains at present in use with cockers; the *long main*, which in general continues for a week, seldom or never longer; the *short main*, of a day or two (both regulated by the same laws); and the *welch main*; in the long main the cocks are generally the property of a joint subscription, or of only two individuals, and the cocks thus collected are chosen for the main, according to their weights, those being preferred, as a medium weight from three pounds eight ounces to four pounds ten ounces, giving or taking an ounce on either side, though they are generally matched to a drachm weight. The cocks which form the bye battles in the main, become the objects of separate bettings and are subject to the same weights and regulations. Cocks whose weights are above four pounds eight ounces, are termed shake-bags or turn outs and are seldom matched against each other by weight.

The short main lasts only for a day or two, the cocks being fewer in num ber, or the numbers are doubled for each day. The welch main is generally fought for a purse, a gold cup, a fat hog, or some other prize; in this main all the fowls are restricted to a certain weight, viz: about four pounds four ounces; these are matched against each other, as shall be agreed upon, the winners again taking the winners, till they are reduced to a pair; then the winner of the last battle gains the prize.

Besides this there is also to be noticed the battle royal, which consists in any number of fowls being put down together in the pit, and the last surviving fowl gains the prize.

Those species of fighting, called the battle royal and the welch main, are known no where in the world, as Mr. Pegge conceives (ubi supra) but in this country; neither in China, where this species of diversion is very prevalent, nor in Persia, nor in Malacca, nor among the savage tribes of America.

The battle of the main always begins with fighting the lightest cocks; it is fair to feed them in any way you please after they are weighed; and those which, proportionately to their bulk, had been previously most reduced, or brought down, now have the opportunity of being fed and brought up again, thereby gaining upon the weight of their opponents; for the lightest cocks are found to be the first prepared by the artifices that are used to bring them to their wind and action.

The following articles are observed by the members of the Cock pit royal for regulating the mains: "Articles of agreement made the   day of   one thousand eight hundred and   , between   : First the said parties have agreed, that each of them shall produce show and weigh, at the   on the   day of beginning at the hour of   on the morning,   Cocks, none to be less than 3lb 8oz., nor more than 4lb 10oz., and as many of each party's cocks that come within one ounce of each other, shall fight for   a battle, that it   each cock, in as equal divisions as the battles can be divided into six pits, or days play, at the cock pit before mentioned; and the party's cocks that win the greatest number of battles, matched out of the number before specified, shall be entitled to the sum of   , odd battle money, and the sum to be staked into the hands of Mr.   before any cocks are pitted, by both parties. And we further agree, to produce, show, and weigh, on the said weighing days,   cocks for bye battles, subject to the same weight as the cocks that fight in the main, and these to be added to the number of cocks unmatched; and as many of them as come within one ounce of each other, shall fight for   a battle; the number of cocks so matched, to be equally divided as will permit of and added to each day's play with the main cocks; and it is also agreed, that the balance of the battle money shall be paid at the end of each day's play. It is also further agreed, for the cocks to fight in silver spurs, and with fair hackles; and to be subject to all the usual rules of cock-fighting, as practiced at the Cock pit royal, Westminser; and the profits arising from the spectators, to be equally divided between both parties, after all charges are paid that usually happen on those occasions.—Witness our hands,   day of   18   .

It is understood on all occasions, that battles for £5 and upwards must be fought in silver spurs, unless the contrary is expressly agreed upon, for this reason, that the battle is not so soon ended in silver, and the fowl has more opportunity of displaying his powers than in steel spurs. The setters of the cocks are not permitted, by the general laws of cocking to take up their fowls after they are put down upon the pit, unless either of the fowls touch the side of the pit, or are entangled in each other, or in the mat; in either case they may be handled and brought to the centre of the pit; if the fowl is thrown on his back with his legs upwards, and not touching the pit, it is lawful to turn him only; but it is not allowed, on any pretence to remove feathers, &c., from the beak or eyes during the fight.

If either, or both cocks, through blindness, or any other cause, cease to fight, "The law is told," that is, a person counts twice twenty, when they may be handled and set to again; this telling of the law is repeated as long as both cocks fight; but ten only is counted at each interval after the first previously to their being put together; either ceasing to pick, is told out by a person counting distinctly and audibly twice twenty, they are then set to beak to beak; and if he now refuses to fight, ten is told, and "once refused," announced; if he continues to refuse, ten more, "twice refused," and so on till he has refused ten different times, when he loses the battle; this is termed the long law. If a cock resumes his fighting at any period during the counting, in that case, in counting again, to begin the tens till the refusals make ten following each other. Should both be disabled, and refuse to fight before the long law begins counting it is a drawn battle and neither wins; and should both refuse fighting during the telling of the long law, it is that cock's battle which fought last; but should he die before the law is told out, he loses the battle, notwithstanding the other did not fight within the law.

If any one desires to stop this telling him out, he may pound him, that is, he bets the cock will be beaten ten pounds to five shillings; in this case he must lay down his hat, handkerchief, glove, or something upon the pit, as a token of the challenge. When the short law is told by a person, distinctly counting twice twenty, and afterwards repeating the words, will any one take it? three times; if no one accepts the challenge during this short law, the Cock is beaten. It is necessary when any one takes the poundage or bet, that he declares it, and also lays down something on the pit as surety; when the cock must fight till death and sometimes most unexpectedly he recovers and wins.

Having described the natural origin of this race of birds, the history of the sport, and its laws and regulations we now proceed to consider the general form and properties of the fighting cock, when in his greatest perfection, according to the ideas we at present entertain.

The general outline of the finest cock, taken as a whole nearly approaches that of a lengthened cone, excluding the leg and tail, the apex of the cone being the head and the base the vent and the belly; under such external form, may exist the best properties of the cock: in describing the beauties of particular parts, the head should be small, the beak strong and pointed, the neck long, and at the same time strong, the girth of the shoulders, chest, and body, broad, feeling broad to the grasp, and tapering again to the rump. The thighs and legs large and strong, and rather long than short; and it is considered a good form if he brings them close up to his body, when held in the hands instead of letting them hang loosely down.

The feathers, to amateurs, also afford a good criterion of judging of the soundness of the bird; where these lie close to the skin, and compacted together, and feel short and stiff to the touch, and shining and glossy in their exterior, such is deemed a sound feathered bird.

The colours most admired are the reds and duckwings; by the red among cockers is understood a cock with a hackle (that is, the feathers of the head and neck) red; with the hackle generally correspond the colours of the rump and saddle.

The red cock varies with a black breast and ginger wing that is, of a gingerbread or tawney colour, and again with a black breast and a dark wing; such are darkreds.

The colour of the wing, as used among the amateurs in cocking, is sometimes taken from the whole wing; as where the wing is altogether of a ginger red excepting the flight, or primary feathers, which are dark, or a part of the wing, as in the duck-wings, hereafter to be described.

The light reds are those breasts wholly red spotted with black or black streaked with red, and these receive their names according to those circumstances, as ginger-breasted, spotted-breasted, streaky breasted, &c.

The duck wing cock derives this name from a bar of steel blue across the greater coverts, like the fascia across the wild duck's wing; in this case it is observed, that the secondaries are exteriorly white, the hackle also white or pale yellow or cream colour, as are saddle feathers which correspond, as we have before noticed, with the hackle.

In discriminating the individuals of this breed, it is farther usual to describe the colours of the breast and the shoulders; the breast may be black or spotted or streaked; the shoulders may be tawney or dark red, or birchen, that is of the colour of the twigs of a birch broom, or silver shoulders being nearly white.

The yellow cock is merely a variety of the duck wing, from which it differs only in having the secondary feathers or those next the flight, dark, instead of white, which is not of unfrequent occurrence; the blue bar in these cocks is sometimes seen to vary to a light brown.

The next colour to be noticed is the dun; these cocks are in reality of a lead or slate colour, and may be wholly so, or duck wings, with the breast, flight and tail dun; or a yellow dun; by flight feathers are understood the primaries, or first and strongest feathers of the wing; the red duns, are red cocks with a dun breast flight, and tail.

Black cocks are so coloured, some wholly so, others with birchen or brazen shoulders, which are almost the only varieties of this cock.

White cocks are either wholly white, termed smocks or white red shoulders, which are termed piles; when these are streaked with any colour in the hackle, breast, rump, or tail they are then termed streaky piles.

If the pile cocks have a mixture of dun (that is lead colour on the breast and shoulders) they are called dun piles; another variety of this fowl is the cuckoo which is deemed rare, that is a white fowl with the feathers variegated promiscuously, or rather barred with black and yellow.

The spangled fowl is particularly rare; it is a red fowl with the feather tipped with white, or sometimes white and black.

There is still another breed of cocks, we have to mention, called hen cocks, from their feathers being short resembling those of a hen; their colour is generally brown, or speckled, they are allowed to fight as well as any other and to be as good game; we are totally unacquainted from whence originates this breed; in fighting it frequently happens that they have an advantage in being mistaken by their antagonist cock for a hen and frequently from this are enabled to get the first blow.

When any coloured fowl has the shoulder, mixed with black such cock is denominated beezy shouldered, a term whose origin we are not acquainted with, probably from the French word *bis*, black or dusky.

The legs as forming part of the description and character of the cock should also be noticed. These are either yellow, blue, white, olive or dark green willow, or light green, black or carp legged, a mixture of black and yellow; the beaks in general correspond with the colour of the legs.

The eyes are also an object of attention, being a point in the match pile; the red or ferret eye (the iris being red); the pale yellow, or daweye; the dark brown, or sloe eye.

Other qualities of the cock remain to be considered; they constitute important properties in the battle, these properties consist in the specific weight of the cock, in regard to his bulk, as a large cock may not only feel light in hand, but weigh light in the scale, his bone and flesh being of a lighter quality, while others, though much less shall outweigh him; and such are commonly distinguished by the phrase, lumpy cocks, while the others are termed corky or light, like cork, which is of more value in the match, as the larger cock has the advantage.

The constitution, or rather healthy condition, of the cock is also necessary to be known; this is more readily ascertained than would be imagined; first by the feather, as we have before stated, being sound, and difficult to be drawn out, short, smooth, hard and shining, his crowing with a shrill and clear voice; his looking red in the face; if white, or pale in that point, or if he pants much, and turns blackish after exercise, it is presumed, with tolerable certainty, that he is diseased and unsound ; that he is unfit for the pens or the battle.

The next consideration in the *fighting cock* is the spur ; to hit well with the spur is as necessary as to have *courage*, or any other good quality, as without this all the other qualities may be thrown away ; this however, is not known from any exterior indication but by actual trial, and is not confined to any particular colour or breed. The piles often are observed to carry a fatal spur, without having so much GAME as the other breeds, especially if the battle be of long duration.

And next of the *game*, or *blood* of the fowl ; for by this term is indicated his *courage*, or rather his endurance of the battle ; this property is so extraordinary in some of these animals, that they *fight* obstinately to the last, and by these means, though apparently beaten *gain* the battle.

Action in fighting, to be excellent, should be rapid without hurrying ; quick but cautious ; to break well with their adversary, that is on the first onset to throw off or parry the blow, and then to hit ; for if they strike and hit together at the onset, it is not unusual to see the *thigh* or *wing* broken, or the spur pass through the body of one or both. It is of consequence also that in the early part of the battle, they should strike without laying hold, and keep a distance, as laying hold in the *beginning* of the battle, is almost useless, but not so when the first efforts are past, and they become a little weary.

It is usual for the cock to aim at the head with the beak, but his stroke is known to be more fatal when he lay hold of the point of the wing, as in this case the spur enters some part of the body or the wing, and disables the fowl more certainly.

A cock is said to fight well at the foot when he has obtained an advantage and follows it up till he has killed his adversary, never suffering him to rise *after being once down.*

THE OLD ENGLISH MODE OF BREEDING.

FROM REES' ENCYCLOPÆDIA.

A well tried breed of cocks being obtained from actual observation of their powers, are to be used as the stock to be bred from, and it should be observed that it has been found injurious to breed from two old fowls; on one side or the other they should be young and three or four hens are fully sufficient for one cock, and, the hens should be all of one breed, and if the colours are somewhat alike so much the better, as they unite the more kindly.

The breeding place should be well aired and kept entirely free from other poultry; clear water, grass, gravel, and lime rubbish, an occasional change of food as barley, oats, potatoes boiled and sometimes a little meat and toast and beer, also to be recommended.

The hen house should be perfectly dry and clean, and the roost with perches rather low, as otherwise the heavy fowls jar their feet coming down and occasion them to swell and become crippled.

The perches should be carefully made of the proper size for the grasp of the foot, not being too large or too small, as in the former case the hind claw as brought forward, and he becomes what is called duck clawed, and in the battle the breast bone becomes crooked.

There are several injurious things to the health of the fowls, which should be carefully kept away from their breeding place, as anything which tends to soil the water they drink; the keeping of pigs, ducks, or allowing them access to coal ashes, or any soapsuds, are found by experience to produce the roop; geese and turkies are injurious to fowls, by continually fighting and battering them, and should not be allowed to be near them.

The nests of the hens many be about a foot and a half from the ground, made in an earthen pan or dish of a proper size and clean straw, rubbed up so as to render it soft. Hay is found by experience to be injurious to the eggs, and to more readily produce vermin; and its faint smell seems also not to suit them.

There should be nests for every hen, and even their number should be rather more than less than the number of hens, as otherwise they are apt to fight and disturb one another from the nests, and break the eggs.

One egg should be always left in the nest for them to lay to, and that should be marked, that it may be easily known. Also the eggs as they are laid should be removed from the nest and marked with the date of their being laid and the hen laying them and be placed in a box of bran and now and then if laid on the side be turned over; they are however considered best placed with the small end downwards, as it has been found by experience that they keep better in this position, and the following reason is alleged for this effect, the shape of the shell which is a reversed cone, forms a support to the yolk, and prevents its descending to the shell.

When a hen begins to cluck or be brooding no more of her eggs should be saved, as from this time her eggs are apt to become imperfect, are frequently within yolks and often without shells; cockers have a notion that the fowl bred from a clucking hen will not show the same game and bottom as those produced by her first eggs.

If two clutches are wanted from any hen in one season it is effected more certainly by putting her first clutch of eggs under a dunghill hen and putting the game hen under a coop where the other hens are about her, till her heat is over, when she may be set at liberty; whereas by removing her she is forgotten, and when brought back to the other hens fighting ensues.

The next or second clutch she might be allowed to set upon herself.

When a cock takes a dislike to any brooding or other hen, she should be removed, as he would otherwise injure or destroy her.

About 12 eggs form a proper clutch, as the hen cannot well cover more, when the first chickens are hatched they may be taken away and placed in a basket with flannel or wool by the fireside, and be fed with crumbs of bread, then they should be placed with the hen at night, as she otherwise might take a dislike and kill them.

The eggs being all hatched, at least, those that are sound and good, the hen and chickens should be conveyed into some dry place, where cats or vermin of any kind cannot get at them.— The hen should be cooped to prevent her from wandering from the brood, and getting into wet, and dirty places.

The chickens are best fed with crumbs of bread and hard boiled eggs chopped up with it, and this occasionally changed with advantage for groats or grits, wheat, chopped raw meat, or new cheese and curds, till they are able to eat barley, as they are apt in a short time to clog with any one kind of food, to pine and die. They should have clean water, at least once a day, and it should be placed out of the sun. About the end of the third or fourth week it is well to set the hen at liberty with her chickens, taking care that she is not annoyed by other hens.

One advantage attends bringing them up under the dunghill hen, which is that she is less quarrelsome or subject to be disturbed by other hens.

It is a false notion of old times, that the chickens brought under a dunghill hen will partake of her properties, which is well known by experienced breeders to be untrue.

It is advisable, when the chickens are at an age that their sexes can be distinguished, as at about six weeks or two months old, to select those intended to be kept and to destroy the rest as the survivors thrive better, and it prevents the brood from being too much distributed, for it is better to purchase fowl for the spit than to keep these to the injury of the rest, unless where the sole object in breeding them is the table.

In about four months it is usual for them to begin to crow, and this is the right time to cut their combs, as cutting them early is thought to prevent their fighing together, and they also lose less blood than if cut later, when the difficulty of stopping it is greater, as it is necessary then to use the cautery, or a styptic, for the cautery cannot be conveniently applied between the two surfaces or lobes of the comb. In about a few weeks after this or when they are sent to their walks, their gills and deaf ears may be taken off, by which term is understood a loose fleshy whitish carbuncle behind the ear. Some cut the comb close, called the "low comb;" others leave an arched portion which is termed the "high comb."

About this period of the young fowl, a disaster frequently happens which should be carefully guarded against; which is, that they will, without any apparent cause fight and destroy each other, and we think we have observed to happen more frequently after rain than at other times; perhaps from their being wetted, soiled and disfigured, they may appear strange to each other, and thus are led to begin fighting; at least this is the most probable reason that has occurred to us.

If this happens before they can with propriety be separated for different walks, it will be found necessary to pursue a certain measure to prevent their fighting; this is usually accomplished by separating them after fighting and keeping them for some time without food; another discipline to prevent this evil consists in holding the weakest in your hand, while the strongest spurs and pecks him till he cries out, or by beating him with a glove or handkerchief he will afterwards be satisfied with being subordinate for a long time; otherwise they are fighting and picking or pulling the skin from the skull often in a way that they never recover from, and such are called peel pates, and are not allowed in a main.

This state of discipline and subordination will be promoted by the presence of the old cock among them who will so interfere in their battles, as to awe them to a more peaceful demeanour, and this the more effectually if all the hens are removed.

They should now, before they are sent to their walks, be marked, and a regular register be kept of them. The marks are generally made in the eyelid, nostril or connecting membrane of the toes by cutting a notch in one or more of them; and are described as right, left, or both eyes or nostrils out or in right or left feet.

Having premised thus far in raising them, it is now our business to speak of the most appropriate walk, which is often among experienced cockers even in some respect not sufficiently attended to. Farm-houses are not always good walks for the reason above mentioned, that the game chickens get battered by other fowls. Poor cottages where they are generally walked, have this disadvantage, that they have not sufficient food; a clear air—good food—pure water, and perfect seclusion from other fowls are the best requisites on a walk of this kind, at any rate it is proper they are taken up for fighting that they should be seen, and such as want it be fed, or, as is called hand-fed.

At about a twelvemonth old they are termed stags, and at two years old they are called cocks. It may be desirable to try the breed while they are yet stags, in which case the least valuable are selected; such for instance as are shorter legged than the rest, or are in any respect deficient in their make; from these trials we may be led to presume upon the courage and action of the rest of the brood, and for this purpose the stag may be fought against a cock of the same weight to ascertain his qualities.

Short silver spurs, in these trial battles are better than steel ones, as they are not so immediately destructive, and a stag that beats a cock of equal weight must have undeniable good qualities even though he afterwards wins no other battle.

At two years old he becomes a cock, as we have observed, and is then fit for fighting in the main, or single battles. It still remains, however, ere we bring him on the stage, to describe the regimen requisite to give him the greatest prospect of advantage, and a successful issue to the contest; as a well prepared fowl will have the advantage of a superior one that is ill fed or not prepared.

The fowl is supposed to come from his walk in good condition; in which case he will be too fat for fighting and will have no wind till he is reduced. To effect this, medicine and abstinence from food are required for seven or eight days before he can be brought to the pit, at least such is the regimen pursued by our first feeders, and is pretty generally as follows: His tail and spurs being cut short, he is put into his pens, and the first day receives no food; Second, he has physic consisting of cream of tartar or Jalap, or both united, in the dose of about five grains of each; or if it be a very fat and large fowl the dose may be increased to ten grains of cream of tartar. These are given him mixed in fresh butter; this generally purges briskly, and scours out the intestines. Immediately after the physic is given him and before it affects him, he is placed on loose straw or a grass plat with another cock and allowed to spar with him, the boots or muffles being previously tied on their short spurs. In this way he is exercised till he is a battle-weary; he is then returned to his pens. Before putting him up it is necessary to examine his mouth to see if he has been picked or wounded in the inside, as such wound is apt to canker. To prevent this, it is washed with a little vinegar and brandy; he now is allowed his warm mess to work off his physic. This is a diet made of warm ale or sweet wort, and bread in it, with a little sugar candy; or bread and milk and sugar candy; a large tea cup full.

He is then shut up close till the next morning, or about 24 hours. If the weather is cold, the room should be made warm or a blanket placed over the pen; if in warm weather he may be clipped out for fighting; but if the weather be cold this is best left till the time of fighting. The windows of the room should also be darkened, excepting at feeding times.

Early on the following morning, that is, about the third day, his pen must be cleaned out from the effects of the physic, &c., and clean dry straw be given him; his feet also should be washed and wiped clean before he is returned to his pen; if his feet feel cold his pen should be made warmer.

He is next to be allowed some cock bread, that is, a sort of bread made of ingredients in the following proportions: About three pounds of fine flour and two eggs, and four whites of eggs, and a little yeast; this is kneaded with a sufficiency of water for a proper consistence, and is sent to the oven and well baked; some add as a great secret, a small number of aniseeds, or a little cinnamon; of this bread as much as would fill a tea-cup, cut into pieces is given to him twice that day; and no water is then given him whatever as it is considered highly injurious at the early part of the feeding.

On the fourth day early in the morning he should receive half a tea-cup full of good brandy, and a little water, in which toast has been steeped some time. Having eaten this, clean his pen, let him be supplied with clean straw, and let his pen be uncovered for about an hour while he scratches and picks the straw. Some think it highly advantageous to prepare the barley for them by beating and bruising it, and thus to take away the sharp points of the barley and the husky shell or covering which is then blown away.

In the afternoon, the same quantity of barley should be repeated, but no water.

On the fifth, or next day, he may have the bread as before, but three portions of it, and no water.

On the sixth, or weighing day, very early in the morning, give him bread as before; he is then to be weighed, and afterwards a good feed of barley and water should be given. Some hold it a valuable secret to give them flesh, as sheep's heart, for this and the succeeding day, chopped small and mixed with the other food.

On the seventh day, or the day before fighting, early in the morning, let him have the same feed of barley; in the afternoon bread and the white of an egg boiled hard, and a little water.

On the eighth, or day of fighting, he may have a little barley, as about 40 grains; some recommend it to be previously steeped in port wine, which we are not assured is at all useful. If at any period of the feeding the food should remain in his crop, no more should be given him till it is removed, which a bit of apple or cheese will assist in digesting; and should the fowl dung loose or purge, when not required it may be counteracted by giving a little hemp seed which some steep in brandy. A little wheat or millet seed may also be added to his food. Repeated trials have taught us that about 2 oz. may be taken away or superceded to the weight of a fowl for one day, by the above means without injury: about eight is as much as he should ever gain or lose in the whole.

He is next cut out for fighting, that is his wing's rounded, the hackle and saddle feathers cut shorter, the feathers about the vent cut close off, and the curly feathers of the tail, leaving only the vane or fan, which is shortened about one half. The spurs are now placed on his legs, and he is fitted for the battle; in placing his spurs on they should not be tied too tight, least he be cramped or too slack, least they get loose; for should they come off or even break, during the battle, they are not allowed to be replaced. The point of the spur should be carefully observed to be neither to the outside or inside of the hock or heel, but exactly behind, and in a line with it; the hunckle or hock is taken as a guide for its direction following that of the natural spur.

There remains for us to make one remark more to render these matters clear, which is, that, although eight days are found to be a sufficient time to prepare a fowl for battle, yet in a main, ten days are commonly taken for the purpose, pursuing a similar treatment to the foregoing. The cocks are weighed on the eighth, and the lightest begin fighting on the tenth day, so that the larger cocks, which are to fight in the latter part of the main, and have been considerably reduced, are brought up again by a greater proportion of food than the medium quantity we have described, and which ought also to be administered oftener in the day,—the success of the main often depending upon the proper management of the latter fowls, which must be left to the skill and judgment of the feeder, who ought to be intimately acquainted with the nature and constitution of the fowl, that he may be enabled to bring him to the battle in the best possible health and condition, neither distressed by medicine or abstinence, before he is weighed, nor rendered inactive by overfeeding afterwards, as, in either case he has not a fair chance for his life.

COCKS AND COCKING IN IRELAND.

CONTRIBUTED BY MARSHALL WHEELER, ESQ.

Owing to the indiscriminate crossing of the various breeds of game fowls native of and imported into Ireland, it has got to be that very many of their fowls cannot be said to belong to any breed, and take their names solely from their various colors. To so great an extent has this crossing been carried, that should a cock be obtained of a certain color which it would be desirable to perpetuate, no dependence whatever can be placed on results, for it might turn out the thing desired and it might not. A brown red cock might turn out a spangled, a gull or a white. It were an almost endless task to name over the different kinds of that country, a few therefore of the most prominent will have to suffice, to wit :

Brown reds,	Black reds,
Thrush breasted,	Spangles,
Piles,	Blue duns,
Duns,	Gipseys,
Gulls,	Birchen grays,
Whites,	Skinners,
Henfeathers, and	

Highflyers, composed of the golden and the silver pheasants. Of all these varieties the brown reds are in Ireland the "first favorites" among most cockers, on account of their general superiority as to health, strength and gameness. The black reds stand next in favor, and sometimes successfully dispute the palm of superiority with the brown reds. Instances of extraordinary good cocks are not unfrequent however among those of other colors, a white cock was once thrown out from a blue skinner; his owner fought him for three successive years against others of all weights from all the surrounding country and never lost a battle. He was finally poisoned. A cock of the henfeather variety in a main in Dublin of 21 cocks, won nine fights in succession and the main. At another main fought at Dungannon, in Tyrone county, one of this breed won five successive battles and the main. Though no positive dependence can be placed on results as to color, yet it is generally true that a brown red cock with a black hen will produce his own color; and the same is also true of a black red with a yellow hen. The thrush breasted varieties are results of a cross between Irish and English fowls; spangles and piles of certain Irish crosses; blue duns are from black or brown red cocks with blue hens; the Gipseys are an Irish cross, and are so called from a certain appearance of their countenances, which are smutty looking and feathers around their faces like a hood; the gulls, come of a blue cock and black hen; so also the birchen grays; whites are usually thrown from the Piles or spangles, though sometimes from other kinds, they are milk white; the Highflyers *it is said* by some enthusiastic sportsmen come of a cross between the Golden or Silver pheasant of Ireland and a game hen, though the tradition is worthless when it is known, that such a cross can no more perpetuate itself, than the mule, being barren; and the Henfeather variety are so called, because the cocks have tails short, like a hen, and the feathers all stick forward.

Thirty years ago cock fighting in Ireland used to be carried on to a grand extent. In Dublin a cock pit was erected enclosing an acre of ground, the roof being entirely of glass. Thither resorted the high and low breed of the land, standing upon a common level, and carried cock fighting to the height of perfection. And in the rural districts cock fighting flourished without let or hindrance, bringing all classes to a democratic level. Noblemen there were who kept the game cock keepers and feeders, as much so as a groom for their horses. Many curious anecdotes might be told of these high ones and their game cock trainers, for be it known, that the latter occasionally took the liberty of using their masters feathered bipeds without any special permission. A noble whom we will call Cook for the nonce, once kept a large number of the purest, best games for fighting. Well, his keeper (whom we will call John), one day took it into his head to bring on a half dozen of Cook's cocks to a fight that was coming off near Dublin. He did so, and bet his pile on them. Just as the fight was about to begin in came Cook, and without knowing his own cocks, put up a heavy sum on them. The fight went on, Cook's cocks came out victorious, and Cook told John to bargain for the lot, as he had nowhere before seen cocks which he thought were so near the equals of his own at home. John hesitated, turned red and stammered out the truth, when Cook was so pleased thereat, (for the cocks had whipped a rival noble's), that he had a coach-and-four got up, and took John and the birds home in triumph, and afterwards employed a painter to take the pictures of the cocks.

The system of feeding for a fight was and is much the same that is practiced in this country. Sometimes in case of sudden necessities, a fat cock whom it was desirable to bring down as soon as possible, would be put upon a swinging rope over night and not allowed a moment's rest, which, together with the usual purgative, usually brought several ounces lighter in 8 to 12 hours, though the practice was not a good one, and never used when it could be avoided.

After the law had been passed against cock-fighting, the practice had to be followed more privately, and many amusing scenes were the consequence. At a cock-fight in Dublin one night, the police came in upon the crowd and "sich a gittin up stairs you never did see" by all of the crowd, except one fellow, who was one of the main men at the main, and who ran about the pit catching the cocks, putting them into bags and handing them over to the police, as if he had just come in with them and was anxious to break up the whole concern. "We don't want the cocks," said the police: "But what the d———l shall be done with them—they will get them and go to fighting them again, if they are left here," replied *the stranger*. "Then we deputize *you* to take care of them," said the chief of the party; and thus did the *proprietor* save his own and his opponents cocks, and they fought them afterwards.

But the palmy days of this sport are among the things of the past. Still cock-fighting may one day revive in all its pristine vigor and glory under new influences and new laws. It shall so be when the people of Ireland as a mass shall so determine.

PECULIARITIES OF GAMES.

When young game cocks begin to feather they generally show their pugnacious propensities by sparring, but this is not long continued before the blood warms up, and a fight is the result. Stags and pullets alike contest the mastership, and only cease as a rule when swelled heads, bunged eyes and physical prostration compel them. In the process of recovery, one or two, yet more pugnacious than their fellows, resume the fight, which ends, after many days, in victory to the strongest or quickest, and then all of that hatch seem to acknowledge the sway of the victor, and willingly assume a position known as "under cow." The youthful victor will remain "boss of his walk" for from four to eight months, if all are kept in the same flock, and no untoward events transpire. Exceptions to the rule are found in the "boss" becoming disfigured in some way, so that his comrades fail to recognize him, and when this is the case a free fight is pretty sure to follow, not unfrequently ending in the death of one or more on the walk.

A good plan is, after young chicks have fought awhile, catch and dip their heads in water, and after separating them until they stiffen from exertion or cold, let them run together again.

At the age of from six to eight months the stags should be put upon separate walks, but if these cannot readily be obtained put two or three upon the same walk, being first satisfied that one is completely boss over his companionis. There is then danger in leaving them long together, for age and blood alike begin to tell, and the policy is to separate at earliest convenience.

When two or more game cocks are placed in the same neighborhood, say not over a quarter of a mile apart, and there are sufficient hens with each, trouble will not often arise, for each will apparently mark out his own territory, and while he will protect it against invasion, he will rarely invade that of his neighbor, unless he be more than usually savage and restless. But there are times when the tamest and most petted games will trespass, and then the sequel is death unless there be opportune interference.

Different strains and breeds have different dispositions, easily made manifest to the close observer. All will see traits of character and marks of intelligence in the game such as are not to be found in any other breed of fowls, and it is reasonable to suppose that games differ in a less degree. We have seen games possessing as much sagacity as many valued breeds of dogs; and know of a hotel keeper in New York who not long ago reaped much profit from having a game cock to mount his bar and sip and enjoy wine with all his admiring customers. A sketch of this noted cock was given in *Wilkes' Spirit of the Times* in 1860.

We could, if it were necessary, give many instances of *tameness* in game cocks, the docility of some being thrown off only in the presence of actual preparations for battle, and we never knew an experienced cocker to esteem this quality a positive fault.

Some cocks are very wild, and will loudly quack when caught, but there are few which will not tame when boxed or prepared for the pit. When they refuse to tame after ordinary care, we are very apt to suspect a fault in blood, and would not run the risk of either breeding from or pitting them, more especially if the " quack" bears any resemblance to the " Squawk," which is one of the marked characteristics of dung-hills. The difference in the sounds is easily distinguished by any one at all familiar with games.

Savage cocks are much admired by many cockers and fanciers, and as a rule, in the rough-and-tumble fight have an advantage. They sometimes, however, when engaged in battle in the pit, turn on their handlers, and by so doing give the opposing cock a chance to recover wind or strike a fatal blow ; so that in view of this danger, they are not more desirable for pit or other purposes than extremely tame ones.

Cocks sometimes become "crowed down" while in keeping for the pit. It is yet a mooted question whether such are games or not. We have seen them tested, after recovering spirit, and they have stood all ordinary tests applied. But we would never advise any one ever to enter such a fowl, and would discourage breeding from him.

There are others again, which will not crow down under keeping, which will enter and carry themselves admirably in the pit, but will, when the battle is over, and when they are cold, and stiff and sore from wounds, cow down and refuse to show fight until such time as they have partially or fully recovered. Then, they are as good as at first, and quite as reliable in a fight. This, perhaps, does not so much argue absence of gameness, as weakness of blood and want of general tone. Well-crossed fowls seldom show this trait. It is at all times an objectionable one, and can only be removed by a change of the mode of breeding, or by carefully crossing with fresh and vigorous stock. It shows the necessity of a cocker having a direct or near control of the breeding of his stock, so that he may at all times be thoroughly acquainted with the dispositions of such as he has important use for.

As regards the peculiarities of stags, there are those of different strains and breeds, which, if they have run boss for but a short time, will stand the steel when seven months old ; but these are mostly confined to small breeds and strains. Others will not stand the steel until nine months old ; and yet others, mostly large breeds, cannot be relied upon until they are twelve months old. All, of any breed or strain, must as a rule be first in good heart before they will stand.

A large sized stag, therefore, should not be condemned until after he reaches the age of one year, and been trained under favorable circumstances. We have had stags, large and apparently overgrown, which, when a year old would assume their natural symmetry, and were then as courageous and anxious for battle as any other.

There is an old saying, rather a superstition, prevalent with cockers and fanciers, "that there is no full cluck of chickens but that one of them will run away."

We pronounce it at best a superstition, unfounded in fact, and wanting in every element of logic. It doubtless arose from the old English practice of refusing to allow the hatching of eggs which had been laid by the hen when in heat, or when nearly approaching her time of setting. But it was the practice to condemn "clucking eggs," not because they failed in any attribute of gameness, but because there were natural causes which argued their lack of vitality, and which made it self-evident, to the thoughts of these men at least, that chicks from such eggs would not be as muscular, compact, or vigorous, as those from other eggs. This idea gave rise to the habit of throwing out "clucking eggs," and the practice, witnessed but not fully comprehended by more ignorant men, gave rise to a superstition which is modified in form, so as to deny the gameness of *one* of a cluck. If it were now true, it was coeval with the origin of games, and it would not be difficult to prove mathematically, with the superstition as a basis, that we have now no pure games, that any such are unknown to the world—a statement which would be classed as absurd in the minds of any one.

If the doctrine of the one egg were true, we would go a step farther, and say that *two* of every cluck will run—the two selected being from the egg last laid before setting, and the one laid immediately after the previous setting—if the hen be in her second stage of motherhood; for the last egg is usually laid after the hen has commenced setting, and the first after the previous setting, before she is done with her chicks. It is usual with old cockers to throw aside these two eggs, some perhaps, from superstitious motives, but intelligent ones certainly from a desire to rear fowls of stong blood and full physical strength.

That which is based upon good reason has thus become miserably perverted. All who know anything of fowls know that while their eggs are in embryo, there is generally a number of them, all more or less connected. These are given embryotic growth by the blood of the cock and hen, are at all times permeated by the blood which circulates within and through the hen, and if one were to be faulty in this respect, all must be.— But the fact that the hen has less generative and less physicial power while clucking, or while feeding her young, is calculated to impair the strength of the offspring, just as we see a child born of sickly parents, but the fault goes no farther than that ; and while the chicks from such eggs are not desirable acquisitions to any poultry yard, they are so for these reasons, and these reasons alone.

We have said that many old cockers are in the habit of throwing aside the cluck egg ; many others refuse to use both kinds of eggs above described, and we justify the refusal, for the reasons stated.

We will also, upon similar grounds, justify the destruction of all deformed eggs.

There is yet another superstition we are anxious to dissipate, and cannot do it more conveniently than by quoting a part of one of the author's letters to *Wilkes' Spirit of the Times*, written over the signature of "Game Fancier," as follows :—

"As a general thing, sporting men are freer from superstitions than any other class, and at first thought, one is almost led to hoot at the idea of any portion of them being guilty of that which their very practice seems to deny. Yet the charge can be successfully maintained in a few instances, and it is a credit to them that they are few, though 'twere greater honor were there none. I have noticed among several cockers, whose experience should teach them better, a practice, which they attempt to sustain by reason and practical results, but which in reality is denied by both. Their custom is this : Never to set those eggs that have been laid after twelve o'clock in the day, and invariably selecting those laid in the morning. They argue the eggs laid after that hour (make the time meridian, or mid-day,) are *weaker* than those laid in the morning. As a clincher to this, and to drive the nail deeper, they assert that hens *always* begin to lay, first in the morning, quite early, and every succeeding day, a little later, until they finally cease ; contending that the first are strongest ; that the powers of the hen are exhausted,

or nearly so, when she has laid the first half of her complement of eggs.—
This is their belief—one which, if not disastrous, leads to great waste, and
chokes the birth of many a gallant fowl. I hold that good game eggs are
too scarce for only half to be used, and am therefore led to inquire into the
truth or fallacy of a doctrine tending to the almost wholesale destruction of
games; and which, if carried out, would rid the world of half its feathered
tribe. In the first place, the idea is rank with error, that all hens *commence*
laying in the morning, a fact sustained by every line of physiology, and upheld by the example of every female thing which has the power to conceive.
Embryo eggs, like the *fœtus* in the womb, have a certain stated existence,
governed by *time* and circumstances, upon which depends its birth; and is
it not ridiculously preposterous to tell us that the time of each and every
hen commences and ends together; that the conceivements which give rise
to the eggs, all took place at the same moment? As well might it be maintained that mankind are all born at the same hour. Any man who has ever
carved a hen can bear me out in saying that frequently a clutch of eggs is
found, all varying in size, and it is reasonable to suppose that each must
undergo a certain time before they are laid, while it is strikingly apparent
that all hens are *not* in the same state, that at least, the eggs of different hens
are not all at the same stage of maturity, and hence it follows, that the first
eggs are as liable to be laid in the afternoon as in the morning. This at once
shows that the belief above alluded to is merely a superstition, unsustained
by physiology, reason, or known results. The opinion that the first eggs
laid are strongest, is equally erroneous.

"The carrying out of this belief will not suit under any circumstances;
but if the hen *by chance* commences to lay early in the morning, and later
each succeeding day, and becomes restive and desirous of setting before
laying a full complement of eggs, it may then be policy to allow her to set,
in some cases, because, if long delayed, the desire may be overcome before
the chicks are hatched, and they become weakened by her leaving the nest
too frequently. But this is merely *chance*, and is not founded on any correct
principle."

Deformed chicks are frequently seen. These are in many cases due to setting eggs that have not had a regular shape, and are sometimes peculiar to the hen which laid the egg, owing to some deformity in her. From eggs, peculiar from the last mentioned cause, only the most perfect ones should be selected and used; though we believe the better economy to be the cooking of the hen. But if their use is insisted upon, because of some valuable qualities in the hen, and you should mix them with other eggs, mark them plainly with a pencil, and watch the hatching and growth, so that like deformities may not extend throughout your yard.

By the same process of marking, the cluck eggs can be detected and removed.

Game hens are not devoid of some peculiarities. We have had them to catch mice with industry equal to that of the cat, though doubtless from a very different motive. Such a hen will seize a mouse with her bill, and holding it up, will strike with the legs until the mouse is killed ; and some of them will afterwards eat his dead mouseship. In early life we once saw a game cock attack a garter snake, and after he had killed it, attempt to swallow it whole. As may well be imagined, we were greatly surprised at so uncommon a spectacle, and watched the result with interest. The cock, with apparent ease, soon had half the snake (small in size, of course) down his throat ; too far down to relinquish his task. After many attempts he succeeded in mastering his snakeship, and depositing him in his crop. The cock afterward picked gravel, as though nothing unusual had transpired. Day after day we went to see him, supposing he would die from the effect, but we never discovered that he was any the worse from his singular meal.

Last year (1868) we had an Eslin stag running on a walk at Mr. Jefferies, on the Brandywine, in Chester county, Penn'a.— One day Mr. Jefferies had occasion to go down to the creek, and while there saw his hens with their heads and necks extended at full length, looking with astonishment at some object, and chattering in their peculiar chicken language. The stag, which was first at some little distance off, was soon attracted by the chattering, which was doubtless fully understood by him. When he reached the position of the hens, he espied the object of their solicitude, which was nothing less than a water snake, twenty-eight inches in length. The stag immediately, and with remarkable strength of bill, seized the snake by the neck, and holding him out, flayed him mercilessly with his spurs, notwithstanding the snake was winding and twisting all the time, in its endeavors to release itself. He thus flayed the snake until it seemed beaten into a soft mass. It was certainly remarkable in a game stag, not a year old, to attack so large a snake, and perhaps nothing but the fear that his hens were in danger, induced him to do it.

It is a well established fact that both game cocks and hens frequently master hawks;—a game hen will at all times turn upon one if she cannot otherwise protect her young.

We once had a game cock, a cross between the Tartar and Strychnine, which was almost useless for all breeding purposes, because of his extreme savageness. He was apparently regardless of, and certainly very inattentive to the hens, most of his time being employed in displaying his pugnacity. He would strike anything and everything that came in his way, whether man, beast or post, and was almost constantly on the rampage. When he could get nothing else to strike at, he would take his wing and tear and batter it, as though he enjoyed the luxury of suicide. This was virtually his ending, for he died from the effects of picking and beating himself. With all his savageness, we never knew him to strike his hens, but in all other respects lacked consideration for them. He was not only useless for breeding purposes, but never could have been satisfactorily handled in the pit.

It is contended by many experienced cockers that no matter how game a cock may be, if struck by the gaffle in his testicles or generative organs, he will not stand. One in whom we place much confidence, at a fight in Wilmington, Delaware, had a cock so wounded, and he ran. He was told the cause by an English cocker present, and after he got him home he killed and dissected him, discovering a mass of coagulated blood in the generative organs, and the marks of the gaffle. He afterwards tested with the steel all the brothers of this chicken, and all of them stood till dead. It is needless to say that he has now adopted this belief. Handlers in the pit, acting under a similar belief, are sometimes rascally enough to squeeze the fowls, not alone with the view to cripple them, but by painfully compressing their generative organs, to place them under cow.

Fowls have peculiarities in fighting, and these sometimes extend to strains and breeds. The rule will not always hold good, as evidenced by the fact that some derived their name from their method of fighting.

SHUFFLERS are so called because in fighting they constantly shuffle, tumble, and strike in a pell-mell, rough-and-tumble way. They generally strike low, as for the body, and seldom reach the head of an opponent. Fowls of this kind should always be fought with a long gaffle, say two, or even two-and-a-half inches, according to the size of the fowl; for the reason that where body blows alone are struck, the gaffle should be long enough to penetrate and fatally wound. It is a good rule, when you are obliged to use short gaffles, to select a cock which strikes high and parries well. Such cocks, with short gaffles, have a decided advantage over Shufflers; but with long ones, the advantage is not apparent, or if so, is in favor of the Shuffler.

Some cocks are in the habit of stooping or squatting when an opponent makes a blow, and as soon as the other misses and goes over him he will wheel about and strike before the other is sufficiently recovered to renew the combat. Such cocks are dangerous, and to many very desirable.

The WHEELERS are so called from their mode of fighting.— Some of them are so addicted to, or the habit is so natural with them, that they will wheel after the third or fourth blow. While they are not desirable, they will often win the majority of battles by their style of fighting.

Others are known as square, stand-up fighters—never dogging or flinching. These fight with a will, and strike with or without a bill hold. They are in all respects pertinacious, and when they get a good hold, they will frequently strike until the force of their own or the opponent's blows breaks it, and when thus broken, will quickly strike again, as though to quickly revenge their mishap, or to prevent the competitor from taking any sudden advantage of the position of affairs. This is almost universally esteemed first-class fighting, not alone for the beauty of the style, but because such cocks generally do good execution, and because they seem the more directly to answer all the needs of true gameness.

There are peculiar marks in shape and station, some breeds and strains being lofty, of lenthy leg; while others are squatty or low-set. Cocks, lengthy in leg, do not always stand well upon them, but many do, and where this quality is well exhibited, it is not alone valuable, but adds greatly to the beauty of the fowl—provided the plumage, in fullness and richness, accords with the stature.

Frequently fowls low set in the legs, stand up well, and hold the body in a position which is beautiful in its elevation. From long dealing in games we find a great majority prefer fowls of good stature and long and strong legs;—we speak of long legs for games, not for shanghiæs. Many believe that the long-legged, high-headed cock has a great advantage in *reach*, and is in most respects the best and strongest hitter in battle, and that they have, as well, an advantage in billing.

It is a mistake to suppose that the high-standing, long-legged cocks have always an advantage over low-set adversaries. We have frequently known high-stationed cocks to be poor hitters, a hesitating or cautious style of fighting giving even a much smaller opponent the advantage; occasionally, also, you will find one a poor biller, and when these two qualities are combined, such cocks are not profitable in the pit, however good may be their blood.

We have frequently seen low-set cocks, when placed in the pit, straighten themselves up to an apparently unnatural height, increasing in stature in the excitement of meeting an enemy.— These fowls are generally very nervous, energetic and excellent in battle.

There is no rule in stature, color, or shape, in selecting a fowl for superior fighting qualities. There is certainly none which can be intelligently described. Much depends upon individual judgment, yet more upon a careful study of the characteristics of your fowls.

All cockers ought to frequently try their fowls by sparring them with the mitts on. A tolerably correct judgment can then be reached of both striking and billing qualities.

A fowl that is tenacious in his hold is desirable, no matter what his size, for the reason that he is apt to be almost constantly fighting, gains much valuable time over his opponent, and follows his blows with exhausting rapidity.

High-standing cocks, quick at billing, sometimes depend too much upon this quality, and neglect that of striking. Frequent sparring and training will often correct this evil, especially when sparred with a cock larger and a better striker than himself at first, and then alternating the sparring with a smaller and yet poorer striking cock. He is thus forced to realize the disadvantage he places himself under, and the change to a contest in which he can practice on the knowledge acquired, is always beneficial.

When one wishes to procure good fighters, and has not the advantage of making a personal selection, he should determine upon those belonging to well-approved breeds or strains ; and if he desires a peculiar style of fighting, the names of several strains will give him an opportunity to select intelligently.

All game fowls should only be purchased from dealers in whom the buyer has the utmost confidence, or where known references are at hand.

Some strains and breeds are throughout noted for their fighting qualities—few of the stock doing anything that will injure a hard-earned reputation. In yet other strains and breeds the reverse is sometimss true, and the quicker the use of these is abandoned, the better it will be for all parties concerned. It is a waste of money to purchase stock—a waste of valuable time to breed from it—and in the pit too much risk is run.

Fanciers and cockers have frequently become entirely disheartened by what they have styled their "bad run of luck," whereas, if careful study had been given to the characteristics and to the breed of the fowls employed, they would have found other and better reasons for their misfortunes.

When a cocker loses his money on a good, hard-fighting cock, he is generally content, for he knows that by his calling he has pledged himself to risk all the ordinary mishaps of battle, and as a rule he does not grudge the money thus lost. No confidence is violated, and his opinion of himself and his fowls remains as before. It is only in contests of this kind that "bad luck" can of right enter.

"Luck" is too much in vogue, especially in the minds and purposes of those who are inexperienced. There is no need in a love of the sport being constantly coupled with imprudence, or with too much risk. "Luck" should at no time enter into a calculation, as long as it can be kept out, for even when it is triumphant the pleasure derived is not half so great as that acquired by a careful study of the characteristics of one's fowls, the training of them, and the realization that the victory attained is ni part due to your own labors.

All fanciers should carefully study the peculiarities of any strain of games they may have in their possession, or of any fowl upon which they place much store; for herein the greater part of the pleasure of the amateur is derived. The advice is of no need to old cockers, for there never was a successful one yet but that intuitively learned its importance, and at all times kept up the practice. It is really their chief pleasure, for many of them, well-to-do in the world, look upon the battle only as a test of their own judgment.

RULES OF THE PIT.

RULES AND REGULATIONS FOR THE BOSTON UNION CLUB COCK PIT.

ART. 1st. All fowls brought to the pit must be weighed and marked down, for those to see that have fowls to fight.

2d. Fowls within two ounces are a match.

3d. A Stag is allowed four ounces when he fights a Cock.

4th. A Blinker is allowed four ounces when he fights a sound fowl.

5th. Fowls being ready, brought to the pit.

6th. Each man takes his station, and sets his fowl to the right or left, as he pleases, there remains till the fowls are in one another, or in the tan, or on his back.

7th. The handler shall not assist his fowl from where he sits him, if he does, he forfeits the battle.

8th. In no case shall they handle the fowls, unless they are in one another, or can count ten between fighting.

9th. The fowls in hand, each man to his station; either counting ten, the fowls must be set, or the delinquent loses the match.

10th. The fowls, set, either refuses to show fight, the last that showed has the count, which is five times ten, and then they are breasted.

11th. The fowls are breasted at every five times ten, after once breasted.

12th. The fowls brought to the breast, the one that had the count counts five times ten more, and then twenty; then he claims the battle, which is his.

13th. In case the fowls show while counting, it destroys the count, and they commence again.

14th. In case a fowl is on his back, his handler can turn him over.

15th. In all cases the parties can select Judges from the company present.

16th. In case there are no Judges, it will be left to the keeper of the pit.

17th. In no cases shall any person talk with the handlers while the fowls are fighting.

18th. All disorderly persons will be requested to leave IMMEDIATELY.

19th. All weighing will be left to a man selected for the purpose.

20th. All matches will be fought with round heels, unless otherwise agreed upon.

21st. A man known to use any other, unless agreed upon, forfeits the battle.

22d. All cutters, slashers and twisted heels are barred from this pit.

23d. In all cases the last fowl that shows fight, has the count.

24th. All fowls brought to the pit that do not show fight, do not lose the battle, unless otherwise agreed upon.

☞ *Gentlemen are requested not to Smoke in this Room.*

NEW YORK RULES.

For the following we are indebted to James Connor, a writer in the *New York Clipper:*

NEW YORK RULES ON COCKING.

Art. 1. The pit shall be a circular pit, at least eighteen feet in diameter, and not less than sixteen inches in height—the floor of which shall be covered with carpet, or some other suitable material; there shall be a chalk or other mark made as near as can be to the centre of the pit; there shall also be two marks, which shall be one foot each way from the centre mark.

2. The pitters shall each choose and judge, who shall chose a referee—said judges shall decide all matters in dispute during the pendence of a fight; but in case of their inability to agree, then it shall be the duty of the referees to decide and whose decision shall be final.

3. Chickens shall take their age from the first day of March, and shall be a chicken during the following fighting season, to wit: From the first day of March, 1859, to the first day of June, 1860.

4. It shall be deemed foul for either of the respective pitters to pit a cock with what is termed a foul hackle, that is, any of the shining feathers left whole upon the mane or neck.

5. The pitters shall let each cock bill each other three or more times, but this is not to be so construed that the pitter of a cock has a right to bill with his opponent's cock for the purpose of fatiguing him,

6. No person shall be permitted to handle his cock after he is fairly delivered in the pit, unless he counts ten, clear and distinct, without either cock making fight: or shall be fast in his adversary, or fast in the carpet, or hung in the web of the pit, or in himself.

7. Any cock that may get on his back the pitter thereof shall turn him off it, but not take him off the ground he is lying on.

8. Whenever a cock is fast in his adversary, the pitter of the cock the spurs are fast in shall draw them out; but the pitter of a cock has no right to draw

his own spur except when fast in himself, or in the carpet, or in the web of the pit.

9. When either pitter shall have counted ten times successively, without the cock refusing fight making fight, again breasting them fair on their feet, breast to breast and beak to beak on the centre score or mark, on the fifth ten being told, and also on the ninth ten being told, shall have won the fight. The pitters are bound to tell each ten as they count them, as follows : once, twice, etc.

10. No pitter, after the cocks have been delivered in the pit, shall be permitted to clean their beaks or the eyes, by blowing or otherwise, or of squeezing his cock or pressing him against the floor, during the pendency of a fight.

11. When a cock is pounded, and no person take it until the pitter counts twenty twice, and calls three times "who takes it?" and no person does take it, it is a battle to the cock the odds are on ; but the pitter of the pounded cock has the right to have the pound put up, that is, twenty dollars against one ; should not this demand be complied with, then the pitter shall go on as though there was no poundage.

12. If a cock is pounded and the poundage taken, and if the cock the odds are laid against should get up and knock down his adversary, then if the other cock is pounded and the poundage not taken before the pitter counts twenty twice, and calls out three times "who takes it?" he wins, although there was a poundage before.

13. It shall be the duty of the respective pitters to deliver their cocks fair on their feet on the outer mark, or score, facing each other, and in a standing position, except on the fifth ten being told, and also on the ninth ten being told, when they shall be placed on the centre score, breast to breast and beak to beak, in like manner. Any pitter being guilty of shoving his cock across the score, or of pinching him, or using any other unfair means for the purpose of making his cock fight, shall lose the fight.

14. If both cocks fight together, and if then both should refuse until they are counted out, in such cases a fresh cock is to be hoveled and brought into the pit, and the pitters are to toss for which cock is so set-to first ; he that wins the toss has the choice ; then the one which is to set-to last is to be taken up, but not carried off the pit ; then the hoveled cock is to be put down to the other and let fight, whilst the judges or one of them shall count twenty, and the other in like manner ; and if one fight and the other refuse, it is a battle to the fighting cock ; but if both fight, or both refuse, it is a drawn battle.

15. If both cocks refuse fighting until four, five, or more or less tens are counted, the pitters shall continue their count until one cock has refused ten times, for when a pitter begins to count, he counts for both cocks.

16. If a cock should die before they are counted out, although he fought

last, he loses his battle. This, however, is not to apply when his adversary is running away.

17. The crowing, or the raising of the hackle of a cock, is not fight, nor his fighting at the pitter's hands.

18. A breaking cock is a fighting cock, but a cock breaking from his adversary is not fight.

19. If any dispute arises between the pitters on the result of a fight, the cocks are not to be taken off the pit, nor the gaffle taken off until it is decided by the judges or the referee.

20. Each cock within two ounces of each other, shall be a match, except blinkers, when fighting against two-eyed cocks, an allowance of from three to five ounces will be made; when blinkers are matched against each other, the same rule to apply as to two-eyed cocks.

21. Any person fighting a cock heavier than he is represented on the match list, shall lose the fight, although he may have won.

22. In all cases of appeal, fighting ceases until the judges or the referee give their decision, which shall be final, and strictly to the question before them.

23. When a bet is made, it cannot be declared off unless by consent of both parties. All outside bets to go according to the main bet.

24. Any person violating any of the above rules, shall be deemed to have lost the match.

RULES OF COCKPITS IN THE SOUTH.

FROM "PORTER'S SPIRIT OF THE TIMES."

Dr. J. W. Cooper, alias "Tartar Cock," "Sergeant Cock," etc., of West Chester, Penn'a., sends us the following, which will be of some advantage to our Southern sporting friends, as we are assured they are used throughout the greater portion of that section of the Union. We commend them to the careful attention of our amateur friends in the South, and can say to our Northern ones, that a better batch cannot well be collected together. Our correspondent obtained them for us, from a leading cocker in the South, and their correctness is indisputable. They were originally extracted from the "*Red Lion Rules*" (by which they used to fight in England), and were first adopted in this country by a party of Virginia and North Carolina gentlemen. These gentlemen merely omitted such of the English rules as did not apply to our mode of fighting; in other respects, they are the same as those of Red Lion:—

RULES TO BE OBSERVED IN CONDUCTING A SHOW OR A MAIN OF COCKS.

Article I.—On the morning the main is to commence, the parties decide by lot who shows first. It is to be remembered that the party obtaining the choice generally chooses to weigh first; and consequently obliges the adverse party to show first, as the party showing first weighs last. When the show is made by that party, the door of the cock-house is to be locked, and the key given to the other party, who immediately repairs to his cock-house, and prepares for weighing. There ought to be provided a pair of good scales, and weights as low down as half an ounce. One or two judges to be appointed to weigh the cocks. Eeach party, by weighing the cocks intended for the show a day or two beforehand, and having all of their respective weights, would greatly facilitate the business of the judges. There should be two writers to take down the colors, weights, marks, etc., of each cock. There ought to be no feathers cut or plucked from the cocks before they are brought to the scale, except a few from behind to keep them clean, and their wings and tails clipped a little.

ARTICLE 2. As soon as the cocks are all weighed, the judges, the writers and the principals of each party, and as many besides as the parties may agree on, are to retire for the purpose of matching. They are to make all even matches first, then those within half an ounce, and afterwards those within an ounce; but if more matches can be made by breaking an even or half-ounce match, it is to be done.

ARTICLE 3. On the day of showing, only one battle is to be fought. It is to be remembered, that the party winning the show gains also the choice of fighting the first battle with any particular cock in the match. Afterwards they begin with the lightest pair first, and so on up to the heaviest fighting, then in rotation, as they increase in weight. This first battle, too, will fix the mode of trimming.

RULES TO BE OBSERVED IN THE PIT.

ARTICLE 1. When the cocks are in the pit, the judges are to examine whether they answer the description taken in the match bill, and whether, they are fairly trimmed, and have on fair heels. If all be right and fair, the pitters are to deliver their cocks six feet apart (or thereabouts), and retire a step or two back; but if a wrong cock should be produced, the party so offending forfeits that battle.

ARTICLE 2. All heels that are round from the socket to the point are allowed to be fair; any pitter bringing a cock on the pit with any other kind of heels, except by particular agreement, forfeits the battle.

ARTICLE 3. If either cock should be trimmed with a close, unfair back the judge shall direct the other to be cut in the same manner, and at the time shall observe to the pitter, that if he brings another cock in the like situation, unless he shall have been previously trimmed, he shall forfeit the battle.

ARTICLE 4. A pitter, when he delivers his cock, shall retire two paces back, and not advance or walk around his cock until a blow has passed.

ARTICLE 5. An interval of—minutes shall be allowed between the termination of one battle and the commencement of another.

ARTICLE 6. No pitter shall pull a feather out of a cock's mouth, or from over his eyes or head, or pluck him by the breast to make him fight, or pinch him for the like purpose, under penalty of forfeiting the battle.

ARTICLE 7. The pitters are to give their cocks room to fight, and are not to hover or press on them, so as to retard their striking.

ARTICLE 8. The greasing, peppering, muffling, and soaping a cock, or any other external application, are unfair practices, and by no means admissable in this amusement.

ARTICLE 9. The judge, when required, may suffer a pitter to call in some of his friends to assist in catching his cock, who are to retire immediately as soon as the cock is caught, and in no other instance is the judge to suffer the pit to be broken.

ARTICLE 10. All cocks on their backs are to be immediately turned over on their bellies by their respective pitters at all times.

ARTICLE 11. A cock, when down, is to have a wing given him, if he needs it, unless his adversary is on it, but his pitter is to place the wing gently in its proper position, and not to lift the cock; and no wing is to be given unless absolutely necessary.

ARTICLE 12. If either cock should be hanged in himself, in the pit or canvas, he is to be loosed by his pitter; but if in his adversary, both pitters are to immediately lay hold of their respective cocks, and the pitter, whose cock is hung, shall hold him steady whilst the adverse party draws out the heel, and then they shall take their cocks asunder a sufficient distance for them fairly to renew the combat.

ARTICLE. 13. Should the cocks separate, and the judge be unable to decide which fought last, he shall at his discretion direct the pitters to carry their cocks to the middle of the pit, and deliver them beak to beak, unless either of them is blind—in that case they are to be shouldered, that is delivered with their breasts touching, each pitter taking care to deliver his cock at this, as well as at all other times, with one hand.

ARTICLE 14. When both cocks cease fighting, it is then in the power of the pitter of the last fighting cock, unless they touch each other, to demand a count of the judges, who shall count forty deliberately, which, when counted out, is not to be counted again during the battle. Then the pitters shall catch their cocks and carry them to the middle of the pit, and deliver them beak to beak, but to be shouldered if either is blind, as before. Then if either cock refuses or neglects to fight, the judge shall count ten, and shall direct the pitters to bring their cocks again to the middle of the pit, and pit as before; and if the same cock in like manner refuses, he shall count ten again, and call out, "twice refused," and so proceed until one cock thus refuses six times successively. The judge shall then determine the battle against such cock.

ARTICLE 15. If either cock dies before the judge can finish the counting of the law, the battle is to be given to the living cock, and if both die, the longest liver wins the battle.

ARTICLE 16. The pitters are not to touch their cocks whilst the judge is in the act of counting.

ARTICLE 17. No pitter is ever to lay hold of his adversary's cock, unless to draw out the heel, and then he must take him below the knee. Then there shall be no second delivery—that is, after he is once delivered, he shall not be touched until a blow is struck, unless ordered by the judge.

ARTICLE 18. No pitter shall touch his cock, unless at the times mentioned in the foregoing rules.

ARTICLE 19. If any pitter acts contrary to these rules, the judge, if called on at the time, shall give the battle against him.

DIRECTIONS FOR KEEPING COCKS.

The following directions for keeping cocks are taken from the *New York Clipper*, to which paper the author contributed them:

The first thing to be provided is such a house or room as will admit of light and air, which is necessary to be given by the feeder in the middle part of the two last days, before the cocks are to fight.

The next care must be to provide such coops as a cock can take exercise in, which ought to be made of thin boards and of the following dimensions, viz :—two feet wide, three feet deep, and three ft. high, with a smooth round roost two inches through, placed in the middle, between the bottom and top of the coops, so that the feeder can take it down or put it up as he thinks proper. The bottom of the coop ought to be made of two thin boards which must be left loose so that they can be turned over when necessary. The coop ought to be placed about three feet off the ground or floor, with a trough in each, made of soft wood, ranged in a line on each side, and numbered so as to have a passage through the middle, which places the whole business in the view of the feeder. If convenient there should be under each coop a small tub or half barrel of straw, for the purpose hereafter mentioned.

The coops being prepared, put up your cocks in the evening. On the twelfth day before they are to fight, carefully separate the fat cocks from the middling (which are those that are not fat yet have flesh enough) and lean; then separate the middling from the lean, which are those that want flesh. The fat, middling, and lean cocks, being placed separately, write under them "fat" or "lean," as the case may be. This being done, weigh each cock carefully and set the weight on his coop. Late in the evening of the same day put muffs on their spurs and spar all the fat cocks on a bed of straw, giving each a little warm sulphur water to drink, and put them in their tubs under their coops; cover them warm till next morning, observing to leave a little opening for air.

On the next morning, early, take the fat cocks out of their tubs and put them in their coops. Then give them the following purge :—thirty grains cream of tartar, five grains refined nitre, molasses and hard soap, rub into a mass and form into Pills, the size of a pea; give two or three of the Pills and carefully put them down their throats, observing to keep their tongues down, which will cause them to swallow the Pills easily. After giving the fat cocks their purge, feed the middling cocks with corn bread and skimmed milk, and the lean cocks with scalded barley, observing to give them cool spring water to drink three times in the course of the day; the same feed must be repeated to the lean cocks in the evening. The middling and lean cocks being fed, the fat cocks must now be attended to. The physic will now begin to operate, which must be worked off with warm toast and water. Take care not to let the water be any time in the trough; if they should drink too much it might be hurtful.

At twelve or one o'clock, the fat cocks' physic will be worked off, when they must be fed with new milk and rice, well boiled (*warm*.) Late in the evening of the same day spar all the middling and fat cocks on straw as before directed, giving them all a little warm sulphur water to drink, and put them in their tubs under their coops, cover them warm till next morning, leaving an opening for air.

On the second morning early take the middling and fat cocks out of their tubs and put them in their coops. Give each of them the purge made up into a Pill as before directed, then feed the lean cocks with bread and milk, and cool spring water three times a day. The lean cocks being fed, now for the lean and fat cocks. When their physic operates give them warm toast and water. At twelve o'clock feed them all with boiled rice and new milk, warm. Late in the evening of the same day, all the cocks must be sparred on a bed of straw (*lean, middling and fat*). A little warm sulphur water being given them to drink, put them in their tubs, covered warm, leaving a little air till next morning.

On the third morning early, take the lean, middling and fat cocks out of their tubs and put them in the coops; give all and each of them the purge made up as before directed, and when their physic operates give them warm toast and water, and at twelve o'clock feed them with boiled rice and milk, warm; give them moderate exercise in the evening by flirting them. Then feed them all with corn mush and milk, warm, and put them in their tubs covered warm, leaving them air till morning.

On the fourth morning early take the lean, middling and fat cocks out of their tubs and put them in their coops; then feed them with oat bread, wetted in warm skimmed milk, and water at twelve o'clock. Give them all the same feed. Late in the evening exercise them all by flirting; then feed them all with oat bread, wetted with milk and water, or barley, warm. Their drink must be barley water three times that day, and let them remain in their coops that night; but they must be kept warm, with much straw around them. Their roosts must be taken down.

On the fifth morning feed all the cocks with oat bread and scalded barley mixed. At twelve o'clock feed them all with barley bread and the white of hard boiled eggs. Late in the evening exercise them by flirting; then feed them all with scalded barley and corn bread, mixed; give them spring water and milk to drink three times that day (a little warm), and they may go on their roosts that night. When eggs cannot be had scalded rice will do to mix with the bread.

On the sixth morning feed all the cocks with oat bread and scalded barley. At twelve o'clock feed them with barley bread and the white of hard boiled eggs. In the evening exercise them by flirting them; feed them all with scalded barley and corn bread. Their drink must be barley water, cool, three times that day; and they must roost in their coops at night.

On the seventh morning feed all the cocks with oat bread and the white of hard boiled eggs; late in the evening exercise them by flirting, then feed them all with scalded barley and corn bread. Their drink must be milk and water (cool) three times that day, and put on their roosts that night.

On the eighth morning feed all the cocks with oat bread and scalded barley. At twelve o'clock feed them all with barley bread and white of hard boiled eggs. Their drink must be barley water (cool) twice. Late in the evening pit the cocks and give them all a little sparring; just a few strokes, to give them a little airing and retain for them the use of their wings and feet. After the sparring is over, feed them all with new milk and rice boiled (warm), and keep them warm in their coops at night, with much straw around them; the roosts must be taken down. On the ninth morning feed all the cocks with oat bread and scalded barley. At twelve o'clock feed them all with barley bread and white of hard boiled eggs. In the evening exercise them by flirting them; feed them with scalded barley and corn bread. Their drink must be milk and spring water (cool), three times a day; and they may go on their roosts that night.

On the tenth morning feed them all with oat bread and scalded barley. At twelve feed with barley, bread and white of hard boiled eggs. In the evening exercise them all by flirting them; feed them with corn bread and scalded barley. Their drink must be barley water (cool), three times a day, and they must roost in their coops that night. Air ought to be given them in the middle of this day.

On the eleventh morning feed all with oat bread and scalded barley; at twelve feed with barley bread and white of hard boiled eggs. Late in the evening feed them with corn bread and scalded barley. Their drink must be milk and spring water (cool), three times a day. They must roost in the coops that night. On this day they ought to be exercised by letting them loose in a room, one at a time, where there is light and air, for the space of but one hour each. If this is not convenient they must be exercised by flirting, and the light and air be given them in their coops in the middle of the day, as before directed.

On the twelfth day very early (being the day of battle) give all the cocks that are to be shown in the main a light feed of oat bread, and in about an hour after give them a drink of spring water and milk (cool); all the rest feed and give drink as usual, but none in the whole course of their feeding ought to have full feeds, except in the evening, when they might bear a little more.

TAKE NOTICE.

Some fat cocks will be sufficiently reduced by two sparrings and two purges, which may be known by weighing and comparing the weight with that on the coops. In this case the third sparring and purge ought to be omitted.

Attention and frequent use of the weights is necessary to discover the order and situation of the cocks.

Fat cocks require middling long sparrings; when much wearied, let them rest and then put them down again; and others in proportion to their flesh and order.

No cock ought to be put into a coop that is deficient in feathers or good health, or is slack of spirit.

With some it will happen that their physic will not operate as soon as it ought. In this case exercise by sparring will sometimes cause it to work, otherwise increase the dose by taking a small bit from a Pill made up, and laid by for the purpose.

It will sometimes happen, notwithstanding the sparring and physic, that some cocks will be inclined to too much flesh, having good appetites and inclined to eat freely. In this case they ought to have more than common exercise, and be sparingly fed with barley bread and scalded barley, and their drink cool spring water.

It will also happen that some will be too much reduced, or will be wanting in appetite, which will cause them to be rather weak and thin in flesh. In this case they ought to be indulged in that kind of food they are most fond of, such as bread made of corn, and sometimes of oat meal, well baked; and they ought to be fed often and a little at a time, and given plenty of milk and barley water (cool); but when they are sick and cannot digest their food, turn them out of their coops.

When they incline to drink much, it is a sign of heat, and sometimes happens towards the latter part of their keeping.— Then they should have a little sorrel or plantain leaf cut and mixed with their food. Give them also milk and cool spring water with a little fine rectified nitre in it to drink, which will cool and moderate their heat. This ought to be repeated till their thirst or desire for drink subsides.

In no instance give cocks cold water immediately after being heated by sparring or otherwise.

When cocks incline to purge, give them new milk well boiled with barley bread (warm), and their drink ought to be warm toast and spring water.

In giving cocks drink observe not to let them have more than four dips at one time, which ought to be about eight and eleven o'clock in the morning, and three o'clock in the evening; and never feed a cock unless his crop is empty. Give him drink and exercise and it will soon go off.

About seven or eight days before the cocks are to be put up to feed, examine them at their walks and take up all the fat cocks-and give them one sparring and one purge, and don't let them out of their coops for two days, which will prevent their taking cold; then put them down on their walks till the day you are to take them up to keep.

This method prepares fat cocks for the coop, by taking off some of their fat before they are taken up; which is a great advantage and help towards getting them in proper order to fight.

Reducing the weight of cocks depends entirely on the size and order when they are put up. Large fat cocks will lose from ten to sixteen ounces, and smaller ones in proportion.—Large ones that are only in middling order will lose from six to ten ounces and smaller ones in proportion. Lean cocks will lose one or two ounces, but will nearly gain it in feeding, and all of them ought to be rather in the rise in weight toward the latter part of their keeping.

They ought to be moved from the place of feeding to the place of battle at least three days before the fight.

If the weather is warm and clear they ought to be trimmed the day before the fight, provided they are kept warm at night. Be careful not to cut their wings and tail too short; and before they are heeled to fight they ought to be let loose in a room where there is light and air for about fifteen minutes.

Care ought to be taken to keep the cocks clean, and shift the straw at least once in two days, which should be turned over once in that time.

Every evening for three days before they fight wash their feet, legs and head in chamber-lye, and every morning in water not too cold, and wipe them dry. This will heal the bruises about their heads and the cracks in their toes.

Stags ought to be put up the ninth day before they are to fight, and ought to have but one sparring and one purge, unless they are fat and strong, and then not more than two at most.— In that case they ought to be cooped one day sooner. They are to be treated in every other respect like the old cocks.

The sulphur water directed to be given, is made by pouring a pint of boiling water on half an ounce of sulphur, and pouring it off as it cools, when it will be fit for use.

The scalded barley is prepared by pouring on scalding water and not letting it stand more than ten minutes, then pour it off and spread the barley on a table to dry. The water that is poured off serves for their drink, which ought to be made fresh every morning; it is best to be weak; a slight taste of the barley is sufficient; when otherwise it is rather heating.

In mixing milk and water for their drink, observe not to put more than one-fourth skimmed milk and three-fourths spring water; when there is a greater proportion of milk it is not so cooling.

The different sorts of bread for feed, such as oat meal, barley and corn meal, must be heated, and ought to be baked the day before they are used. They are made in the following manner: Take equal measures of the white of eggs and milk, beat them well up together, then add as much flour as will make it bread; which must be well worked up and baked. Care must be used to let it be soaked without burning the crust.

In no instance must sour milk be used, for it will cause them to purge, which will be very hurtful.

When tubs cannot be had to put them in after sparrring, it will do to put them in bags with straw in the bottom, leaving air for them. Next morning take them out of the bags and put them in the coops. Good bottomed and strong fowls in fighting order, with proper heels well put, will insure success.

The following, from the *Edinburg Encyclopædia*, is sent us by our valued friend " J. E. S.," to whose labor we are also indebted for many of the compilations from *Rees' Encyclopædia*.

The fowl is supposed to come from his walk in good condition, in which case, he will be too fat for fighting and will have no wind till he is reduced. To effect this, medicine and abstinence from food are required for seven or eight days before he can be brought to the pit, at least such is the regimen pursued by our first feeders and is pretty generally as follows: His tail and spurs being cut short he is put into his pen, and the first day receives no food; second, he has his physic, consisting of cream of tartar or jalap, or both united, in the dose of about five grains of each; or if it be a very fat and large fowl, the dose may be increased to ten grains of cream of tartar. These are given him mixed in fresh butter; this generally purges briskly and scours out the intestines. Immediately, after the physic is given him, and before it affects him, he is placed on loose straw or a grass plat with another cock and allowed to spar with him, the boots, or muffles, being previously tied on their short spurs. In this way he is exercised till he is a little weary; he is then returned to his pens. Before putting him up it is necessary to examine his mouth to see if he has been picked or wounded in the inside, as such wound is apt to canker. To prevent this, it is washed with a little vinegar and brandy; he is now allowed his warm nests to work off his physic. This is a diet made of warm ale or sweet wort, and bread in it, with a little sugar candy; or bread and milk and sugar candy, a large tea cup full. He is then shut up close till the next morning, or about 24 hours. If the weather is cold the room should be made warm, or a blanket placed over the pen; if in warm weather he may be clipped out for fighting; but if the weather is cold this should be left till the time of fighting. The room should be kept dark except at feeding. Early on the following morning, that is about the third day, his pen must be cleaned out from the effects of the physic, &c., and clean dry straw, which should be done every day. His feet should be washed and wiped clean before he is returned to his pen. If his feet feel cold his pen should be made warmer. He is next to be allowed some bread; that is, a sort of bread made of ingredients in the following proportions: About three pounds of fine flour and two eggs, and four whites of eggs and a little yeast; this is kneaded with a sufficiency of water for a proper consistence and is well baked; some add, as a great secret, a small number of aniseeds, or a little cinnamon; of this bread, as much as would fill a tea cup, cut into pieces is given him twice that day, and no water is then given him whatever, as it is considered highly injurious at the early part of the feeding. On the fourth day early in the morning he should receive half a tea cup full of good barley and a little water, in which a toast has been steeped some time. Having eaten this, clean his pen, &c., and let his pen be uncovered for about an hour while he scratches and picks the straw. Some think it highly advantageous to prepare the barley for them by bruising it, and thus to take away the sharp points of the barley, and the husky shell or covering which is blown away. In the afternoon the same quantity of barley may be repeated, but no water. On the fifth or next day he may have the bread as before, but three portions of it, and no water. On the sixth or weighing day, very early in the morning, give him the bread as before; he is then to be weighed, and afterwards a good feed of barley and water should be given.

Some hold it a valuable secret to give them flesh, as sheep's heart, for this and the succeeding day, chopped small and mixed with the other food.

On the seventh day, or day before fighting, early in the morning, let him have the same feed of barley; in the afternoon bread and the white of an egg boiled hard, and a little water.— On the eighth or day of fighting, he may have a little barley, as about 40 grains.

Aside from this, says " J. E. S.," I would recommend regular exercise of the cock, flying him every day and keeping up the exercise as long as he does not pant—and carefully rubbing the legs every day with the hand, stretching them out, &c.

BREEDS AND STRAINS.

THE COUNTERFEITS.

In briefly describing this strain, we will speak of the manner in which it gained its name.

A battle was fought in Baltimore county, one cock being matched against a more noted one, the one of less celebrity winning with apparent ease. The man who lost the battle claimed the conquering cock as his own, and charged that it was stolen from his yard; but it being shown to his satisfaction that this was not the case, he replied, "Then he is the best *counterfeit* I ever saw." In this way the winning cock and his progeny were christened Counterfeit, and after the battle alluded to he came into the possession of a man named Goss, who besides breeding with him, fought several battles, until finally he was conquered by a Gray Eagle cock.

The Counterfeit has been styled the champion strain of Baltimore for many years.

The strain was first derived from a dark red cock, weighing five and a half pounds, with fine *rosy* comb. The colors run into black reds, reds with blue breasts, and dark legs. They are proud in bearing, well feathered, and have generally rose, with occasionally a single comb.

There are *spurious* counterfeits (by the way, not a repetition in meaning) in the market, having been so named because they well answer the general description, especially in having rose combs. Such are at best but three-quarters game, and have generally been obtained by crossing with half-games.

Genuine Counterfeits are good and rapid fighters, strong in leg, well built, good for pit purposes; and, where the oddity of a rose comb is not objected to, excellent for breeding purposes.

THE SERGEANT STRAIN.

The following is a brief history of the Sergeant strain of game fowls, and the cause of their celebrity as fighters :—

Some forty years ago a man named Good, then residing on the "Neck," in Philadelphia, had a good strain of games said to be imported from England. He and some countrymen from the neighborhood of what was then West Philadelphia, all of them being known as "country boys," frequently fought mains against the city proper, and almost invariably won. The Philadelphians, to repair their losses, attempted to purchase fowls from the countrymen, but the latter refused to sell upon any terms, fearing that they might be made to suffer from their own games. Many of the Philadelphia sportsmen then gave up the contest as a hopeless one ; but not so with one of their number, who was determined to win even at the sacrifice of honesty.— This man was a Sergeant, at the time engaged in recruiting troops for the United States army. He had a great passion for cock-fighting, was too proud and persistent to acknowledge his city conquered, and being unable to obtain a good strain by any means at hand, resolved to steal and finally succeeded in carrying off one of the very best cocks belonging to the "country boys." Hence its name, the "Sergeant," from the fact that it was stolen, trained and fought by this man. The battles were soon renewed, and success inured to the Philadelphians. The strain was cultivated with much care, and for several years it was the recognized champion of Pennsylvania.

The strain was afterwards very much prized by some of the prominent sportsmen of the State, among whom we may mention Dr. Jamison of York, Graves of Philadelphia and Wilson of Harrisburg. The last-named gentleman went to much pains and expense in raising these fowls, and could at any time produce from his stock a number of excellent fighters. Jamison, Graves and Wilson, on the part of Pennsylvania, challenged the State of Maryland to a contest, they intending to use the Sergeants. The challenge was accepted by the latter, who presented the Tartars.

The battle was fought at Hagerstown, Md., and those acquainted with the opposing strains, can readily imagine its severity. The bets on both sides were numerous and heavy. The main resulted in the success of the Tartars.

The Sergeant strain (if its origin could be traced it might be shown to be a distinct breed) is still highly valued by the cockers of Pennsylvania, but it has been imprudently crossed at different times, and is now so mixed up that it breeds a variety of colors.

The original color was red with black breast, willow leg, beautifully feathered, with proud and lofty bearing.

The cocks are pure game, good fighters, but somewhat inferior in strength and make-up to the Tartars, as shown by many battles. They are, however, a great acquistition to any cocker's yard, as their qualities can be relied upon.

THE VIRGINIA GRAYS.

SOMETIMES CALLED "MEXICANS" AND STRYCHNINES.

The Virginians have a breed of game fowls, originally purely Mexican, which they now call "Strychnine," from the severity with which they fight—striking rapidly and with great force.—This stock, though hailing from the country of the notorious Santa Anna, differ widely from the General in an essential particular—courage.

The Strychnines have fine, long and glossy feathers, mostly dark gray, with black intermingled, with large bones, and tall, commanding appearance. Their eyes are full, heads small and finely shaped.

It was a large cock of this breed which the author sent to Europe, to "CENSOR," the London correspondent of *Wilkes' Spirit of the Times*, and received in return the celebrated "Clipper" fowls. The cock in question was accompanied by three Tartar hens, the object being to allow "Censor" to cross them on English soil, and by their progeny show some of the English cockers that crossed games, well and carefully bred, could show qualities superior to those attained by the process of breeding in-and-in, so prevalent in England. The Strychnine cock weighed about seven pounds when he left our chickery, the largest in our possession, and for that reason was selected, notwithstanding he was somewhat older than we would have otherwise preferred. The exchange was entirely satisfactory to both parties.

The Virginians greatly prefer fighting their Strychnines to

selling them, and are fully of the opinion that nothing less than a shower of burning cinders from the crater of a volcano could induce them to leave the field of battle.

Their reputation extends through many of the States, and wherever the breed is kept they are highly valued. In a recent main between Baltimore and Philadelphia, the Baltimorians won by using this breed, having one fine dark gray which won great distinction.

They are valuable in crossing, because the immediate progeny as a rule (when crossed with red or darker fowls) show distinctly the colors of either the cock or the hen, there being little or no mixture. This result is frequently sought by men who wish to retain the strength of their stock, and who have not the facility or means to obtain a fresh supply of Strychnines to breed with their own.

THE CLIPPER BREED.

OR BLACK AND BROWN REDS OF ENGLAND.

This breed, or strain (we hardly know which to call it) of games, for many years noted in England for their extraordinary courage, and almost universal success in battle, was presented to us by "Censor," the well known London correspondent of *Porter's now Wilkes' Spirit of the Times*. We had previously made him a present of a Strychnine Cock, three Tartar hens, and a trio of Baltimore Top-Knots, and he returned two trios of Clippers, from which we are now rapidly and steadily breeding. The following letter from "Censor," gives a true and graphic description of the breed:—

"J. W. COOPER, M. D.—*Dear Sir:*—Allow me to thank you most cordially for your kind and handsome present of Game Fowls. They reached me in safety a few hours after I had put a notice in *Porter's Spirit*, saying they had not arrived. I am sending you by Saturday's steamer, *two trios of as good birds as ever flew*. The cock on the left, (that is to say, on the left of the other when both are looking through the bars,) has won two fights, and is slightly lame. You will find him a nice bird to handle and very tame. He was bred by Mr. Cobden in Sessex—within three miles of Goodwood Race Course. Whenever a main is fought in the South of England his birds are sought for, and odds are sure to be laid on the party in alliance with Cobden. This bird would, I fancy, make an excellent cross with the Tartar hens. The two hens with him were got by a brown red Nottingham cock, out of hens of our late celebrated jockey Frank Butler, of the black breasted red sort. He had an immense number in all parts of England, and won an enormous quantity of mains. The other cock was bred at Epson by Mr. Heathcote, part owner of our famed Epsom Race Course. He is a thorough sportsman—he keeps a pack of stag hounds, and breeds none but the best game fowls he can procure. I liked him better than a stag I thought of sending, brother of the hens in this pen—they of the Staffordshire stock, where more cocking takes place at present than in all the rest of England put together. You will, if they reach you in safety, have two sets of hens, no relation to either cock, and no relation to each other—excepting that the pair of hens are sisters.

The Baltimore Top-Knots are nice birds; but I infinitely prefer the Tartar hens, and shall next year cross them with a Staffordshire black-breasted red; that *must* be a good cross, I think."

Allow me to remain, dear sir, very faithfully yours,
"————————," alias "CENSOR."

The following extracts from *Censor's* letters to the "*Spirit*" show the way in which this desirable exchange was made:—

January, 15, 1859.—"One word about game-fowls; I have been at that game too, amongst my other youthful accomplishments. A cross breed I have always found to be fine fighters. Much as I may be against in-and-in breeding, I have found chickens from a son with his mother the quickest birds I have seen fly; from them I would not advise breeding again.—Breeders of game-fowls in this country are fond of adhering to "feather." I really cannot discover any reason for it, any more than I should for selecting a sire of the same color as the dam of the colt, with which I hoped to win a (?) fortune. I should much like a clutch of eggs from those tartar and strychnine gentlemen, which are mentioned as excelling in beauty, strength, and fierceness, all ever seen by "Tartar Cock." He does not date his letter, but if he resides in the vicinity of New York, and has more eggs next Spring than he wants for hatching, he might send me a few. Half of them, or nearly half, would hatch after their voyage, and I would find a friend, or be there myself, to meet them in Liverpool, so as, if possible, to set them there, and avoid land carriage. I tried the experiment with French eggs—bought in a shop—and succeeded in getting eleven chickens from thirteen eggs. Those eggs I picked out of about three dozen. In return I would send him a box of *clippers*, not one of whose family were ever known to "show the white feather." I will now bid you farewell, dear SPIRIT, with a hope of seeing a bushel of eggs, a match at billiards, and a two-country horse-race.

"Should such a glorious race be run,
May I be there to see the fun."

March 19, 1859.—"In former days, there used to be some prime cock fighting before the races—then, a main of cocks was made by two magnates, and they fought for large stakes; the case is now altered, and a bit of fun of that kind must take place on the sly. A capital main was fought yesterday in London, but I must not tell you *where*. The black breasted reds showed a decided superiority, nearly every bird winning his battle. Should there be any performance of this sort at Liverpool, I am certain to hear of it, and shall put myself under the *wing* of some old bird of the locality, and get a peep at them. Please tell "Tartar Cock" that I have not forgotten him. I have a stag and two hens ready for exportation, and shall inquire about the conveyance he advised me of to-morrow. I shall, most probably, send them from Liverpool next week, and shall address them to your office."

March 26, 1859.—" I had a sad misfortune the week before last (whisper it to Tartar Cock, though I fear he will not believe it)—it was thus: The black-breasted red stag I intended taking with me to Liverpool, *en route* for New York, got loose, and had a fight with his own father; the old 'un killed him. I am the more sorry because he was "a ripper." He was bred by Mr. Heathcote, owner of the race-course at Epsom, master of a rattling pack of deer-hounds, and a man who will have nothing on his premises that is not game. I have two prime hens, and shall endeavor to replace this bird from Newmarket, to which town I wrote on Monday ; and, having placed the affair in the hands of one of my allies, who handles his own birds, I have little doubt of his sending me one of as good blood as there is in England, and no relation to my hens. I fear that at present, with this bad luck against me, I must not venture upon a transaction with Old Dominion."

April 9, 1859.—" I would have said something about game-cocks, but have this day seen so wonderful a performnace in the animal magnetism, by a boy and girl, sister and brother, that I really do not seem to have anything like " a heart that can feel for another." Give my compliments to both "Tartar Cock" and " Old Dominion ;" thank them very much, indeed, for the flattering letters, which reached my hands on Tuesday last, and say that I feel the kind manner in which they speak of, and have addressed a stranger, far more sensibly than the handsome present of fowl which I am expecting to receive every minute."

April 9, 1859.—" I am sorry to inform you that my game-fowls have not yet arrived. I shall go to-morrow to Messrs. Lansings' office, and make inquiry about them ; I much fear they have died on their passage. This will be very vexing, as I have been doing an immensity of " game-talk" lately ; I shall crow no more—my comb is sadly cut. What will they say in our cocking-districts of Staffordshire ? They will no longer place any faith in poor, crest-fallen*   CENSOR.

April 16, 1859.—" My game-fowls arrived safely on the day after my last letter. I will write privately on Tuesday. I shall send back the pens, *full*, by ship from Liverpool, on Saturday. The Virginians have already commenced laying. Mine will show more *family* even than the beauties so kindly and so handsomely presented to"   CENSOR.

---

* They were not due in England at the date of your letter, having left New York on the 9th March.—ED. PORTER'S SPIRIT.

May 7, 1859.—" My basket of eggs reached me in safety, and uncracked, in about ten minutes after I posted my last letter. They are now under hens which will sit on a brick-bat rather than not sit. Should any of them be hatched, I shall talk of the chickens a few ! The eggs are larger than those laid by the birds I sent over will be found ; if the fowls are superior they will be miracles. I will write to Mr. Grant by Tuesday's mail. Please tell the European Express Company, with my love, that they are as clever as any party of my acquaintance, or they could not have delivered a delicate basket of new-laid eggs at my door, so safely, after a trip of 4,500 miles.— It is my belief that, if the "poultry" does not come to life, the fault will be that of Pickford's Van (our great carriers) and not of the Express Company. The live fowls are going on capitally. I think I owe Mr. Miller a letter, but I have lately been so busy, and so little at home, that I have had no time to look into my affairs of fancy."

"I must now say farewell, for I have spun out my yarn. Please tell "Tartar Cock," I will answer his letter on Tuesday before I go to the Liverpool Races. He has set me a difficult task. Black-breasted reds are not to be gathered from bushes, but I will stir my stumps for him."

The clippers, two cocks and six hens, were afterwards received by us, all in good order, some of the hens having laid in their box while *en route.*

The Clippers breed black-breasted reds and brown-breasted reds. The older cock is low set, but very powerful and quick, notwithstanding his lameness. The younger one is large and tall, strongly built, savage in appearance, active and strong.

Few if any finer fowls can be found in the world. We have used the utmost care in keeping a number pure, while the *cocks* have been used part of the time in crossing with other valuable kinds.

We have never, with the steel, tested the two cocks sent us, because we valued them too highly ; but have made some of the stags pass through very trying ordeals, which they bore with the highest bravery. It is unnecessary for us to recount all these trials, as they were similar to those practiced by all experienced and careful cockers, who wish to ascertain, by every known test, the purity of their stock. We cannot refrain however from presenting an account of a stag fight between a pure Clipper and a full Tartar, written by a friend to *Wilkes' Spirit.*

It may appear *far-fetched*, and we confess *must*, to those unacquainted with the characteristics of the fowls combatting, yet there is ample proof of its truth. It illustrates, in the highest manner, the indomitable pluck of both. The letter was published as follows :—

A STAG FIGHT.

Delaware Co., Penn'a., Nov. 8.

DEAR SPIRIT :—I am no chicken fancier ; so far from that, I do not know how to distinguish between the true game, the mixed breeds, and the common dunghill fowls, much less to what particular breed they belong, or what name they bear. Indeed, I have always been a skeptic in the game fowl belief, and looked upon them as something different only from the common breeds because some individual had seen proper to christen them with a new name. This whole race of feathered bipeds were to me nothing but fowls "of low degree," christened according to some one's fancy. I have seen the same thing elsewhere, and I thought this was but another exhibition of it.

Meeting with my friend, Dr. Cooper (who is known throughout this country and Europe as a celebrated cocker), of course we had a dispute on the matter. Now the Doctor, by the way, appeared to me to be a genuine monomaniac, and game chickens were all he could think of or talk about.

In order to convince me, the Dr. offered me a dozen eggs from his chickery, all numbered and labelled as carefully as medicines in an apothecary shop, which he proposed that I should take home and place under a hen, and observe what kind of stock they were. I accepted his offer, and accordingly in due time I was the proprietor of eight of the Doctor's game chickens. This event took place about three months ago. I now give you a slight episode in their history : Now I had carefully watched my brood, and observing nothing belligerent about them, but rather the reverse, I had just concluded in my own mind that there was no game there, when, one morning, I observed a something astir among the three stags, that indicated that there was not the most amicable feeling in this feathery household.— True, they had often, after eating, indulged in a little set-to, probably for the sake of promoting digestion, but at this time there was evidently some malice in the act.

One of the stags was a large black with a powerful beak and heavy limbs, and the other was a little " John Bull," much his inferior both in weight and limb. Finally, after some preface, at it they went with a will, and during the half hour I watched them, I could not see which was getting the worst of it. Thinks I, there is some grit there, and I will let them settle the matter to suit themselves. On returning at noon, I found them still fighting, and having torn each other considerably I thought proper to separate them, by putting one into an adjoining inclosure. But when I returned in the evening, judge of my surprise to find them fighting through the pales, each one with a bare neck which his antagonist had made a clean thing of.— You may believe I began to believe in game chickens somewhat. I then took one of the stags and threw him to the other, concluding that inasmuch as they had apparently ruined each other, they might fight till they died.— From this till dark they kept it up; but despite the entreaties of my wife, I let them " go." At nine o'clock I found them on the ground, with the head of one under the wing of the other. They had evidently not retreated, and, as yet neither one was master. Early in the morning, before day had appeared very brightly, I arose and went to look for my chickens, expecting to find one or both of them dead. Judge of my surprise, to find them just commencing again the battle of yesterday. Sore, and torn, and cold, they never faltered, but again pitched in, with a determination to do or die. Well, thought I, this is rather severe fighting for stags not three months old, and it is a pity that they should use themselves up in such an ignoble fight.— Some of my neighbors, who had manifested much interest in it, declared they should fight no longer, and so after about twenty hours battle, I separated them. Upon an examination of the chickens, I found them both much torn, so much so that I did not think they could recover. They could not stoop to pick feed from the ground, and the flesh was completely torn from the windpipe of the smaller stag. His crop was torn open, and I had to sew it up. The larger one was, to use a fighting phrase " bunged up," and there was no sign of an eye, an hour after the fight. Thanks to my skill as a surgeon, they are now getting well, and though not in good trim, I will put either of them against any stag of his age in the State. They may kill him, but they cannot make him run.

To conclude—I will say that the Doctor's setting of eggs has converted me to be a believer in game chickens, and if any one wishes to have them in their purity, Dr. Cooper can supply them with the article.

I look upon my stags as juvenile specimens of a "feathered earthquake," and woe to the dunghill of low degree that crosses their path. Who can beat my three month old stags ?   Yours,   J. A.

THE TARTAR STRAIN.

This is a strain that has acquired great celebrity in the United States, and has even extended to Europe.

Thirty years ago it was the champion, and would have continued so, doubtless, had sufficient care been taken in its propagation. It first originated in Martinsburg, Virginia, from a dark red cock (whose history was not fully known), weighing six and a half pounds. This cock was the hero of many battles, and became so celebrated that toward the close of his life no matches could be got against him. He was strong, remarkably savage, and noted for his indomitable perseverance in battle, fighting with renewed energy and strength just at the moment you would think the combatants should be fagged out. A main for $3,000 and the championship was fought between the Tartars of Virginia and the Sergeants of Pennsylvania, then a justly noted strain. Not a cock in this main, and the many preceding it between the parties, "showed the white feather," though nearly all the Sergeants were killed in the $3,000 test. In the palmiest days of the Tartar, we, then a resident of Virginia, procured a quantity, and have bred them ever since, supplying northern and southern sportsmen with them. They breed black reds, reds with black breasts, blue reds, and brown reds, and green, blue and yellow legs. They have an elegant carriage, stand up well, with full breasts, large eyes, and move with a princely step. Their wings are full and strong, and their necks are plentifully covered with hackle feathers.

The author has carefully bred the Tartars ever since he obtained them in Virginia, and in such a manner as both to keep the strain pure, and enhance its fighting qualities. Within the past few years the popuarity of the pure Tartars has revived, and they are now acknowledged as second to no strain or breed known. We can give ample testimony of their pureness, and herewith quote a letter taken from *Wilkes' Spirit of the Times*, as follows:—

TARTAR GAME FOWLS.

Honesdale, Penn'a., August 8.

DEAR SPIRIT:—Through the kindness of our mutual friend, Dr. Cooper, of West Chester, Penn'a., I have obtained by exchange, a trio of the celebrated Tartar game fowls, a large black-breasted, dark red stag, and two (almost black) brown pullets of good size. They came by express, and notwithstanding they had been cooped up in a small box for three successive days, pounding along over some hundred and fifty miles of rail and turnpike, well soaked with muddy watter at that, both of the pullets laid the next morning after their arrival, which was about 10½ o'clock the previous evening, and they never ceased until, having laid twenty-three eggs, they went to setting. I put thirteen under one, and ten under the other; the one with thirteen hatched every egg, the other comes off this week. So much for the perservance and pluck of the pullets, and now for the stag. I sparred him with a three year old cock of my breed, which has fought several battles here and elsewhere, and proved himself to be a number one customer. Well! that brush was "some" to see! More active and savage fighting I never witnessed. Several times the Tartar stag knocked his adversary heels over head, and would inevitably have killed him, had he been "armed and equipped as the law" (of the pit) "directs." I found the breathing apparatus of the Tartar to be much the best, for while the old cock has as broad a breast as the Tartar, still it is nothing like so full. Indeed, I have never seen so full a breast on any other breed of games. Where "a long pull and a strong pull" is required, this fact gives the Tartar breed an immense advantage, for their is nothing like breath in such cases. Judging from the Tartars, I should pronounce them a very hardy breed of games, not liable to disease or to feel a rugged winter much. The stag "stands well up on his pins," which are very strong and well set. His voice is full and sonorous. His eye large and bright, with a very hawkish "cut of its jib." He is decidedly bold and familiar in the presence of "humans," not caring to step aside to let one pass. The other day a large hen-hawk made a swoop for one of my young chickens, but missing his stroke he cleared out with the gallant stag rushing after him. I would have given something to have seen them meet! In conclusion I have but one thing to say, and that is: take the Tartars "all in all," they are the best breed of games which has come under my notice, and I would recommend them to the attention of both cockers and fanciers, for they are both brave and beautiful.

Yours, truly, M. W.

A majority of the cocks fought in the great New York main against the "Daffodil Cocking Club of Portchester," were of the Tartar Strain, or had Tartar blood in them, there being some crosses with Rattlers, &c,, all, however, supplied by the author. The "Daffodil" undoubtedly owed their success to the quickness and *endurance* of the strain they used. They have sent the following official report for publication in this work.—

Friend Cooper :—Hearing of your intention to write a book on the subject of cocking, as well as the breeding of game fowls, and having some years since fought a large number of your fowls both singly and in mains, we have taken the liberty of forwarding you the annexed account of one of the numerous mains fought and won by us, feeling assured it will prove interesting to a large number of your readers, many of whom must know by experience, the thorough game and bull-dog ferocity of the fowls raised by you for the pit, as well as the beauty of feather of those raised by you for the purpose of supplying many gentlemen with fowls, for the adornment and embellishment of their country seats, and to whom "a thing of beauty is a joy forever." These latter, although opposed to the practice of cock-fighting, yet loving as they do, the elegance of plumage, and the proud bearing of the cock, the motherly qualities of the hen, both as a setter, and the taking care of the chicks, as also the unrivalled qualities of both fowl and eggs for table purposes. have not suffered themselves to be carried away by the new fangled mania of parties for gray and buff Cochins, Brahmas, Crevecombs, and La Flechis, paying the most outrageous prices for fowls during the " last sensation," the same as we recollect years ago, they ran after the leggy Shanghæs, the Black Spanish, and Dorkings; the excitement for all of them dying out in a short time, and the same ecstacies being gone over again at the introduction of a new specimen. But these gentlemen have still kept in all their purity the different strains of games, the Dominiques, Irish Grays, Spangles, Strychnines, Seftons, Counterfeits, Tartars, Rattlers, &c., many of which strains, if I remember correctly originated with yourself. The main of which we write was fought in a small village near New York, on the part of the residents of said village known as the Daffodil club, and a number of their friends, from the Empire City. The club obtained all their fowls from yourself, mentioning when ordering them, they were to be fought in a main, and even to this day, we bear in mind the feelings of delight we experienced, when looking over the seven stags sent us ; all in the flush and vigor of health, the lightest of them nearly five lbs. in weight, showing you had not detereorated the size of your stock by breeding " in and in ;" but by judicious crossing and selecting the finest and hardiest birds, had kept your fowls in the finest condition, and to appearances in their pristine purity. The stags were placed in the hands of an experienced heeler and handler of our place—a man who takes pride in bringing them to the battle ground in the finest condition, looking upon the labor bestowed as a labor of love, and they consequently came to the scratch in the heighth of condition (with one exception) and ready to do battle for a man's life, if such were necessary. A full account of this main was published in "*Wilkes' Spirit of the Times*" shortly after it was fought and the high praises bestowed upon the birds, for their unflinching gameness, and quick fierce fighting qualities, were well deserved, as no amount of praise was unmerited, and you, yourself, should feel proud of being able to send forth such fowls from your breeding walks, to do battle for your reputation as a raiser of games, excelled by none, and equalled by but very few :—

FIRST FIGHT.

A brown red Tartar of ours against a black red of New York, heavy weights, five lbs. eight ounces. They were brought in by their handlers, duly examined, the regular inch and a quarter heels (which, by the way came from yourself), pronounced correct ; the usual amount of billing without the cooing, allowed, when the judge gave the word and they were placed on the score; they eyed one another for a few seconds, when our bird not liking the waste of time, went to work, and for a few moments, nothing could be seen but a cloud of feathers and the noise heard of contending pinions, when finally the Tartar, caught a good hold, and struck five or six times without letting go, when upon separating ; the black red, was found to be desperately hurt, and it only required a short space of time to settle this fight in favor of the "Daffodil." Won in a single heat, time eight minutes.

SECOND FIGHT.

Another brown red Tartar on our side, seemingly a brother of the first one, and a Pyle shown by the party from New York ;—weight four lbs. eight ounces, the light weights. This fight was literally snatched, "as a brand from the burning." After the usual preliminaries had been gone through with and the fowls scored, our bird being a very savage one, turned upon the handler immediately, and while with his back to his opponent, the Pyle rushed up, and catching hold rattled away with such effect as to break a wing of our bird ; the odds were instantly ten to three upon the Yorker, but our bird being "strong as a horse" upon his feet, managed to give better than he was obliged to take, until a lucky blow, laid the Pyle dead upon the carpet. Many long faces were pulled, as well as plethoric pocket books, which by the way grew much lighter for the New York party, and exclamations arose around the pit, "is this your style of bird ?" "if we had known this we would have remained at home, &c." Time of this fight forty minutes.

RIGHT HIND.

A black red Tartar, shown by us and a duck wing of New York, weight five lbs. five ounces, a noble pair of birds ; and although we were unfortunate, in as much as we lost the fight, we were almost as well satisfied as if we had won, as you, although you lose your money, would much rather have a fowl fight till the last than walk off like a quarter horse, carrying your little pile with him. We had a bad send off, as our fowl did not appear to take hold (he had just caught and was suffering slightly from the rattles) but being stung pretty hard, he woke up and they had it, hip and thight until we had a throat cut, when of course the betting which had been in our favor turned round and the odds were on the duck wing. Our bird fought savagely, striking whenever he caught hold, head wing or tail, it made no difference, but losing so much blood finally told upon him, and after a fight of some thirty minutes duration, we were forced to succumb, draw our fowl, beaten but not disgraced.

FOURTH FIGHT.

We again showed a black red, (cross of Tartar and Rattler) green legs, a perfect picture, so much so, that before cutting a feather, we let him run in the pit, when they commenced betting at once ten to seven on the "Daffodil" and right well did he deserve their approbation. But the story will tell. New York showed a blue hackle, weight five lbs. three ounces.— After allowing the customary time for the betters to lay their money, the birds were put on the scratch and loosed, when they flew at each other as quick as the lightning's flash ; both were quick hardy birds, and "give and take" was the order of the day. When they came together it resounded through the room ; you know "when Greek meets Greek then comes the tug of war." This fight was one of the finest we ever witnessed, calling forth the expressions, "there's a drummer for you." "Skunk and Rattlesnake again !" and many more that I do not recollect. Suffice it to say, that we, although two ounces the lightest, won this fight in a canter, and made the betting on the main ten to five, in our favor.

FIFTH FIGHT.

We showed a Dominique fowl, a muff. New York a brass back, weight five lbs. one ounce, this was a deceiving fight ; our bird was declared a "dung-hill," "an old fashioned Dominicker," "King of the dung heap," &c., &c ; but "let those laugh that win." Upon being placed upon the score, to it they went pell-mell, now our bird down, now their's; we finally had a wing broken ; "told you so," &c. &c., went round the pit ; two to one on the brass back, but you well know odds in money never won a fight yet. We managed to give blow for blow, and struck as hard with brass back's hold, as we did with our own ; but brassy fought fast and furious, and struck us now here, now there ; he was in fact a rattling fighter, when just as we were on the point of giving it up, master Brass Back caught it, just between the shoulder. He did not like it much, and upon some more of the same sort, being administered, he proved the quarter horse, mentioned before, and left. Cries now arose, "where's your dung-hill now?" "got any more of that sort," &c., &c. It being now twelve o'clock, we all adjourned for supper to mine host's dining room, but feeling anxious as regards the settling of the main, we merely satisfied the inner man, quaffed a mug or two of ale, and then left the dining room for the Pit, where already had assembled the numerous spectators, who had merely left for a drink and a cigar, and were impatient for the resumption of the ending battles of the main.

SIXTH FIGHT.

The Duffodils showed a gray Strychnine, the New Yorkers, another blue hackle. This was another telling fight, first one, and then the other, weights even, four lbs. thirteen ounces. I can assure you, they were a pair of clippers, never waiting for a head hold, but striking wherever and whenever they could catch; when an unlucky *coup* blinded us. It would have seemed as if this would have finished us; but no, we fought the more savagely, and the bystanders shouted out, "there is one of the old Jacksons," (a breed of great celebrity in years gone by, and having the reputation of fighting better, after losing their eyesight) and which comparison, was considered by us as a compliment. We fought of course, a long way up hill, but our opponent had been much hurt, and did not press the fighting, seeming more inclined to fight it out on his handler's line, than to force us; but as we were continually picking, as you know a good blind fowl will, we at last got him where we wanted him, and finished the thing in a jiffy. This set our opponents to thinking. They had caught a Tartar, and we think they came to the conclusion, it wasn't so soft a thing to beat a lot of countrymen as one of them confessed. One had left word at his place of business, he was going in the country to clean out a few wood-hogs; but they found the tushes were too sharp, and he was glad to get back to Thirty Fourth Street, minus his watch and jewelry which he had raffled off to put him in funds.—Time of this last fight, forty-three minutes.

SEVENTH FIGHT.

Weights five lbs. two ounces; ours a blue red, Tartar and Counterfeit. New York another Pyle,—the best fowl they had shown by all odds. They got under way, and fought long and well. It was some thirty-three minutes before victory perched on the banners of the "House of York," and we congratulated them on having at least one good fowl, paraded by the residents of the Empire City. They took all our badinage in good part. We wished them better luck next time, and we cordially asked them to call on us again (remembering that to the victor belongs the spoils), which they declined doing that season; and then the war broke out, and fierce battles were fought by many of those present, and many a gap was made in that little circle of acquaintances who met, were entertained and defeated by the "Daffodil Club" of Westchester County, in the winter of 1860 and 1861.— We have said enough, and only trust the next time a main is fought by your fowls, that we may be there to see, and again chronicle the battles, and victories which we feel assured would result, if they were equal to those sent us and fought by us on the memorable and never-to-be-forgotten occasion. Wishing you a long life and much success, in the breeding and raising of game fowls, we remain

                              Yours most truly, the
                       "DAFFODILS OF PORTCHESTER."

Portchesther, N. Y.,
January 1st, 1869.

The above is one of the prominent mains wherein the Tartars established their claims to general superiority. It was a main which won great attention at the time, not alone from the amount of money which changed hands (some ten thousand dollars) but the celebrity of the cockers engaged in and present at it. If we remember aright the first intention was to fight in New York City, at one of the largest pits near Broadway, but the door-keepers became too largely interested in the sale of tickets, which commanded high premiums, and undue publicity was thereby given the affair. When the hour was reached the house was so crowded that it was found impossible to proceed, the main was adjourned, and finally came off as above described.

We regard the Tartar strain as our standard variety, because it is not only always true in battle, but possesses a strength and hardness uncommon even in games. Few of them (and these we never again breed from) have small, thin and weak-looking legs; but are in limb strong, thick, well set, with knees that tell of bone, and of muscle to back it.

Many of the strain are remarkably savage, while others, under kind treatment and free from annoyance, are just as remarkably tame. They are very polite and attentive to the hens, good and frequent treaders, and are in all respects just what ought to be expected in large and vigorous games.

They owe their origin, doubtless, to an early acknowledgment of the benefits of crossing, and to its most judicious application. At this time very few cockers or fanciers acknowledged the utility of crossing, and the men who then did it evidently had its monopoly. The result was their triumph not through the superior gameness of their fowls, but by the pure force of bone and muscle.

We have carefully bred the Tartars for thirty years, and have never been without the pure stock. The demand for them has always exceeded that of any other strain, save perhaps, the first season after the receipt of the Clippers, when men from all parts of the country wrote us for eggs and chicks and stags and pullets. The prices offered were exorbitant, but the system of sale was not materially changed, and before the demand was half supplied the war broke out, cutting off one section of the Union, and for a time greatly decreasing the interest in games. Since the war the demand for the Tartars exceeds that of the Clippers somewhat—mainly because of their greater size and strength; but both crosses, as well as originals, are greatly sought for.

We believe the reputation of the Tartars has extended throughout civilized North America, and they can be found in almost every State of the Union, in the possession of the most noted and most successful cockers and fanciers. They have in many places completely supplanted varieties dependent only upon local reputation, and we know them to have won important mains in almost every prominent city of the Union.

They very in weight from four and a half to eight pounds, and from this strain more shake bags can be obtained than any other strain known to us except the Prince Charles. All are firm of chest and strong of limb, wing and bill. Some of them have not as small and as pretty heads as other game varieties, but the clearness of the eye, well set and almond shape in the lids, tells of good blood and high spirit.

While their purity is preserved, or their crosses carefully made, they will maintain a first-class reputation, and be constantly sought by all lovers of games.

THOMPSON WHITES.

The original of this breed of game fowls was imported from China by a gentleman of Virginia, under the name of the China Pheasant Games. [Why the word "Pheasant" was attached, we are at a loss to say, as no Pheasant marks or traits distinguished it. The only accepted reason is, that it was at that time popular to attach the word to varieties of fowls, and in some cases to varieties of games.] A main was made to fight against the late Bradford Thompson, then the most successful cock-fighter in the State.

Amongst others the imported China Pheasant game cock was matched, but when he was brought into the pit, Mr. Thompson offered to forfeit the match if the cock could be bought for fifty dollars, which offer was accepted.

Mr. Thompson kept the cock for a breeder, and by running with him a selection of his finest hens, and reserving only those that took after the cock in color, he very soon established the color and peculiarities he desired, besides, one of the best breeds of game fowls ever known in the Southern States.

It was a boast of Mr. Thompson's that though he had made a great number of mains with his white cocks, they had never disappointed him, as he had never lost a main with them, and rarely even a single fight.

After Mr. Thompson moved to Alabama, he was not personally engaged in any main, though he would let his friends have cocks, who fought them invariably with success. It is easily discovered how these fowls dropped the original name of China

Pheasant Game for the more appropriate one of *Thompson Whites*.

Up to the time of the death of Mr. Thompson he raised no other fowls on his place in Alabama but the Thompson Whites, and would let no one have the stock to raise from, as the cocks he let out to fight were to be returned if not killed. By judicious crossing he kept them constantly up to the mark, not only in size but also in gameness.

After his death some of the stock got into other hands, and for the purpose of keeping them pure, they have been bred in-and-in too long, as the size—which was originally small—has been still farther reduced, though in point of gameness they are as good as ever.

These fowls are easily described. Both cocks and hens are pure white, with bright yellow beaks and legs. When they were in their prime, in the hands of Mr. Thompson, the cocks would weigh from four to five pounds. For fowls of this size they were remarkably well bodied, and very strong. They were quick, active and savage, and would often win the fight before the other cock would begin.

The author was presented with a trio of the Thompson Whites by a friend in Georgia, obtained directly from the widow Thompson. They were very pretty, but not much larger than the largest sized Bantams. We placed the trio on a walk for the purpose of breeding from them, and afterwards testing their qualities, but the cock, after numerous battles with neighbors of "low degree," was one morning found dead, his head crushed by a brick, thrown doubtless by some one who had received injury or was envious of the qualities he displayed. The experiment was not pursued further, as the stock had been bred in-and-in, to so great an extent that the fowls were unfit for other than quick fighting, and had lost bodily vigor. The description and history furnished above comes from the gentleman who presented us with the Thompson Whites, and who at the same time sent some Claibornes, with their history and description.

THE CLAIBORNES.

SOMETIMES CALLED MOBILE.

This is a variety of the black breasted red games, and takes the name of Claiborne from the gentleman who successfully bred and fought them for a number of years.

Mr. Claiborne was a constant patron of the pit, not merely for profit, but from a natural fondness for the sport. He was in the habit of importing fowls from England and Ireland, Spain, and from any other country whence he thought he could obtain a good breed of game fowls.

Probably no one in the South was more successful in raising fine fowls, and when carried to the pit, they amply repaid the care and attention bestowed upon them. In having such a variety of superior fowls, he could cross, as judgment dictated. By a judicious cross what may be called a "hit" was made, and the strain in question—the Claibornes—was established.

They are thought to be a cross between a good English and a good Spanish breed, as they resemble both in different particulars. The hens of this variety are a rich, beautiful, deep buff or dark red, small, thin head, long neck, full breast, broad, short back, and a tail wide and fan-like. But as in almost all of the feathered tribe, the cocks of this variety have by far the advantage of the hens in point of style and beauty.

In courage, bravery and style, they have no superiors and but few equals. From head to tail and foot, they show every faculty that is requisite for a thorough-bred game cock, and those who have fought them for several years have yet to say that one of the strain ever left the pit—dead or alive—unless he was brought out.

When they are backed with any amount, a man has the satisfaction of knowing that if he loses, it will be by a scratch or a decided superiority of the opposing cock, as the Claiborne may be killed but not whipped. They never run.

The cock has a beautiful, small, round head, clear, brilliant and fiery eyes; neck full and well hackled; breast black, broad and full, and very strong; tail full, wide and sickled; wings broad, full, long, and hanging low on the shank, thighs long and large; shank, short, wide and strong.

Both cocks and hens of this strain have either a white or clear yellow beak, legs and claws. The hens have generally long, keen spurs. This they probably get from the Spanish blood, as there is no other breed where the feather is so universal. The long, keen spur of the cock is a suitable weapon for the pit with naked heels, though they will carry a three or three-and-a-half inch gaffle with as much ease and sprightliness as an ordinary game cock a pound or pound and a half their superiors in weight.

The variety is a medium sized one, the cock weighing from four and a half to five and a half pounds.

As a general thing both cocks and hens have a slight top-knot—though not always.

A fine trio of this strain was sent the author in 1859 from Georgia, (the donor being the same who sent the Thompson Whites), the gift being accompanied by a letter from which we extract the following:—

"The cock of this strain will be two years old next Spring. He is the one I wrote about in a former letter. I send him instead of a stag that you may see a specimen of the breed fully grown and developed. He is one of the finest I have ever seen. Schley says that if anything out of the pullets by any sort of a good cock ever runs, he will forfeit all he has got. The pulletts he presented—the cock I bought. He says that you may know something of the blood of the pullets, as their sire has been in several fights without receiving a scratch, and for two years he stood with five hundred dollars on him, without being taken up. He says that the cock I send is as good as they can make them. He yesterday saw him in my yard. Let me know if you have, or ever saw a finer trio of games than the Claibornes, *for beauty, style and gameness.*"

The fowls above described came to hand safely, and the first year were carefully bred by themselves, the product being large. The second year, with the cock and Claiborne hens, were placed Tartar hens, and the third year Clipper hens—the eggs all carefully marked, and the result of this was an additional number of pure Claibornes, and a number of crossed Claibornes, Tartars and Clippers.

We have since regularly bred from them, always maintaining the pure strain, and at the same time so crossing others with approved breeds as to increase their size and strength of leg.

The promises of our friend have all been realized, and the Claiborne's withstood bravely all the known tests. We have since sent them to various parts of the United States, and the accounts we have received tally with the original impression.

While we do not wish to disparage the fondness of our friend for the Thompson Whites, we must pronounce the Claibornes immeasurably superior to them in general make-up and all the more rude but valuable attributes of game fowls.

We agree with him in the belief that the strain owes its origin to both Spain and England, and if we were to guess the English fowl to which it owes part of its blood, we would say the Lord Sefton, for in many characteristics can this cross be traced. Or they might be a sub-cross of the Baltimore Top-Knot. In any event, the strain is first-class, and equal to any of its size we know of.

Our possession of it has always been a source of pride, and we may say of profit, and our gratitude to our Georgia friend (who must here be nameless) is yet as fresh as when the old trio first greeted our eyes.

We may mention that the Claiborne's have long been known

in the South and West, and have always maintained a high reputation particularly in the South. They are there regarded as the equal of the "Stone Fence" variety; but are more valued, because more rare. All the cockers of Mobile are familiar with their traits and history, and most of them place implicit reliance on the strain. The same is true of Florida, Mississippi and Louisiana. Their reputation has extended to the remote parts of Texas, New Mexico and California.

Though chiefly raised, prior to 1860, in the South, and long inured to the climate of the Gulf States, they are thoroughly hardy, and breed and live and fight as well North as South. We have sent some as far north as Maine and the Canadas, and we have yet to hear of any want of hardihood shown in any case.

The reason of this is found in their history, their blood, and perhaps the larger part, being due to the north of England.— Games, properly treated and understood, are the hardiest fowls known to the line of poultry, and we have never yet known a good variety but that could safely withstand all the ordinary changes of the climate—especially all the changes known to the United States.

OLD NICKS.

In the counties of Nash and Halifax, in the State of North Carolina, certain wealthy planters have had a breed of game fowls which have had a local fame ever since the Revolution. One particular strain, called the Wagoner, has been known by tradition for two hundred years.

The Carolina birds have been repeatedly crossed by other games, and are now owned and kept in their purity in Nash county by some members of the Arrington family.

In 1858 a main was fought by N. Arrington, Esq., at Memphis, Tennessee, and several years before in Georgia, for large stakes, in both of which he was the victor.

These chickens were also owned by a gentleman in Davenport, Iowa, who christened them Old Nicks (we believe in honor of Dr. Van Meter, of Bowling Green, Kentucky, a noted gamefowl fancier.)

They are of various colors, are fair sized, well shaped, strongly built, good flyers, and good billers. The hens lay very large eggs for their size, so much so as to render them valuable to farmers, independent of their fighting qualities.

The strain or breed has great celebrity, in North Carolina, Tennessee and Kentucky, and where known is universally admired. It is also known to the Shenandoah Valley and in Western Virginia.

We have recently succeeded in obtaining some of them, and shall carefully breed from them. They have no prominent mark to distinguish them from good English or American game fowls and doubtless owe their sole origin to England, coming from the hands of some of her nobility, and passing into the possession of wealthy Southern planters, who will frequently give, but rarely otherwise dispose of a pet variety of games.

PRINCE CHARLES BREED.

This breed of fowls is a cross from an imported brown red cock from England and blue American hen selected for the many fine points she possessed. She had a good bearing, was a good layer and setter, and her chickens were remarkable for their courage. The cock weighed six pounds, stood up well upon his pins, had fine large tail and hackle feathers full and long. His feathers were compact, healthy, beautiful and glossy; and his legs a willow color. He was the hero of seven battles, and always came off with little damage to himself. This was owing to his powerful fighting; he was savage when pitted and fought with the ferocity of a bull-dog. It mattered not whether he or his antagonist had the hold, he was constantly fighting. So great was his strength that when his adversary had the hold, he would rise and strike, and thus break his opponent's well directed blows. A fowl having this quality will always have the advantage in fighting, for not only does he break his adversary's blows, but when he gets the hold he makes good use of his time, which generally gives him an easy victory. When he has a cock cut down he shows no quarter, darting upon him like a hawk; if down lifting his head and striking as hard as though the other cock were resisting. This is the way all game cocks should fight, and would, if care were taken in selecting and breeding them.

The name Prince Charles was given him owing to his having been imported and having such princely appearance. The stags and pullets of this English cock and American hen are beautiful, and fully partake of the qualities of their parents. They breed brown reds, blue-reds, and dark-reds. This is a breed of fowls that every cocker should have. He could not make a better selection than this stock to cross with, or to have the breed as it now stands, a cross between English and America. We have tried the cross with many varieties—with small to increase the size and make-up—with large to add characteristics wanting in others. Our success has nearly always repaid the trouble.

We have had cocks of this variety to weigh as much as eight pounds, and proportionately well built.

The hens commensurately share the size and strength of the males, are of good feather and very pretty. They are blue, red, brown, and sometimes so light as to approach the appearance of Piles.

The variety is tame as a rule, the cocks being easily made pets of, and the hens quiet and sedate looking. They are very productive, the hens generally being both good layers and setters, and are very motherly in the care of their young. All of them are hardy, and in this respect are second only to the Tartars. They seem to breed equally well North or South, and have the faculty of making themselves at home wherever they are.

We have known shake bags of the Prince Charles variety to bring very high figures, and many of them have been victors in a series of battles.

They are at all times reliable, and their product, under favorable circumstances, is nearly always abundant.

Their reputation is confined to no locality, but is especially recognized in some of the northern States, where large fowls are as a rule in greater demand than in the South.

BALTIMORE TOP-KNOTS.

This is a large and beautiful breed of games, first known to a gentleman by the name of Goss, of Baltimore County, Maryland. Mr. Goss acquired much celebrity throughout Maryland by their use, and his fowls, in frequent contests against the city of Baltimore proper, established a reputation that has since become more than local.

The celebrity of the stock reached the author many years ago, and he effected an exchange with the owner, and has since, to a great extent, bred the Top-Knots, and found their praises well warranted.

They are mostly red-feathered, with yellow legs, while some have blue breasts and tails. They are lofty, stand up well, but some are too slim in body for our taste—superior strength and endurance being found in superior compactness of body. They lack the round, plump appearance of some other varieties of games. The top-knot of the hen is frequently rather large, but that of the cock is invariably confined to a few feathers back of the comb. They breed large, say from six to seven and a half pounds—are quick hard-fighting fowls, and have generally excellent bills.

They are frequently taller than other fowls of equal weight, and in this respect acquire some advantage in fighting, especially in billing—which they are skillful enough not to lose.

We have frequently seen their gameness tested with the steel, and invariably, when vanquished, they stood until death.— We once saw a Top-Knot stag cut down, with both eyes out, and under the hold of his opposing fowl, yet he raised, struck, and killed his adversary.

The breed is a fine one, and well worthy of propagation. We take it that it is a distinct breed, in the absence of any knowledge to the contrary. Mr. Goss was one of the number of cockers fond of keeping his own secrets with regard to his own fowls, and we were never able to obtain a satisfactory history of the variety.

We sent some of the Baltimore Top-Knots to "Censor," in London, and while he seemed highly pleased with them, he preferred the Tartars.

THE RATTLERS.

Rattlers are so-called because of their mode of fighting, and owe their origin to the author of this work, being the result of a cross between an imported English gray cock, with a small Counterfeit hen. The original cock had a blue breast and blue legs, and considering his variety of colors, was very pretty.

Rattlers, for fancy and color have few equals. The cocks are hard fighters, and handle their legs like drummers beating the reville—hence their name.

They breed a variety of collors, but mostly have blue legs. In size they run from four to five and a half pounds, and are always counted light weights. They are greatly superior in fighting qualities and general vigor to some of the pure-blood English varieties, because they are the result of a judicious cross, and are fresh and hardy. Where small weights are wanted we know of no variety better, unless it be the Clipper—and these are mainly preferred because their descent is more directly English, the idea prevailing to some extent that the more recent the importation of game fowls the better and purer ought the blood to be—a rule that does not always hold good.

The Rattlers show in feather, size and all outward appearance that they are the result of cross—that are of mixed game blood, but this should not be an argument against their general use for fighting purposes. They are thorougly game, strong and long-winded, and as quick as it is possible for fowls to be. The stags mature early, and at an early age can be trusted in the pit. The following, which transpired in 1860, is descriptive of the exploits of one of the Rattler stock:—

GALLANT-COCK-FIGHT IN LOUISVILLE, KY.

The city of Louisville, Ky., is at all times a great place for cock-fighting, and no more gallant battles are known in the Union than some of those which take place within its limits. Yet, of all days dedicated to this sport, Easter Monday is the most popular; and almost every game in fighting condition is then brought to the "scratch." On the last egg anniversary, the 25th ult., it was hinted around among the cockers of that city, that a certain sporting gentleman, known there by the alias of "Jim Scarp," had a cock raised by Dr. Cooper, of West Chester, Penn'a., and of a cross of his great Rattlers and Tartars. The size was not known, and nothing further could be learned. The Southerners, always ready for a "match," nothing daunted, cooped up their fowls and carried them to the gentleman's yard, where they separately challenged him to bring forth his game and fight. There were all sizes, from eight lbs, to four, if occasion offered to test the rattling powers of the half-tartar. But, one of the large number present matched the Tartar, and he weighed two ounces over, and was armed with $2\frac{3}{4}$ inch drop-socket gaffs, while "Jim" had nothing but two inch ones. Still he was determined to "pitch in," notwithstanding the disadvantage his fowl labored under. $50 was staked by the principal parties, and at least $500 used in side bets. The fight commenced, and a more gallant one was never witnessed It continued eight minutes, during all of which time the Rattler rattled into his opponent as though he were beating a drum. Had he flagged a moment, he would have been killed by the long gaffs of his gamey and strong opponent. As it was, the little six lb. four oz. half-Tartar and Rattler, literally cut the old champion of Louisville to pieces, and "Jim" and his friends pocketed the $550, as gallantly as they had bet it.

7

EARL DERBY.

It is said that for more than one hundred years this variety of games has been carefully bred at Knowsley, the seat of the Derby family, and by skillful crossing and breeding, they still maintain their high reputation.

D. S. Heffron, of Utica, N. Y., some years ago contributed a careful description of this variety of fowl to the *Country Gentleman*. We quote it in full:—

"In Mowbray's Poultry," a recent reprint of much merit, printed and revised by L. A. Meall and F. R. Horner, M. D., the following language is used when speaking of this breed : "*Black-breasted* Reds, the purest and truest breed are those known as the "Derby Strain," having been very extensively reared by the late Earl, at Knowsley, where they have been kept for upwards of a century; the greatest care being taken, during the whole of that time, to prevent the slightest deterioration in the stock, for which purpose they have at occasional intervals been crossed with the strains in the possession of Lord Sefton, Lord Germain and other fanciers. The same authors give the characteristic markings of a true bred Derby, as distinguished from other black-breasted reds, to be "white barred shanks of the leg, and claws the same, and a striped or streaky white bill."

And now that we have inadvertently introduced the peculiarities of this family, we will quote a few other foreign authors on the subject of the color of the legs. The Rev. Mr. Dixon, M. A., in his "Ornamental and Domestic Poultry," says: "The famous breed of game fowls belonging to the Earl of Derby are black-breasted reds, and do not differ from other birds of the kind, except it being a select family." And when describing the Derby cock, in the language of the Earl's game keeper, Thomas Roscoe, he says : "The legs are long and white ; in both insteps ; claws strong ; nails long and white." Of the hen he says she has "white legs, toes and nails."

In the "Poultry Book," edited by the Rev. W. Wingar and G. W. Johnson, Esq., page 142, we are told that the "Derby Red" have "legs, feet and nails white."

And in "*The Illustrated Book of Domestic Poultry,*" edited by Martin

Doyle, and published in London in 1854, page 143, the author says: "The black-breasted reds have branched into families known by the color of the legs. The white legs are Lord Derby's breed. The others are yellow legs, olive legs, blue legs, and dark legs, but "happily no black legs."

Here then in this sub-variety of game fowls, the black-breasted reds, we have distinct families, each distinguished by the color of their legs. According to the authorities quoted, and others that might be given, no game bird is ever admitted abroad as belonging to the Derby strain, except it has *white shanks, feet and nails*. In this country however, there is great looseness on this subject, as different breeders claim that their respective birds are pure Derby, though the legs may be yellow, olive, blue, or dark. We greatly offended some poultry fanciers at the State Fair last fall, because we happened to state that their game birds were not Derby, though so entered, as one trio had yellow legs, and the other dark. And if we rightly remember, the yellow legged birds took the second premium for Earl Derby, when a Devon cow might as well have taken a premium for an Ayrshire or an Alderney. In justice to the judges, however, we freequently admit that we presume their award was made through ignorance, but we have reason to believe that it is not always that the breeder retains the name through ignorance.

Nearly two years ago, and article of ours appeared in the COUNTRY GENTLEMAN under the head of "*Pure Bred Fowls—Experience*." Among other things we referred in that article to our experience in trying for three or four years to obtain pure Derby fowls, without success. But we did not give it up then. Early in 1858 we procured a cock and two hens, with assurance that they were true Derby, but when we came to breed them only a small part of the young had pure white legs and feet; while some had yellow legs, some olive, and some dark. Experience makes us feel sensitively on this subject perhaps, but we exonerate the parties who sold to us from all blame, as they were no doubt themselves deceived.

But the "tables have turned." The last spring we procured, at considerable trouble and expense, a Derby cock and four hens. Though we have raised but few chickens this year, we are jubilant over our success, as every fowl that has been hatched from this stock has borne the characteristic Derby marks of white legs and feet.

D. S. HEFFRON.

Utica, N, Y.

The writer above quoted shows throughout his fondness for breeding to a feather and retaining all the distinguishing merits of any breed of games. If the Derbys were to be propagated with the sole view of retaining these marks, they would soon lose value for all purposes, and this is why, even among the best cockers of England, it is difficult to find what are called Derbys.

The stock, in order to maintain its celebrity and be a source of profit to its holders, had to be crossed, and while the stock was saved from deterioration, the gameness was not in the least impaired.

We have imported Earl Derbys from parties who would not deceive and were not themselves deceived, and while our experience was much the same as that of Mr. Heffron's, we cannot confess the same degree of disappontment, for we knew the varieties of Derby crosses, and were satisfied if the game blood was pure.

We agree with the authorities quoted that white shanks, feet and nails characterized the original Derbys, and were doubtless the cause of much pride in the then Earl of Derby, but we will not join in condemning those not having these peculiarities.— It is possible to take a hen with white legs, and breeding her with a cock of green or yellow, ultimately produce her characteristics by selecting for after breeding such as best bear her marks; and a skillful but unscrupulous dealer could with equal ease produce a variety of fowls with all the marks of the original Earl Derby, and yet they would be farther from the original breed than any of the crosses thus named, and valued more for their good qualities than their oddities.

The Derbys are a standard variety in England, and have always been held in high estimation in this country. They are well known in all parts of the civilized world where games are valued, and prior to the introduction of some of our hardier strains were thought unequalled anywhere. They yet are valued above all others by some sportsmen—the admiration being most strongly developed in England, where pride of country has some share in the estimate.

We have raised them for thirty years, but never pursued for a long time the policy of breeding them to feathers, as we have always been of the opinion that, if deficient in anything it was in strength of bone and muscle, and this we cultivated in most cases, at the expense of peculiarities which were more fanciful than valuable.

Their weight runs from short of four pounds to five, and sometimes, though rarely, to six pounds. They are fine feathered, with long and brilliant hackles, and have every appearance of gameness.

THE IRISH.

The best Irish breeds are not known by any distinct names, and in treating of them we fully endorse the remarks of our contributor "M. W." Their choice must depend upon the judgment and experience of the buyer and the credibility of the seller.

The variety of Irish fowls which find their way to this country are almost legion. Some of them constitute our best games, while yet others are fit for no purpose but such as dunghills are noted for.

We have bred them, and prefer far above the others the blue reds, or such as produce red cocks with blue breasts, and blue hens. This variety, when obtained pure, is always reliable, and exceeds in size, strength and general make-up that of any other—excepting alone the black and brown breasted reds, which, when imported from Great Britian, we have always thought ought to be classed as English fowls. This classification is due more to the prevalence of these colors in England, and the taste of Englishmen for them. The Irish care little or nothing for color, but are a confident and not a calculating race. If they have pride of country behind them in a battle, they will as a rule unhesitatingly lay their pile on the cock representing their nationality, without caring for or thinking much of winning characteristics. They are mostly naturally fond of the sport, but make it less a study than others, and this in a measure accounts for the mixed up condition of their games. They will trade, exchange, buy or sell, with equal freedom. They were among the first of the nations to recognize the necessity of crossing, but many of them pursued the plan without study or system, and without previous knowledge of all the characteristics of the fowls which they employed. They yet, however, produce many good games, and as cockers or fanciers, they are not by any means to be "sneezed at."

PITTSBURG DOMINICS.

The Pittsburg Dominic (or Dominique) is a large strain originally from a seven pound Pittsburg cock, which had won several shake-bag fights, and a Virginia hen of excellent game qualities. The cross maintained all the fighting qualities of the father, and do up to this time.

It is the best strain known to deceive those not fully acquainted with it, the cocks, under only a cursory examination, looking very much like dung-hills—the mixture in feather doing more than anything else in aid of the deception. Many professional cockers prefer this strain on account of its appearance, as it frequently gives the owner a chance to gain odds in betting and in weight. A man can make a nice thing of it when he can get two to one bet against him and extra weight in his favor, and most any one would give it if he thought he was fighting against a dung-hill or half-game.

We have long raised the Dominics, and have always had faith in them. In testing the first which came into our possession we put short gaffles on a White Hackle cock of equal weight. The Dominic much of the time had the best of the battle, knocking his opponent crazy two or three times, but the gaffles were all too sure, and he gradually yielded his life, fighting to the last.

The Pittsburg Dominics are of all known dominic colors, being so called because of their mixed colors. They are of all sizes,—the stock from which we have been breeding being large, the cocks ranging generally from five to seven pounds, and occasionally producing good shake-bags. The strain is a very popular one in the western part of Pennsylvania, especially in Pittsburg, where they have long been in use, and in Maryland and West Virginia. They have long been successfully raised in York county, Pennsylvania. Their reputation is more than local, but until within the past twenty years was mainly confined to the belt of country named above. Since, they have been pretty well introduced into all the States, and we believe they have everywhere maintained their reputation as good games. Cockers before afflicted with the "feather prejudice," believing that only such fowls as have all the marks of original breeds are pure games, have been compelled to acknowledge that the Dominics have shown the fallacy of their old theory, and by many such it now more "honored in the breech than the observance."

THE WHITE HACKLES.

This strain or breed of games was formerly very popular in Philadelphia, where it was for a long time considered No. 1, it having won many matches and mains. Its fame was ably contended for in the columns of the New York *Clipper* by an easy and racy writer who assumed for his *non de plume* that of his favorite strain, and contended spiritedly against all comers—persistence finally leading to a "fowl" controversy with the writer of this work. There were certainly few better fowls than the White Hackles when in their prime, or when under the careful treatment of a Philad'a gentleman known as "Billy Beard," from whom they also took their name. He for some years maintained their strength and other good qualities, but afterwards they fell into other hands, and as they were chiefly raised in the city of Philadelphia, without the advantages of good country walks, they became unhealthy and finally unsafe to breed from. Some of them, however, were procured by gentlemen who could give them all the advantages of good walks, and these doubtless yet have them in full health and vigor. Indeed "White Hackle," in a communication to the *Clipper*, of date June 4th, 1859, described their extensive propagation at "Bright Side," the residence of Col. Hoe, of inventive fame; and arrangements were then made for their annual sale in New York city, but we believe afterwards discontinued.

The White Hackles breed brass backs, reds with blue breasts and tails, the feathers in the neck cutting out *white*, hence the name White Hackle. They are not large in size, running from four to five and a half pounds, and are generally esteemed light weights.

Their origin is unknown to us; but we believe them to be English fowls bred in this country to a feather.

THE WARRIOR.

This strain is the result of a cross of fowls selected because of size and endurance, and without regard to name of blood.—They have their origin mainly in the Tartars and Prince Charles. They generally breed dark blues, mostly with blue legs. They have plenty of bone and muscle. They fight with remarkable energy, skill and strength, and are in every respect reliable.

The writer has recently sent a few noble specimens of this strain to leading sporting gentlemen in Tennessee and Kentucky, by whom they were greatly admired. One of them was sent to Dr. Greenfield, the intention being to match him in a main as a shake-bag. He was seen by Mr. Cheek, a noble hearted Southern sportsman, who came all the way to West Chester with a view to purchase some Warriors and Strychnines. He carried with him some $13,000 (his habit being to constantly carry with him large amounts of money), which he said he was willing to stake on the fowls procured. Messrs. Cheek, Greenfield and Yancy then united in a main, and easily won it, using mainly Warriors and Strychnines. Mr. Cheek was subsequently murdered in Arkansas, the temptation to the outrage doubtless being the heavy funds he was always known to keep about his person. He was widely known in the Southern States as a true-hearted sportsman, and his death greatly regretted.

The Warriors are comparatively a new strain, but are gradually winning their way in public estimation. Many of the prominent cockers and fanciers of the South possess them, the object in their purchase being not only their known fighting qualities, but their use in crossing and giving general tone to smaller varieties of games which are favorites for pit purposes. They well unite the characteristics of the Tartars and Prince Charles, and show quite as many shake-bags as either of these strains.—The hens are fair sized and good layers of large eggs.

MEXICAN HEN COCKS.

Some twenty years ago two cocks and a hen of this breed were imported from Mexico by a noted Southern cocker. One cock was then killed, he unflinchingly standing all the tests applied. A fine cock and hen, and doubtless some of the progeny, are now owned by John Graham, of Davenport, Iowa.

The hens are black; the cocks black and black reds. They are fair sized, but not larger than the Rattlers, running from four to five and a half pounds—rarely the latter mark. Their chests are finely developed, large and broad, carriage erect, and of very game general appearance.

The long wing feathers of the cock project so far behind as almost to meet, and from this cause they possess the flying qualities of the game cock in an eminent degree.

The sickle feathers of the cock are very short, the tail rather broad, and hence the name hen cocks, or hen feather.

They are not, as sometimes believed by those not familiar with them, deceptive in appearance, and have not the general appearance of ordinary hens.

They are greatly in vogue in all the Mexican States, in Guatamala, South America, and the West India Islands. The people of all these countries are very fond of cock-fighing, and there the sport may be described as a national one, for it takes precedence and is more frequently practiced than any other.— Wherever Spanish blood prevails there cock-fighting and game fowls are popular, and so assiduously has this been cultivated that they seem to possess a variety of breeds not generally known in other parts of the world. The Spanish taste in games lead to the white or light colors, and in the cock pits of Cuba, attended equally by ladies and gentlemen, the white cocks.

are always greeted with applause. We have no reason to believe that they are better than others, just as we have no reason to question their gameness.

In Mexico the Strychnine is the most popular breed, and it shows the contrast of white and black and gray. But the hen feathers always come in for their share of admiration. These and the pure white, furnish the best specimens of the Spanish mode of breeding to a feather. The result is continued gameness in their fowls, but loss in size, limb and strength.

The popularity of the Hen Feather variety has extended to some of our Southern cities, and some years ago that were in great demand in Austin, New Orleans and Mobile. They are always reliable against fowls of equal size and make-up, but cannot withstand the strength of bone in some of the smaller American varieties and crosses. A Rattler or a Clipper would have greatly the advantage in a contest of equal weights.

LORD SEFTONS.

These, like the Derbys, derive their name from the Lord of their original manor. They are larger than most English breeds of games, and are different colors of red—producing black reds, brown reds and blue reds, mostly with yellow or willow colored legs and bills. They have for years contested against the Derbys in England, and have as a rule held their own. They are finely shaped with prominent, well developed breasts, and full, strong wings. They have not the same strength of bone as some American varieties, nor have any of the purely bred English fowls.

In early manhood we came into the possession of imported Seftons, and have kept and bred them ever since. No one disputes their gameness, and all admire their beauty of feather.

Those best hitting our taste are the deep black breasted reds with yellow legs and beaks, these characteristics generally being accompanied with the finest color and growth of feather. They seem also to reach a larger size, and, to the fancy alone, are in many respects preferable. We know of no difference in gameness or fighting qualities which can be distinguished by colors, the brown breasted reds being in these respects fully the equal of those with black breasts, when of like size and weight.

There are duck-wing Seftons, just as there are duck-wing Derbys, but none with white legs and rarely with green.

What is known as the Morrissey strain we believe is the result of a cross by that gentleman of duck-wing Derbys with white legs, with fowls found in New York, and of Sefton descent, though crossed with the blue Irish. They won much local elebrity in New York State, and gave Morrissey some renown as a game fancier. They were afterwards matched against Long Island, we supplying the latter with a variety of fowls, all the result of judicious crossing. The result was that the Long Islanders won the first six battles and the main very easily —the fowls they showed being pronounced the strongest fighters ever seen in a New York pit. This main was published both in *Wilkes' Spirit* and the *Clipper*. Reference can be made to those papers for a full account of it.

ENGLISH GAMES.

Next to running horses, cock-fighting may be called the national sport of the English. Most of them are passionately fond of it, and only at a late day have laws been passed in any way restricting its practice. Many of the English claim that to their country is due the origin of game fowls, but that belief has few supporters in these late days. None of their authors claim this, though they hold up the fact that cock-fighting was a proverbial past-time at the time of the invasion of Cæsar.— There are many game fowls, of pure blood called "English Games," no more definite name being given them. We know of no distinct breed claiming a monopoly of that name, and we presume the practice of so-calling them was obtained in this country from the importation of games which were known to be simply English. Such fowls are the result of crosses, made on British soil, the marks of a distinct breed having disappeared by mingling of blood. They have a general good reputation, but men in purchasing or importing them depend altogether upon the credibility of the seller or importer.

These fowls have been thus generally named because they are known not to be distinct English breeds, but strains, and strains are there in such great variety that it would be difficult to find names for all of them. On British soil they go by the name of the breeder, but when they reach here this name is frequently lost or dropped, and the word English is deemed sufficiently descriptive.

We believe these strains, in number and variety, have been mainly produced by the English operatives and the very poor, who could aford but few fowls, and were compelled to keep up their stock as best they could, for nearly all of the English, when they have the means and the opportunity, are great sticklers for distinct breeds, and for breeding to a feather. Their habit in this respect is just the opposite of that of the Irish nation. English breeders have often been known to discard good fowls for no other reason than that they differed too much in plumage from that which they had fixed as their standard.— The brown and black reds of both cocks and hens are the favorite English colors, and they give preference to willow colored legs.

The cocks in Pennsylvania, brought here by emigrant English operatives, have these general marks, and while by others called simply " English Games," they are among the operatives known by the name of the breeder. Most of these fowls are excellent for both breeding and pit purpcses, and the stock is improving in strength just as the practice of breeding in-and-in is decreasing.

Some of the English operatives living in the vicinity of Philadelphia have won great local celebrity through their fowls, and have engaged in mains against many of our eastern cities, and generally with good success.

Most of these cocks are small and well-bodied, being deficient only in strength of leg. They win many battles, but we are persuaded that they owe the majority of their victories to the skill employed in their training, feeding and gafting. Nearly every English cocker has some secret in these arts which he will part with only to his partners in a main, and rarely then. Most of these secrets can be reduced to mere superstitions, but some of them are valuable, and we believe all that are worth the showing, are given under their proper headings in this work.

We have long enjoyed the acquaintance of many English cockers, and attach more importance to the supreme care with which they attend to every detail in training and feeding fowls for battle, than to any assumed mystery. They permit nothing to remain undone upon which may depend the slightest chance of victory, and when the day of battle comes they are as a rule found ready in all respects, with nothing neglected, and no chance forfeited. They bet courageously, and while they display much pride in their fowls, they show yet more reliance in themselves, and in their skill to meet emergencies. Some of their heelers are noted for their quickness and skill, and all of them hold in high estimation the art of successful heeling.— The rules for gafting, elsewhere given in this work, are complete, and embrace all worth knowing on the subject. The plan given is that pursued by the most intelligent and skillful English cockers.

English games are to be seen in every part of our country where Englishmen congregate. We have pronounced them generally good, as they owe their pureness of blood to breeders who will suffer no alloy to enter, and who are mostly very manly and truthful in all representations affecting their own fowls.— So careful are they in this regard that they keep a truthful run of the pedigree of each cock and hen, no matter how frequently crossed, and detail it with as much interest and carefulness as though it were a thorough-bred horse. To this pride and care are the English indebted for the almost universal good name which they enjoy on all questions affecting the value of blooded stock of any kind.

An English Game, coming directly from the hands of an English breeder, and having his recommendation, can generally be relied upon and risked in battle.

BOB MACE ENGLISH GAME.

This strain is a beautiful red, with black breast and yellow, or green legs, and is distinguished by white dominic feathers at the root of the tail. It is beautiful in color, red, shining and lively feathered. The cocks are plumply built, stand pretty well on their pins, have good breadth of chest, short and rather broad backs, with more strength of leg than generally characterize English fowls.

The original cock and hen were of English importation, the cock being the hero of nine hard-fought battles. In his last contest he was a blinker, and was matched against another blinker of equal celebrity. The fight came off in Philadelphia, and caused some excitement among cockers who knew the history of both. The friends of each backed up their favorites, and bets were frequent and for fair amounts. The cocks fought with little intermission for over one hour, and was decided by the count being in favor of the Mace cock; but both were so cut up that they soon died.

The product of this original has well maintained the first reputation, and all of them are now highly valued, not alone for courage and fighting, but general beauty. They are in some respects equal to the Clippers, and generally superior in strength and quickness to the Derbys.

The strain has as yet but a local reputation, its originator still living; but is rapidly winning its way throughout Eastern Pennsylvania.

It of course takes its name from its breeder, Mr. Robert Mace, of Chester county.

BOB MACE SHUFFLERS.

The cock of this strain was obtained from Goss of Baltimore. He was a fine red, blue-bottomed cock, with yellow legs, and weighed six pounds;—broad, compact, well made, full chested and with rather short and stout neck. His stature was only medium, but he was very rich in feather. He was valued because of the battles he had won, and at the date of this writing is yet alive, quite a patriarch in his way, having reached his twelfth year.

He was bred to a set of red hens from imported English stock, and the result was a lot of very pretty stags, some blue reds with yellow legs, and some red with yellow or green legs —an occasional one tending toward a pile color.

These cocks have for the past seven or eight years been the terror of the Wilmington (Del.,) cockers, an occasional one having there won two battles in one day. None of them have ever shown the white feather, and thus far few of them have been unsuccessful fighters.

They are named because of their shuffling way of fighting, keeping themselves at all times busy and on the move, and having remarkably good wind.

Their reputation is but local, having been mainly used by some of the cockers of Eastern Pennsylvania. The stock is well known to Chester county, and has by it been frequently used against Wilmington, with almost invariable success. The Wilmingtonians soon tired of combatting this strain, and now acknowledge it to be superior to strains heretofore highly valued by them.

The most marked peculiarity in their shuffling mode of fighting is found in the fact that they make a close fight, always near or mixed up with their opponent. As a consequence they force the fighting, and herein is the reason of their success.

We are breeding the strain, and deem it mainly valuable for pit purposes.

THE WHITE-EYED GAMES.

This strain of game fowls sprang from a white-eyed game cock, crossed by Mr. Charles Twaddell with some red English hens. The father had won much celebrity in the pit, and was greatly valued. The first result of the cross was a large ginger red cock, with yellow legs and a yellow or buff eye, nearly white. He was very pretty, and won universal admiration. Twaddell and Mace soon had the stag in partnership and took him to Wilmington for the purpose of giving battle to the best that city could produce. They fought him four straight fights, and at the commencement of the last one he had his wing broken, when he was taken home. The writer afterwards procured him, put him with some of his best hens, and the result is as fine a lot of stags and pullets as any would wish to look upon. The white eye could not of course be retained, but the color now reached is quite as pretty, and we believe the stock is stronger and better.

Mr. Twaddell, to whom we are indebted for this strain, is a whole souled and wealthy sporting gentleman, given to a fondness for gunning, horses, &c. He is a patron of Mr. Mace's, and when he has anything new and valuable in the fowl line shares his luck with the latter.

We have been unable to trace the origin of the old white-eyed cock, but presume his peculiarity was the result of a pet fancy in the mind of some careful breeder, who obtained the result by gradual approximation and by a system of crossing. We know of no distinct white-eyed breed, either in this country or elsewhere, and in the absence of any such the peculiarity must have come from the course suggested. This result would be yet more easy and sure of attainment than breeding to a peculiar hackle or tail feather, and this fact makes our theory more than plausible.

The weights of the strain run from four and a half to six pound cocks and fair sized hens. They have good, strong legs, and are quick, restless fighters.

THE CAMERON STRAIN.

For a history of this strain we are indebted to Mr. Banjamin F. Shields. The original cock was bred from an imported Irish cock, and presented to General Cameron, he giving it to Mr. Duffy, he to John Shields, Esq., (a brother to Benjamin), and he transferred him to the author. While in the possession of Mr. Shields we sent him three very fine hens, to breed with him, after which he sent us the original, and at this writing we still have him in our possession.

From the original, we obtained several very fine stags the first season, and from these selected the most inferior one, and gave him to Robert Mace, who wished to fight him in a scrub match against his old opponents in Wilmington, Del. He took him there, and made a challenge to fight regardless of weight—his own stag weighing six pounds. He fought him four battles in succession, with odd weights against him, winning all with ease ; and wished to continue the sport on this basis, but though there were both English and Irish sportsmen present, they refused to continue it. Mace then declared he would give them further evidence of the gameness of this stag. He then took the heels off the stag and placed them on a game cock of his raising, and cut the stag down. This operation required an hour's time, the stag dying while it had hold of the cock's wing.

The father was one of the hardest and most savage fighters we ever saw. When his hold was broken his bills would come together with a snap, in very savageness and spite. His blows were hard and strong, and as frequent as the emergency demanded.

We have yet got two full brothers of the stag that was cut

down in Wilmington, finer in shape and stature ; we bred from them last year, and intend to keep them for that purpose so long as they can prudently be used.

The stags and pullets from the old cock and the brothers are finely made, strong and large fowls. We recently sent one of last season's stags to Mr. Benjamin Shields, and while on his walk he soon turned upon a Virginia white game, which had been classed No. 1, and in a short time killed him.

The old cock was a light red, with black breast, yellow legs, and a small top-knot. He stands beautifully upon his pins, and ordinarily is very tame, but when teased or annoyed becomes very savage. We first bred him exclusively to large hens, and the cocks from him are generally six pounds strong weight.— These we continued breeding to large hens (this being the second generation) and the result shows itself in stags which when full grown will show seven pounds. One, particularly noticeable, is a dark red, with black breast ; another is a perfect model of the old cock in appearance and disposition.

So highly do we value this stock that we purpose in the near future crossing it with many of our most valuable hens. We are this season producing blues, blue reds and brass backs.

THE BEARDS.

This strain of fowls sprang from a very beautiful brown red cock that William Beard kept for some years as a breeder.— He was afterwards procured by Benjamin F. Shields, who presented him to the writer. His plumage was very fine, both wing and tail long and full. He seemed possessed of much intelligence, was remarkably tame, and fond of being petted.

While on Mr. Miller's walk, near West Chester, temporairly running with ordinary hens, he was observed to stand out at the base of a tree, guarding his hens (which stood affrighted in a clump of bushes,) against the aggressions of a hawk hovering near. He stood out in bold relief, motionless and still, but very watchful, and when Mr. Miller approached him, and the hawk had flown, he suffered himself to be petted—thus showing that he was not the victim of any nervous trepidation.

His original owner was a noted game fowl raiser of Philadelphia, the originator of the White Hackle strain. For years he had the reputation of producing very fine fowls. He was, we believe, a strictly honest fancier and breeder, and had the confidence of all in the line who knew him. The Beard strain perpetuates his fair reputation, and all that we have seen are a credit to his name.

They exceed in health and vigor, in strength of body and limb, the White Hackles, and are better preferred by us for all purposes.

We bred the old cock to some Baily English brown red hens, and now have a fine and large lot of stags and pullets, bred almost to a feather, which run in weight from five to six and a quarter pounds. They well fill the taste of any one for brown reds, being rich in color and of very full plumage. Their heads are small and snake like, with necks looking somewhat larger than they really are because of this fact. They are greatly admired by English cockers in Eastern Pennsylvania, and are almost invariably thought exact duplicates of the Bailey stock—one of much celebrity hereabouts.

They are remarkably hard and fast fighters, and are throughout reliable. They will adorn any cocker's yard, and be a source of pride to any game fancier.

THE SHIELDS STRAIN.

It takes the name from Mr. Benjamin F. Shields, previously mentioned, and from him we directly procured the stock. The strain show fine black-breasted reds, with green legs, lofty in stature, of fine plumage, and excellent make-up.

About three years ago we sent a Shields stag to Mr. Cheek, who in company with Dr. Greenfield and Mr. Yancy, fought a main against Alabama, they repesenting Tennessee. The main came off near Clarksville. The stag was pronounced one of the fastest and best fighters of the main, and easily won his match. The parties were so pleased with his performance that they afterwards kept him for breeding purposes.

Similar accounts of the doings of the Shields stock could be given *ad libitum*. Nearly all of them are energetic and rapid fighters, and we have yet to see the first one show any signs of the white feather.

Mr. Shields has the reputation of being one of the best judges of game fowls in the State of Pennsylvania, is a careful breeder ; and strictly honest in all his dealings. The love for game fowls seems to run in the family, all of his brothers being skilled fanciers. We have frequently exchanged strains and breeds with members of the family, and invariably found their representations true to the letter. They are all well known to Lancaster county, and while they have never bred for sale, they are courteous in giving information, and will occasionally exchange with parties of fair repute, and with fowls of known gameness.

The Shields strain has been the favorite of the family for a number of years, and has always been carefully and skillfully bred. The stags and cocks have acquired a reputation which has become general in Pennsylvania and Maryland, the latter frequently suffering from contests against them.

Their origin is English, and we believe them to be an improvement on the Lord Seftons, for they bear many of the marks of this breed, yet are stronger, more compact, better limbed, and generally more suited for pit purposes.

We have carefully bred them for several years, and they meet our idea of a fowl more nearly than any pure English breed we know of. They produce fair sized hens, and cocks running from five to six and a half and even seven pounds.

THE BAILEY STRAIN.

The original of this strain was brought by Mr. Bailey (now of Delaware county, Penn'a.,) from England. The old cock was a pretty brown red, six pounds in weight, the hens brown and black. The strain now shows all brown reds, being very nearly to a feather—cutting out black in hackle.

Bailey has been very successful in battle with this strain of fowls, and has frequently won very important mains against Philadelphia. He is associated with another Englishman, named J. Elise, who is one of the best feeders and trainers we ever saw. He is in these respects much superior to any the Philadelphians can produce, and those of that city who know the fact, and have no especial interest in the main will bet five to four on the Bailey fowls—not alone because of their confidence in the stock, but because they appreciate the skill of the man who sent them to battle.

Both of these gentlemen are fair and straight-forward men, and neither has ever been known to stoop to any mean or unfair act in the pursuit of their favorite sport. They share losses with imperturable humor, and pocket winnings as a matter of course.

Some years ago we were present at a main of the Bailey against the Philadelphia fowls—each party showing fifteen.— Bailey had but six of his brown reds present, having selected the others from factory neighborhoods in Chester and Delaware counties. Bailey reserved those fowls of his own stock to the last, and when they were reached he was five fights behind in the main—the six remaining fights having all to be won in order to secure the main. We were only a looker-on, but our sympathies were all with Bailey. His cause was a desperate one, and the odds seemed to be worth a hundred to one against him. He showed, one after another, his six brown reds, all so much alike in color that they could only be distinguished by their weight. The betting ran two to one against Bailey, that he would lose the main ; but his fowls went in and won the needed six straight fights.

We closely observed the style and fighting of the brown reds, and they appeared to win not from any fierceness or quickness in fighting, but by skill and what we can best call intelligence. They seemed to fight with deliberate judgment, the secret of their success lying in the fact that they seemed to always meet and break the assault of their opponents. If the other cock had the bill and was about to strike, the Bailey cock was sure to meet and ward it off; but if the other cock lagged for a moment, the Bailey, ever on the alert, would force the battle with telling effect.

The Bailey stock are very highly valued in Eastern Pennsylvania, and have until recently been very difficult to procure, the parties holding refusing to sell.

The partner of Mr. Bailey also has what he claims to be very fine imported muff games, but we are not conversant with their origin, history or characteristics.

Before dropping the Baileys we must tell of a single encounter against one of his fowls which was somewhat amusing.— During the war Bailey visited the writer at West Chester, and while on one of the walks saw some students from Cuba fighting games, in Cuban style, and with natural spurs. One of them had a little stag procured from us in which he took much pride, and wanted to find a match for him. He asked Bailey if he ever fought, and receiving an affirmative answer, challenged him to a single match for $10, the parties agreeing to meet on the following Saturday. Bailey started for home to put a cock in order, and the Cuban immediately commenced pulling all the hackle feathers out of his stag's neck, and twice a day would put whisky in his mouth and squirt it over the stag's bare neck and head; so that by the day of the fight the skin was almost like sole leather, and of a deep scarlet-red color.— Bailey put in his appearance with one of his brown reds in first rate order, and when he saw the Cuban's fowl asked what had been done with him? The answer was that "that was the Cuban style." Bailey confessed that he did not like the appearance of things, but concluded he would fight, especially as his cock weighed a pound more, and had been well trained and fed; while the other had been penned up for a long time, and had been kept on corn and water. We were called upon to heel for the Cuban, he never having seen a gaffle. To this Bailey demurred, but allowed the arrangement to proceed under the proviso that we would hold for him while he heeled his own. The first gaffle he put on was in imitation of our plan, and if the other had been set in the same way he must have won, but the other he put on in the old Philadelphia fashion. We warned him of his error, but he refused to acknowledge it, and when the fowls first went to work the Bailey did all the fighting, with little or no execution, and after a time the Cuban's got in two quick blows and killed him. Bailey still remains unconverted on the question of gafting, and whenever this fight is referred to says that the cause of his loss was the manner in which the Cuban had *tanned* his stag's head and neck. He affirms that the skin was so tough that his cock could not get and keep a hold. There was probably some advantage to the Cuban in this, but we yet believe that the Bailey cock must have won an easy victory if he had been scientifically heeled.

THE ESLIN STOCK.

We procured one of these fowls from Jonathan Dorwarth, of Lancaster, Pa., he getting him from one of the Eslin family, residing near Washington, D. C. Before purchasing we met the younger Eslin in Philadelphia, and made inquiry as to his qualities and gameness. We were told that he was one of the finest fowls, in the narrator's belief, in America; that he had fought him in Georgetown, D. C., against a very fine cock, and when pitted the two rushed at each other, met about three feet above the floor of the pit, and rattled down like Kilkenny cats. When they landed on the floor the other cock was dead. This recommendation determined us upon securing him, and the first year we bred him to some fine hens, sisters of the six Bailey cocks described as deciding the Philadelphia main.

The result was some very fine brown red stags and pullets, which afterwards proved dead game and good fighters.

Mr. Elise, (Bailey's partner) is now breeding from one of the cocks got by this cross, now six years old, and combining within himself all the good qualities of the Bailey and Eslin.

The original was seven and three-quarter pounds running weight, and was a well feathered brown red with green legs.—His station was excellent, his movements very graceful, and he seemed at all times not only to recognize his own importance physically, but to realize that sagacity was also a prominent trait. We succeeded in breeding from him three years. He was a pet at times, and savage at others. We kept him for a time running in the yard attached to our residence, and when he died put one of his most savage stags in the same place.—Visitors made frequent calls to see our games, a few of which, ready for boxing, we are in the habit of keeping in the stable the stags cooped up. These of course kept up a constant crowing, and were a source of irritation to the stag outside. He not only watched the stable, but was always on the look-out for our enterance, and when near the open door would peck and strike our own and visitors legs in a way far more energetic than agreeable. We afterwards sent him to a walk in the country, in care of Thomas White. He kept a number of large bronze turkeys, to which the Eslin stag took a great dislike, and never let slip an opportunity for a general melee. At times the turkeys would concentrate against and tramp and peck him, when he would be partially released by Mr. White driving away all the turkeys but one, when the stag would soon prove the victor. This was repeated three or four times, when early one morning the same general engagement took place, and upon Mr. White starting for the gound the stag run and met him half-way, as though to encourage him in his ideas of fair play, and when all but one of the turkeys were driven away, he repeated the threshing operation. This show of intelligence was frequently repeated, and in other ways he displayed sagacity equal to that of a dog.

After we bred from this stag one year, he was sold to W. W. Lyons, of Jackson, Tennessee. He was extra fine in all respects, and weighed seven and three quarter pounds, and would fight at not much less.

The same strain was afterwards crossed with the Jack McClellan stock, the result being in some cases the very largest game fowls now in our possession—some of the cocks having reached as high as nine pounds in weight.

We also procured a cross from the stag described with our finest Tartar hens, the result being black, brown and blue reds, generally with green legs—all of fine plumage, remarkably deep chests, broad, short backs, and very strong in legs and bill. The cross seemed but a repetition of the finest Tartars, and the similarity led to further inquiry with regard to the origin of the latter; and we may here state that the younger Eslin claims for his father the honor of originating the Tartar stock, and denies the claim set up by Martinsburg, Va. The information with regard to the origin of the Tartars, given in the first or pocket edition on game fowls, was derived from a landlord of Martinsburg, but as the great battle for $10,000, fought by this cock, came off in Washington city, there is probably a good foundation for the claim. We are ourself now sixty-five years of age, and in early youth we remember hearing of Mr. Eslin as a noted game fancier and cocker. His celebrity in this line extended throughout the country, as a cocker exceeded that of any one we know of. England and Ireland may boast of men more widely known, but they owe part of their celebrity to other causes. We believe that the Eslin fowls would have all the chances in their favor as against any nationality, and we can say without boasting that we could, if necessary, select from our own walks fowls which could champion the cause of America against any nationality in the world.

The English sent the writer a challenge through the New York *Clipper* to meet them in a main at the Paris Exposition— the main to last a week, only a triffling sum being staked, the object being to test national superiority in games. We paid no attention to this challenge for several reasons, the first and main one being, that we had quit cock-fighting, and determined not to again resume it. But had we wished to accept, the insurperable objection would have existed, that America's fowls would have suffered in the voyage far more than those from England. The challenge was evidently not a very earnest one, else the amount stated would have compensated the trip, and it would have been made soon enough to allow some preparation on my part. Our impression was at the time that these parties mainly desired the publication of these names in our sporting papers.

In a national contest the Derbys and Seftons could not successfully contend against some of our best American crosses, which are of harder muscle and bone.

But to return to Mr. Eslin. We pronounce his claim to the

ownership of the original Tartar cock a reasonable one, and leave it an open question between Martinsburg and he. Many years ago we knew them to be bred in both Martinsburg and Hagerstown, Eslin claiming that he supplied those used in the last named place. The cock now known as the Eslin is in many and all essential points like the Tartar, and if all the truth could be reached at this late day, might be shown to be the same in origin.

THE JACK McCLELLAN STRAIN.

John McClellan, of Gettysburg, Penn'a., just before the opening of the late war, sent to us four cocks and a number of hens, each representing a separate strain. He foresaw the incursion of troops, and did not wish to lose all of his stock.

One cock when he arrived, was trimmed ready for battle, and was described as the winner of nine fights. He was a Pile, blue, lead and white in color. The second was a beautiful black with yellow legs; the third, a red saddle back Pile, with yellow legs; and the fourth a white cock, with light colored brass on his back, and with green legs. The last was from McClellan's favorite stock, known as the Old Whitey.

We bred all of these strains with their respective hens; with excellent luck, but found that few of them would even generally adhere to the original color, showing that they had been produced by crossing. While none of the cocks weighed over six and a half pounds, and all of them were over five and a half, some of their progeny reached eight pounds in weight.

We do not know the separate history of each, nor does Mr. McClellan, who cared more for gameness than name of breed, and was always a liberal crosser, and whose habit it was to have games of all colors. Their history being unknown they took the name of the owner, and in Maryland and the Southern borders of Pennsylvania were always so known.

The stock from these originals which we yet retain is first-class in all fighting respects. They are strongly built, with firm well-set neck, head rather large, bones very strong, and all of them possessing plenty of muscle. They are thoroughly game, and will show fight under any and all circumstances.— We have frequently seen them, when very sick or bruised, still anxious for battle, and still lustily crowing.

With these fowls Mr. McClellan and his partner in mains frequently whipped the Marylanders. In one main between these parties and Westminster, Md., the famous Ned Hall of

Baltimore, backed the latter, and entered one of his shake-bags in their behalf. Notwithstanding this, McClellan's fowls won every fight save one, and it was disputed. Each party showed nine fowls. McClellan's partner frequently entered Virginia in the winter season, and would keep himself engaged in mains for several months. He was an adept in the art of training, feeding and heeling, and always a very successful cocker. His father (whose name slips our memory) was the game keeper of Mathew Wilson, of Harrisburg, a noted cocker in his day.

We have lately effected a very fine cross between the Eslin and the McClellan fowls, selecting the largest and best hens and cocks of each. The object was to secure pit fowls, without regard to color. Size, bone and muscle were wanted, and we succeeded in obtaining all remarkably well. The cross shows pretty much all colors—some are fine black brass backs, while others show blues, grays, blue reds, pile and reds. The fowls are, we believe, not exceeded in size and strength by any in the world, and most of them are hard and furious fighters. Their principal use is as shake-bags, and for cross-breeding with a view to bring up the size of smaller strains.

Thus far the cocks have been very successful whenever fought, one of them having won a somewhat noted forfeit in the hands of Bailey. The Philadelphians, knowing his strain of fowls to be small in size, challenged him to a shake-bag contest, the forfeit being one hundred and fifty dollars. Bailey accepted, put up the forfeit, and then came to us and borrowed a large cock of this cross, gray in color, and weighing eight pounds.— When he was shown in the city, the Philadelphians could produce none as large as the dominic (they calling him by this name) and consequently forfeited. Bailey afterwards fought the cock for small amounts, won two fights with him on that day, and returned the fowl in good condition.

This cross notwithstanding the size and weight of the cocks, shows some tolerably fast fighters. All of them are hard strikers. They are objectionable to a fancier, because they will breed no previously known colors, but we esteem them among the most valuable shake-bags in the world.

THE BAKER PILES.

This is a strain propagated by Mr. Philip P. Baker, and one which owes part of its origin to the Lord Sefton games. They are very pretty piles, with either yellow or green legs, are fine statured, and as game a fowl as ever entered the arena. Baker raised these fowls for a number of years in the vicinity of Lancaster, and they have from time to time been used in all parts of Pennsylvania and Maryland. They have a good local reputation, and are well esteemed by all who have used them.

We have for a number of years been in correspondence with Mr. Baker, and have lately reproduced many of the strain, in order to meet the taste for pile colors, we regarding them as among the first of their kind. They show birds of very pretty plumage, with long and strong wings, and gracefully flowing tails. Their heads are small and hawk-like, and have firm and smooth bills.

In filling an order for piles we sent some of them to Tennessee, to some leading sporting gentlemen, and they were soon used in a main against Alabama and Kentucky. They had very fair success, and were both quicker and stronger than the Southern fowls against which they contended. They have since been frequently used in the same localities, and are now gradually winning their way as favorites among those who prefer medium-sized fowls. They have never been bred to a feather, and never in-and-in for any considerable length of time, yet there has always been some discrimination made in order to retain the pile colors. This plan has kept up the vigor, activity, freshness and strength of the strain, and prevented its deterioriation. The objection to too many piles is that which is common to all fowls bred to a feather. Men strive to retain all of the colors or as many of them as they can combine, and do it at the risk of health and strength. Piles can be well bred, and well crossed, and still remain piles, and this can be safely done by procuring those of similar color, distinct from and not related to your own, and thus breeding from both.

DELAWARE DOMINICS.

This strain of dominics was introduced into this country by Mr. Henry Browser, of Delaware State, and have long been noted for gameness. We cannot ascribe to them qualities superior to any other games of equal size, though a trial and breeding of nine years has convinced us of their gameness.— We never showed the prejudice against dominics shown by some cockers, nor yet the extravagant admiration shown by others. They are for pit purposes only superior to other games because of their deceptive appearance, and feathered dung-hill look.

We obtained some of the Delaware Dominics, in the year 1860, and one of the cocks was thoroughly tested by our game keeper; shortly afterward one of them won two battles in a single day, in the last fight having an eye cut out and a wing broken, but notwithstanding these disadvantages he won. The next day he was of course, stiff and sore, but showed a willingness to do battle.

These dominics are of very fair size, and produce cocks ranging from five and a half to seven pounds, are well feathered, and of good station. The hens are generally large, and closely and compactly feathered. If we were to judge of gameness by appearances alone, we would decide in favor of the hens.

While breeding these dominics we made a singular discovery, which may be true of all dominic strains. You may put a full dominic hen to a cock of entirely different color, and the progeny will show pullets which take after the cock in color, while the stags will be all or nearly all dominics; but if you put a dominic cock to hens entirely different in color the result will be both stags and pullets which are dominics. We have several times repeated the experiment with a like result, and find our experience confirmed by Mr. La Rue, a game raiser of Virginia.

As a rule we do not prefer crossing dominics with strains decidedly different, but prefer crossing two dominic varieties, unrelated—for pure dominics in color soon accustom themselves to the eye and taste, and though seldom admired at first, frequently become a standard in the cocker's fancy.

We believe the Delaware Domincs equal to any other similar strain, and as the variety is not common to the country, is therefore the more useful for breeding with other dominics.

RED STRYCHNINES.

This variety sprang from the old original gray Strychnine cock, sent to Dr. Greenfield of Tennessee. The strain was obtained by putting this cock with some choice Tartar hens.— The result showed grays and dark reds;—then, in order to keep the colors distinct, we put the grays and the reds to breed separately, the latter showing what are now called Red Strychnines. Some of the red stags, grandsons of the old Strychnine, were just as large and fine as the original, and he was so superior in all respects that he afterwards became celebrated throughout Tennessee, and elicited much attention and admiration. The stags were dark reds, and they well maintained their color and general characteristics; whereas the grays show all gray colors. They are, however, not the less fine games.

The Red Strychnines show black reds generally, with an occasional brown blue and ginger red. Their cross is shown more distinctly in the color of their legs, these being blue, turkey, green, and rattle snake colored.

They are of remarkably strong bone, good stature, finely

feathered, and are among the most desirable fowls for pit purposes extant. We have produced Red Strychnines which are as beautiful as any games we ever saw, the hackle feathers being rich and large, and the tail full and flowing.

Some of them fight savagely, and are fearless of man or beast, while others are tame save only when annoyed, or when a battle is in prospect. They carry well the leading characteristics in fighting of the original Strychnines and Tartars, and we believe fully equal either of these in the pit. They are especially desirable to cockers who want fowls for a substantial, present purpose, and upon which they can confidently stake their money at any and all times. They are bred for pit purposes, purely and simply, and while they must ever remain unsupported in pride of pure breed, they will not be the less valuable in the estimation of those who value fowls most for their performance, and care little for distinguishing marks which are of more ornament than use.

GEE DOMINICS OF GEORGIA.

This is a breed of dominics for many years cultivated in the State of Georgia, and has won celebrity in nearly all of the Southern States, some of their more enthusiastic admirers claiming that they are unequalled in the world—a position very unsafe to assume, however good they may be. For more than twenty years we have heard stories of their prowess, and perhaps to this variety, more than any other, we are indebted for the breaking down of the old prejudice against the gameness of dominics. Many letters from that section have described their sterling qualities, most of these being parties upon whom we could place entire reliance.

The Gee Dominics are a heavy set, compact, round bodied fowl, and characterized in color by a brownish yellow tinge, somewhat resembling that seen on some species of hawks.—

Their legs are yellow, and their appearance throughout strikes one at once as very singular.

We last season had a cock of this breed on a walk about two miles from West Chester. While there a hawk swooped down upon one of the chicks, but before he could raise with his tender burden, the Georgia Dominic was upon him, and a severe struggle followed in which the hawk was crippled, but not so badly as to prevent him flying into the apple tree which shaded his combat. From his perch here he complacently watched the angry and excited game, and in the oppinion of the party who was a witness to the scene, apparently wondered if he had not made a mistake, and if the Dominic, with his peculiar tinge, was really not of his own species. The fowl had no time to waste on marital speculations, but impatiently tramped the ground under the apple tree, almost incessantly crowing, and bantering his enemy to come down for another round. But the hawk had had a taste of his sharp spurs, and wisely concluded that prudence was the better part of valor. We never yet heard of a good game fowl, not under cow, fearing the presence of a hawk, but have often known them to attack, and sometimes to kill. They are each masters of their kind, but the game fowl will neither yield nor leave, while the hawk in a battle of life or death, has often been known to prefer the former, and to " take wings and fly away."

The Gee Dominics show running weights from four to six pounds, and are the prettiest fowls of their kind, in our estimation. We obtained some through Southern friends a few years ago, and have carefully bred them. They are quick and skillful fighters, and seem to well sustain the deeds which made them so popular throughout especially the Southern seaboard States.

THE HENNY COCK.

In describing this variety of fowl we wish to start out with the distinct declaration that as sold and bred it is entirely distinct from that variety known in the South as the "Hen-Feathers." These have not the general appearance of hens, being marked only by a few hen-feathers, and from these deriving their names. On the contrary the Henny Cocks, sold as game by fancy dealers, very much resemble a hen in appearance, the hackle feathers of the neck are quite short, like those of the hen, and the tail is void of all sickle feathers, and consequently much like that of the hen. They are said to have had their origin in Mexico, probably because their feathers came from there. We do not know, and think the place of origin unimportant, for we believe them to be "*a fraud*." We have received almost countless letters of inquiry in relation to these Henny Games, and in some cases orders and money, but the taint is not upon us of ever having raised any. Many of the letters were unanswered, and we hope the experience here detailed will serve to convince all of their worthlessness.

We have seen very many of what are called Henny cocks, and have yet to see the first which will stand in a death struggle with steel gaffles. Judge Grant once sent us a very pretty black one, said to be of the pure breed by the party from whom the Judge obtained him; but upon being tested, he ran. We once purchased a very handsome one, said to have been imported almost directly from Mexico. He was seven pounds in weight, (the Hen Feathers only averaged four), was well feathered, compact, and when standing in the sun his feathers seemed of the color and richness of satin. He had certainly the finest gloss that we ever remember having seen on any fowl. He had a game appearance, and acted as games act when held in your hands—being wirey, restless, and full of motion, as though he cared only for fighting. With natural spurs he was good at sparring, and apparently always willing and ready, and it was my belief at that time that he was game. Before he was thoroughly tested, however, we were induced to part with him to Mr. Wingate, of East Rochester, New Hampshire. He was accompanined by a hen of the same color and breed. Mr. W. bred from the two, the progeny showing variegated colors—none of them pure black, like the originals. This was of course not to his taste, and when the stags were old enough, he put them to the steel, and one after another fled the ordeal. He wrote us, and we ascribed the fault, innocently enough, to the hen. He then killed her and all her offspring, and concluded to risk the old cock in a main. He was put in as a heavy weight, and while feeding he seemed to be in good condition, but when the sparring came he ran, and could not be induced to fight again.

This experience tallies with that of other parties. We herewith copy a letter from a Canadian gentleman:

Hamilton, Canada West, Feb. 24, 1869.

DR J. W. COOPER:—Dear Sir:—Enclosed find $10, for which I want you to send me a pair of game fowls. I leave to yourself as to what you shall send. I want them to breed *fighters*. I have been breeding here for the last three years, and have not succeeded in getting any game birds yet, so that I am now quite disgusted. I have now in my yard some of the Henny Cock breed, and as good ordinary fighters as any man ever saw, *but they are not game*. In the main fought yesterday at Toronto, the father of them fought, and after having the battle all his own way, ran away, as did also his full brother. I can tell you they won a lot of money on the two fights, as we thought them the best we had. Out of nine fights we only won two, and had three bad ones. So, Sir, you see how much we are in need of good games. I do not care for the color, size or shape, only let them be game and fighters. The old Top Knot hen my brother got from you is dead. We prized her very highly, as she threw good birds and game ones. I have your letter of last year before me, mentioning all the different breeds, but I do not feel safe in picking any. I leave it to you, sir, and I feel that you won't send me bad ones.

Yours very truly,
G. N. H———.

Hamilton, Ontaria, C. W.

There are many men in the United States, who have had the same confidence in the Henny Cock as the writer of the above letter, and found themselves victimized. They will do for poultry fanciers, but not for fanciers of the game. They should be classed with the Samatra, Malaga, Indian Pheasant, but never with true games.

BLACK REDS WITH WILLOW LEGS.

This is a fine strain of game fowls, and finds a general description in its name. The cocks are of good station, stand well up, with head erect, full breasted, broad across the shoulders and tapering gradually to the tail. The wing is long, and almost meets at the points, the tail full and flowing, and carried at a medium height. There are two long and shining sickle feathers, and a number of side sickles of fair length and color. The breast is full and black; the hackle and feathers on the back and rump of a dark turkey red. The head is small, with dark gray eye, and most of the cocks have a loud, bold and savage crow. The weight runs from six up to seven and a half pounds—the strain owing its origin to a desire to increase the size of the black reds.

We this spring sent a noble stag of this strain to Walter B. Peck, of Woonsocket, R. I. The high price of $20 was paid for the stag, his weight being six pounds and two ounces. The same buyer this year took the first premium with our large brown reds at the first exhibition in the Institute Hall at Woonsocket, held March 16th and 17th, 1869. The fowl last sent him can with equal ease take the premium as a black red. The hen from which in part this strain of black reds was derived, was a black English, of high station and well built in every respect for a model breeder. Her brothers in the same cluck had been fought and tested day after day, when cold and stiff from previous fighting, and the fowls from which they descended were equally good, and many of them had been victorious in hard-earned battles. The father was a three-year old cock, a black red with green legs, high station, with a small and finely shaped head, and a short, loud and savage crow. He was quite savage. and could only be held with great difficulty.

This stock of fowls was so well liked by those fully acquainted with them that they were greatly sought for breeders, and for exhibiting at fairs. Mr. Wright, of St. Louis, procured one for exhibition, he taking the premium, and afterwards in a letter declared him to be the most magnificent fowl he had ever seen.

For the strain we are entirely indebted to a process of judicious crossing, the cock being originally half English and American, and, as we have said, the hen full English. Their general carriage is very fine, and while they have no odd and curious marks or habits, they exceed in beauty and will win more attention than any breed of fowls not game, when upon exhibition. Their fighting qualities are first class and their gameness indisputable.

Black reds are the special favorites of a great many cockers and fanciers, and run foul of the taste of no admirer of games—the color being a standard one.

THE SUSQUEHANA REDS.

This strain of fowls was first bred on the banks of the noble river from which they derive their name. It has been favorably known for many years, and successfully fought in several prominent mains between Pennsylvanians and Marylanders.

In appearance they are very fine, with bright red color, black breast and rattle-snake colored legs. Their plumage is long, fine and glossy, are well stationed, and though not lengthy in the leg, are long in thigh. Their hackles and tail feathers are full and long, and those of the saddle rich in color. They sometimes breed brown and ginger reds, but generally black breasted. We have not the name of the man who originated the strain. They have long enjoyed a marked celebrity among the river raftsmen, many of whom are addicted to cock-fighting. The strain, when purely obtained is a good one in many respects, and thorougly reliable.

BLACK-EYED BLACK REDS.

This strain of fowls sprung from a black-eyed black red blink cock, got from Dorwart, and a black-eyed dark brown hen, got from Welch of York, Penn'a. The cock was selected as a breeder because of his hard-fighting qualities, he having the faculty of striking extraordinary blows for his weight, which was five and a half pounds. The Welsh hen was selected for her good breeding points. The progeny proved to be generally black reds, but occasionally a very dark brown red—the legs either blue or turkey colored. The Stags are especially fine for pit purposes, and are hard-striking, rapid fighters. One of them while yet young had a leg broken, and as we thought him of little use in this condition, parted with him, he finally getting into the hands of a noted cocker in Eastern Pennsylvania, who took care of and reared him, and when he had sufficient age fought and won several battles with him—all won with little effort. He then took him home for breeding purposes, but changed his mind, the fear coming over him that perhaps he owed his victories to luck. He then tested him against a good brown red game, the black holding his own with his naked stumps against the gaffles. This induced his owner to apply yet severer tests, and while fighting him cut off his toes, and stabbed him with a knife. The stag did not yield under this inhuman treatment and died fighting, when his owner both regretted his imprudence, and confessed his shame at the brutality exhibited. He had heard of such tests being applied in extreme cases, and resolved upon it in the excitement of the fight.

We have continued breeding the strain for the past ten years, and we have never greatly improved their size. They run well in weight for matches, showing from four pounds twelve ounces up to six pounds and four ounces.

When handled they are what we call "close fisted,"—that is, they draw their legs well up to their body, and tightly close their toes, being wirey, full of motion, and ready at any time to leap upon an adversary. In battle they fight actively and almost incessantly, striking with or without bill-holds. They generally make short work of a battle when in good order, and wherever known are esteemed to be winning fowls.

We have another strain of fowls with which the same peculiarity in eye known as the Breniman Black-Eyed Black Reds. They are a good strain of games, and have stood the test of twelve years service to our own knowledge. They are rapid and desperate fighters, and have been known to win battles in quick time. The following generally describes them :—

They are very beautiful and rich in color, having shining hackle and back feathers of a bright deep red, they have shining black breasts and blue legs, of medium height and station, with flowing tail. Their heads are small, the marked feature being a full, bold, jet-black eye. In weight they run from five to six and a half pounds, are wirey, full of motion, and most of them great *talkers* (a term, the appropriateness of which, all game fanciers will recognize) when in hand. They are also "close fisted." They are not in any way related, that we know of, to our own black-eyed brown reds, and yet are alike in most respects. In point of beauty they frequently exceed our own, and win general admiration. The two strains are good for breeding together, as the general characteristics can be preserved without breeding in-and-in. Breniman was a somewhat noted and very careful game breeder, and we believe kept no other kind of fowls.

THE BLACK BRASS BACKS.

This strain was originated about seven years ago, from a cock noted as a shake-bag, weighing nearly nine pounds, and a hen weighing close to six pounds. The progeny show fowls which must invariably win the favor of the admirers of this color. The stag we are now breeding from is eleven months old, weighs seven pounds and two ounces, and if all goes well will probably exceed eight pounds when two years old. His build is remarkably fine, is lofty and stands up as though he were lord of all created fowls. His legs are heavy and strong, of a golden color, head a medium size, with a bright yellow or dun eye; a long and shining jet-black hackle, bright yellow back and shining black breast, the hackle feathers yellow, those of the saddle long and light yellow, with a good, flowing dark tail. He is broad breasted, short and broad backed, tapering to the tail, where his black-tipped wings almost meet. His crow is quick and savage, and his general demeanor proud and game-like. The strain has been frequently tested, is quick and hard-fighting, healthy and vigorous, and is greatly valued by all whose ideas lean toward brass-backs. The cocks are as a rule used only as breeders and shake-bags.

THE BLACK BIRDS.

This strain originated with Major Hambright, of Pittsburg, who bred it from a black game cock and black hens, the latter procured in Lancaster. The progeny shows black reds with red on the tips of the wings, some with green and some with blue legs. A chance one will have a brass color instead of red on the tips of the wings. They go by several names, being known in Pittsburg as Black Birds, in Lancaster as Hambright Blacks, and in other places as Black Games. The strain is valued in some parts of Pennsylvania, and has maintained a good reputation. The colors are not at all times rich, and the sizes have little uniformity, the cocks running from four to six and a half pounds.

NED HALL GAMES.

This strain is very popular in Baltimore, and takes its name from its breeder. The cocks are heavy set, dark reds, low in stature, but frequently heavy in weight, some of them being known to reach as much as seven pounds. Some are green and some blue legged, and all of them are well feathered. They for a long time held the championship of Baltimore, and won many battles in other parts of Maryland. They are still well liked, and retain many admirers in their own locality. They are not a *breed* but must have been obtained by crossing, as they show no fixed color, save that of red, and are only characterized by their low-set, muscular stature.

THE TILTHAMMERS.

This is a first-class strain of fowls, bred with an especial view to size, weight and action. It is a sub-cross, derived from Tartars and other noted games previously bred with a view to the qualities mentioned, and called Tilthammers because of the steady and hard blows which they strike. They show black reds and dark brown reds, with legs blue, turkey colored or green. They are well stationed and of fine plumage, are broad across the shoulders, taper well to the tail, and are broad-breasted and short-backed. They are powerful in bone and muscle, and run in weight from six to nine pounds.

They are terrible in the pit, and so savage that the handler must watch them very carefully. They seem at all times to force the fighting, having remarkable wind, and, notwithstanding their size, are frequently as quick in movement as five pound cocks. They strike well with or without hold, and savagely follow up their blows, repeating them with a rapidity surprising in such large fowls. Their blows often tell with stunning power, and their battles are generally short. The strain is a new one, only brought to its present perfection within the past two years, but as we know all of the blood embraced within it to be of the purest game, we can readily class it among the finest of large game fowls known to the world. The progeny combines many good fighting qualities in an eminent degree, and while there is no marked characteristic in color or leg, the fowl will not the less win an admiration which must soon be general among those who wish shake-bags or large breeders.— They are throughout vigorous, mostly savage, and the first mark strikes the eye of the cocker is the thickness of leg and thigh, and as his glance ascends he sees the physical proportion well carried out in chest, back, and general make-up. They have a quick, short and savage crow, are remarkably attentive to the hens, and when on a walk it is best for cocks of a low degree to keep a safe distance. One of them seems strong and active enough to go through a neighborhood of fowls without weariness. For scrub matches they are especially desirable, but as a rule can rarely me matched, only as shake-bags.

MUFF GAMES.

This is a variety of games with which we have been familiar from childhood, though now they seem to be far less plenty than twenty years ago. Few of the strains now in use are reliable, as they have been bred by fancy dealers and irresponsible parties until the stock is more or less mixed. It already shows all colors. Many cockers still claim to have good muffs, and to admire them greatly ; but, while we have occasionally had them we have not for years bred any, fearing a contamination of other and better stock. We have no disposition to contradict the claims of all muffs to gameness, for we have known them to be true; but the bad have so increased that the experiment of procuring them is at all times rather dangerous.

THE JERSEY NUBCOMB.

It is said, with what truth we cannot judge, that this was once a popular breed in Ireland, and was first brought to New Jersey by an emigrant, who settled and raised the stock there. The cocks run from five to six pounds, and have been well valued for pit purposes ever since one of them decided a main between Philadelphia and Baltimore, he winning his second fight that day. They have long been in use in Philadelphia, and are the favorites of some of the cockers there Their peculiarity is a nub-comb, their heads shaped somewhat like the Sumatras, but we believe that they are not in any way related. There is this difference between a nub and a pea comb: Both are short, and extend but a little way back on the head, but the nub, though somewhat twisted, is single; the principal part of the pea is tripple, with a small addition coming from each side. The Jersey Nubcombs have latterly become scarce, having in Philadelphia become somewhat mixed, so that now most of them are doubted, and only those full known are trusted.

THE IRISH PILE.

This is a fine feathered, imported Irish strain, of good station, proud bearing, and excellent in action. They show all kinds of pile colors, and are evidently the result of a cross originally made in Ireland. Some of them have slate-colored, and others white legs. They show varied weights, from four to as high as six pounds. They are excellent for pit purposes, and have many warm admirers. We have bred them to a greater or less extent for many years, and never had any bad accounts of them.

IRISH STEEL GRAYS.

This breed is imported Irish stock, the general color being well described in the name. They are roundly and tightly built, rather low in station, but are when in hand wirey and tight-fisted. Their hackles and saddle feathers are steel gray in color, with fine flowing, dark tail; are all well feathered, and take high rank for beauty. They were imported by us many years ago, and have always shown pure gameness; most generally run small weights, from less than four to a little over five pounds—the hens just as small in proportion as the cocks. They are nervous and rapid fighters, and among fowls of equal weight, are remarkably successful.

A few years ago we sent an Irish Steel Gray cock and four pullets to Mr. White, of St. Louis, Mo. The cock, because of his extraordinary beauty, won much admiration, and a cocker seeing him pronounced him too pretty to be game, and offered to back his opinion with $10. He was told that it wouldn't pay to ruffle the feathers of the fowl for that amount, and subsequently a match was made for $100, the gray showing his pluck and winning the fight. He is yet alive, and Mr. Wright thinks him the finest and best cock of his size west of the Alleghanies.

IRISH REDS.

These are low-stationed games from imported stock; they are round and compactly built, and have yellow or green legs. Their sickle and saddle feathers are full and of shining red color, with full, heavy tails. They are pure game, but are not as rapid and vigorous as they might be. They have probably been too long bred together, and judicious crossing would be a great benefit, as the blood is undoubted. The variety shows black, brown and blue breasted reds, and is very common to Irish fanciers in this country.

THE BAKER WHITE LEG.

This strain first acquired note in the hands of Philip P Baker. One of the finest of the variety came into our hands, he having the recommendation of Benjamin F. Shields, who had seen him in several encounters. We penned him with four fine hens, with a view to breeding, and after succeeding in getting a number of eggs, were compelled to separate him from the hens, they having hen-pecked him of nearly all his fine plumage. While he was in this condition an urgent letter came from St. Louis, saying that a match had been made for shake-bags, and the cock before relied upon had died, and one of like weight must be immediately procured. This was early in the fall, when all the fighting cocks had been disposed of, and there was no other resort but to send the Baker white-leg. A letter accompanied him, making no apology for his condition, and only saying that he was probably a winning cock, and as good without as with feathers. If any excuse was made, we feared the parties would lose confidence in the fowl, and yield the forfeit. His weight was five and a half pounds, and when he left our yard he was a sorry sight, with nearly all of his hackle, saddle and tail feathers gone, and in some places with his breast bare;—his condition must have been even worse after his long journey by rail to St. Louis. The parties received and concluded to continue the match, and the result was an easy victory to the half-naked Baker white-leg, and an offer after the fight of sixty dollars for the fowl—the offer being refused.

This cock was thoughout a rough customer, and very savage at all times, whether in hand or running in the yard. He had all the marks of the full-blooded white leg Derby, but had too much strength and endurance to be one. We take it that he resulted from an auspicious cross with that breed, for fowls bred to a feather lose that savage courage which characterises some crosses, and it is reasonable that they should lose it. In-and-in breeding lessens the strength of the blood, reduces the size of the fowl, takes from his physicial conformation in every way, and of course modifies his disposition and temperament.

The Baker cock was, then, a half-bred Derby, retaining the white leg, and gathered his hardihood and vigor from his cross. Just what the cross was, is only known to the man that made it. We are satisfied with the progeny as it is, some throwing white legs, others willow-colored, and consider it equal to any original imported stock,

IRISH BLACK-BREASTED REDS.

We pronounce this the handsomest of all Irish strains of fowls, because it best meets the general taste. They breed well to color, and run from four to five and a half pounds in weight.— They are reds, with shining black breasts and green legs, black tail, and white down feathers at the base of the tail. They are round, plump, tightly built, tight fisted and of good action.— Indeed, they have few superiors in battle against fowls of equal weight, being tough; quick, and long-winded ; they strike well and their blows are hard and effective. We have long bred them, and while they are convenient to match, they are always reliable.

We cannot knowingly call them a distinct breed, but believe they have for a long time been bred to feather without or with less regard to breed. This is a habit with some Irish cockers. Where you meet with one whose fancy leans to color, he will not avoid crossing, but will so cross as to retain as nearly as possible favorite peculiarities, and will care little for distinct blood, so it is game. This is a prudent plan, and as a rule is preferable to indiscriminate crossing, for the system should only be practiced with some well-defined object in view ; and the retention of color warrants experiments to retain it when the blood used is known to be equally good in all respects.

The Irish black-breasted reds, at least the variety we are now attempting to describe, is not common to this country, and few Irish cockers have them. The hackle and saddle feathers are very pretty, the station good, the neck of reasonable length, the legs of large bone, and the thighs muscular and heavy. They are in all respects well developed small fowls, well suited for either breeding or the pit, and an acquisition to any cockers or fancier's yard.

THE BOWMAN FOWLS.

This strain takes its name from its breeder, who had a good reputation as a game raiser. The cocks are large black brass backs, showing from five and a half to seven pounds. We have long used them, and always found them as true as steel.— Where brass backs are admired, they are excellent to cross with, as they show remarkable vigor, strength of bone, muscle, and good wind. They are well feathered, and of good general appearance, stand up well, with head (neither too large or small) quite erect, are attentive to hens, polite and proud, and good talkers. The strain is very much admired in certain parts of Pennsylvania, particularly in Lancaster and Harrisburg, but has only a reputation in given localities.

THE IRISH BLUE GRAY.

This is an imported strain or breed—we hardly know how to characterize it. They show blue breasts, with gray hackles, saddle feathers, and reddish backs; some with blue and some black tails, and all with yellow legs. They are pretty fowls and of good game blood, though not equal to the Steel Grays in either action or feather. They show light weights, running from three and a half to five pounds. The hens are small and well set, and good layers of small, well-shaped eggs. They have been too long bred in-and-in, and need physical increase more than anything else.

THE COOK BLUE REDS.

This strain of fowls we received from Judge Cook in 1854, (the Judge being the party who fought the Prince Charles, of which more will be said in recounting our first personal experience in cocking.) We visited the donor in the year named, and although very aged and in feeble health, he still retained his love for game fowls, of which he had several first-class varieties. His yard was the resort of the fanciers and cockers of Pittsburg. Among his favorites were the Rigdon and Gad (peculiar to Fayette county, Pa.,) the Prince Charles, Marksman, Spangles, Greys, Barkers—and the Gwinn's—called after their breeder, a blind man of Cumberland county, Md. The Judge at an early day recognized the utility of crossing, and through him we believe the plan was first explained to McClellan, Wilson and other noted Pennsylvania game fanciers and cockers.— His views confirmed our own, and from him we derived much valuable information. The Cook blue reds are a strain produced by skillful crossing, and first won celebrity in a main fought by Mathew Wilson (first of Chambersburg, afterwards of Harrisburg) against Dr. Dorsey and other gentlemen of Hagerstown, Md. The latter fought a white breed of games, with white legs, and small top-knots—a breed that is now either extinct, or has lost its identity in the white games of the South—the blue reds winning most of the fights, and showing much greater strength, endurance, and activity than the whites—all of which, however, proved to be game.

The Cook Blue Reds have breasts of dark blue, the hackle a dark red, as also the saddle feathers; the legs green, the eye a dark hazel with a black margin around the lids—a good mark in the eye of an experienced cocker. They were rich in feather, of good station, leg of medium length, short, broad chest, broad across the shoulders, tapering nicely to the tail, with full and long wing. They are excellent in the pit, mature early (that is, the stags are fit to use in the pit at an early eage), fight rapidly, and have good wind and endurance. We have always taken much pride in them, as indeed we have in all the strains produced by Judge Cook, who was an educated, high-toned gentleman, and one of the best judges of games in his day.

THE WILD IRISH.

This is a strain formerly bred in the mountainous regions of Ireland, and is so called because of its wild and savage appearance. It shows throughout good cross-breeding, this being much more prominently apparent than in most Irish games.— We have long had some of the strains, and cannot, by any characteristic, even approximate their origin. They throw a variety of colors, and seem to the result of sub-crosses, long pursued, of many of the good Irish breeds. One of them won much praise in a main between Maytown and Lancaster, wherein he whipped an active Counterfeit cock after a very gallant fight.

THE COOK GRAYS.

This was one of Judge Cook's favorite strains, he having for a long time bred it to a feather. We have frequently heard him class it as only second to the Prince Charles. The original was imported by the Judge from Ireland, and the progeny under his breeding showed yellow-grays in color, with snake colored legs. They throw gray stags and gray hens, the latter being somewhat darker in color, as usual with hens. They have long been popular among the cockers of Pittsburg, and are still retained by some of them. The cocks run from four and a half to six pounds, are finely feathered, of rather low stature. Their gameness has often been well attested.

THE MARKSMAN.

This strain of fowls was successfully propagated by Judge Cook, being originally obtained from Mr. Gad, of Fayette County, Penn'a. The first cock took his name for a peculiarity he exhibited in fighting, that of measuring and taking aim at his antagonist before striking a telling blow. He was intelligent, and seemed to act very deliberately under any and all circumstances; was very much petted, and bore it well. The progeny are heavy set fowls, of medium station, round, compact body, and in color light blue reds, but of varied color in leg; run from four and a half to six pounds.

They well retain the peculiarity of the original, and are sure hitters and effective fighters. They are of course neither very rapid or savage in battle, but can at all times be calculated upon in a long heat. Against fowls of equal slowness they have an advantage in well-directed aim and deliberate action, and could be made good use of in fighting against weight. The hens are motherly and domestic, good layers, and finely built. The stags do not generally mature at an early age, and will sometimes remain under cow until nearly or quite a year old. They might be classed as a slow-blooded game, but have many qualities which are good, and which tell well in the long run.

THE GAD MUFFS.

This breed of games came from Gad of Fayette, and from the year 1820 until the death of Judge Cook maintained an excellent reputation in Western Pennsylvania. They showed different colors, and run from five to seven and a half pounds. They were sometimes successfully used in mains between Pittsburg and West Virginia, and Adams and Westmoreland counties, and were often successful. The muff at that time struck cockers as an oddity, and those who had little faith in it ever accompanying gameness, would bet more freely against it, and sometimes to their cost. The strain is now nearly extinct.

THE COOK BLACK GRAYS.

This strain was long bred by Judge Cook, was a mixed black and gray, with a steel colored or light gray eye, exceedingly savage in look. All of them showed dark colored legs, black and full breasts, thick iron gray hackles, and somewhat lighter saddle feathers. In back and tail they were jet black, deep breasts, broad and short across the back, with a pretty taper to the base of the tail. The hens are very pretty, having shining black bodies with steel gray hackles. They also carry the peculiar savage light in their gray eyes, just as the cocks do.—The strain has always been admired, and has been so much a favorite with us that we have bred it, to a greater or less extent, for forty years.

THE COOK SPANGLES.

This strain of fowls originally came from Gad of Fayette county, Penn'a., but was afterwards adopted, and for a time raised almost exclusively by Judge Cook. Nearly all of the colors are combined in one fowl, and the plumage is very rich. The hackles are long and full, and the fowls might with propriety be called shawl-necks. Their tails are very long and full, and well set off with glossy sickle feathers, wings long and almost meet back of the tail, small, snake-like head, some of them showing a nub-comb. Their eyes are grayish in color, with a black margin around the lids—a peculiarity much culivated by Judge Cook. The spangles are found in the hackle feathers. For variety and richness of color there is no prettier game extant than the Cook Spangles, and they are just as game in action as they are in appearance. For very many years they have been well known in western Pennsylvania and eastern Ohio, and they always enjoyed a good reputation. While esteemed good fighters, they have no peculiarity in this line.

THE COOK WHITES.

This breed of fowls was somewhat cultivated by Judge Cook. The original was a large cock, seven pounds in weight, and almost as white as snow, with white legs and beak.— Years ago the strain was much cultivated by some cockers and fanciers. We have frequently seen them tested, and witnessed one main between them and the Barker fowls, the latter winning by pure power of muscle and long-wind. The Barker fowls were then among the most celebrated in Pennsylvania, this being in 1830. At a main in Greensburg, Westmoreland county, which we witnessed, a seven pound white was employed against a Barker of equal weight. The white was handled by Rigdon, a somewhat noted cocker and gafter, the Barker by Peter Drum. The whites had previously been frequently shown in single matches against the Barkers, but though they showed gameness, they had theretofore lost. In this fight the white cock at the first blow cut out the eye of the Barker, and so soon as the fact was ascertained, the hopes of the friends of the white went up above par. The Barker cock became furious at the loss of his eyesight, tore up the tan in the pit, and struck very wildly; while doing this the white advanced, took hold, and both fowls raised, the Barker under the hold of the white. Blows were rapid and sharp, but so much superior was the strength of the Barker, that he literally cut the white down and won his fight. This Barker cock was a pretty fowl, with gray hackle, black breast and tail, and yellow legs.

THE RIGDON BLACK REDS.

This was a strain of games which won local celebrity in the hands of Rigdon, the cocker and heeler already referred to. They ran as high as seven pounds, and were pure black reds in color, with blue or slate colored legs. Thirty years ago they had many admirers in the western part of Pennsylvania, and though frequently used, none of them were ever known to run.

THE MARSHALL WHITES.

Of this breed we are only partially familiar, a very pretty six pound cock having been sent us by Marshall Wheeler, Esq.—He was in most respects like the Cook Whites, cultivated in 1830, and, save his superiority in size, like the Thompson Whites of Georgia. Very poor success attended our efforts to breed from these games, the chicks being very tender and liable to disease. We soon lost all we had from various causes, and at last concluded that they had been so long bred in-and-in that they no longer possessed any recuperative power. They could not be crossed, without destroying the color, and they could not safely be long bred together. We take it that all of these white games, described in this book, were more or less related. While we do not dispute their gameness when bred in good hands, we cannot recommend their use for the reasons given.

THE DR. STOWEY STRAINS.

Dr. Stowey flourished in Fayette County, Penn'a., and beside being noted for his skill in medicine, for a long time enjoyed celebrity as a game fowl raiser. He was one of several gentlemen of that county who kept up the reputation of Pennsylvania for good games, and participated in many mains. Rigdon, first of Washington City, settled in Fayette, and he and Stowey formed a partnership in games, and they for a time held the field pretty much to themselves, owing mainly to superior training and heeling, until the Barker games came into play, and then the tide of battle was turned. The following briefly describes the strains and breeds propagated by Dr. Stowey, at the time (1825—40) well known throughout Pennsylvania, Ohio, Maryland and Virginia :—

STOWEY BLUE REDS.

A very pretty, well stationed strain, with white and blue legs, blue breasts —average weight of cocks five and a half pounds. Good and rapid fighters and dead game.

STOWEY BLACK REDS.

Pretty fowls in every point, of good station, plump, round and of fine black red plumage ; legs blue and slate colored—some with black and red and others with savage gray eyes. They ran in weight from five to seven and a half pounds, the hens also being large. This strain is still in use.

STOWEY STEEL GRAYS.

Similar in nearly all respects with Cook's, save that they were not so nicely distinguished by the dark rim on their eyelids. They were well built, close fisted, wirey and full of action, both in hand and when engaged. They were good talkers, and less savage than Judge Cook's; still good and reliable games. We yet retain some of the strain, and know parties in Pittsburg who have it.

STOWEY BROWN REDS.

In color a dark brown red, green legs and black eyes, averaging from four pounds ten ounces up to six pounds. They sprang from imported English stock, being afterwards crossed with Barker brown reds. They were quick and effective fighters, the blood being improved by the cross ; well stationed, strong and long-winded.

STOWEY GINGER REDS.

Low in stature, but otherwise well built, wirey and courageous—their anger increasing with injuries received. They fight more savagely at the close than the commencement of the fight, and are good for long heats.— Weight from four to six and a half pounds. No distinguishing mark save a ginger red color. Plumage ordinary.

STOWEY BRASS BACK BLUES.

A peculiar and rather pretty strain, the result of a cross of Irish and brass backs. The cocks showed breasts sky-blue in color, dark blue hackle, with a yellow brass-backed back, and yellow legs. They well attracted the fancy, were fine stationed, broad shouldered, full breasted and with short back.— The eyes ran into red and dun color. These fowls were frequently shown by Stowey and Rigdon in mains, and seemed to be equally favored by both of them. They are still in use, some of the strain being on our own walks.

STOWEY PILE.

Of red and white mixed color (of course), with green legs, and in weight averaging five and a half pounds. We have known one of these cocks to win two hard-fought battles inside of three hours. Most of the cockers of Pennsylvania having Piles procured this strain to cross with their own, for at one time they were very plenty in Fayette county; so that the celebrity of the Stowey Piles extended throughout Pennsylvania. It was pure game, and showed hard and rapid fighters.

THE BARKER GAMES.

Barker, from whom several strains took their name, was for many years a noted Pennsylvania cocker, (a resident of Westmoreland county) having won many mains in Ohio, Kentucky, Maryland, Virginia, and his own State. He bred fowls entirely for his own use, and rarely if ever sold. With intimate friends he would exchange approved breeds, and in this way his fowls soon fell into many hands, and were for a time pretty generally propagated. He and Peter Drum, another noted cocker, frequently joined funds, the latter generally acting as heeler and handler. The following briefly classifies and describes the more noted Barker breeds and strains:—

BARKER BLACK BREASTED REDS.

A No. 1 strain, running as high as seven pounds in weight, throughout strong and well made, of good wind and quick, savage action. The cocks are deep chested, broad shouldered, small headed, dark and dun-eyed, green, blue and willow legs, and excellent plumage. They first won celebrity in the hands of Barker and Drum in a main at Salem, several of them being shown, and each winning his fight. They met our taste in all respects and we then resolved upon and finally succeeded in procuring some, having bred them, with occasional black breasted red crosses, for thirty years. They still retain their beauty of feather, size and fighting characteristics, and still hold the same place in our estimation as when first seen in action over thirty years ago.

THE BARKER WHITES.

Miscalled we believe, for it was in most respects the same as the Cook Whites, and Cook was somewhat before Barker in the game field. Barker, however, seemed to have better luck with them than Cook, and occasionally won a well-contested battle. A seven pound cock in which he took most pride was a dusky white, not pure and yet not pile. He was evidently crossed with a pile, and was healthier and stronger than any of the pure whites. The stock soon ran out, in Barker's hand, for he bred mainly for pit purposes.

THE BARKER SPANGLES.

A cock of this strain was the third fought in the Salem main, and was smaller than those preceding him, being less than six pounds, a low, heavy set fowl, but well made in point of muscle and bone. All of his toes had been frozen off, and those who had their money against him thought they had a sure thing of it. The battle was a hard one, but the Barker won, greatly to the surprise of those who saw his crippled condition. Barker was the owner of salt works in Westmoreland county, Penn'a., and our intimate acquaintance sprang from the fact that we were neighbors, his works almost adjoining those of a brother-in-law, for whom we then clerked. These Spangles were much like those held by Judge Cook, and were probably related in some way. They won equal celebrity, and have long been greatly admired.

THE BARKER BLACK GRAYS.

This strain of black grays had greater success than any known to us, save perhaps Cook's, up to 1830. The original in the hands of Barker was a fine stationed fowl, broad breast, broad shoulders, and in weight nine pounds. His color was what in the parlance of cockers is called a black gray—having black breast, dark gray hackle and black tail, with lighter gray saddle feathers. His legs were a dark green, nearly black; his eye large, protruding and jet black; his "countenance" being dark, sombre and of general savage appearance. When in hand he was full of motion and closefisted. Notwithstanding his general ferocious appearance, he was a pet, and was only savage when actually preparing for or engaged in battle. He was too large to be readily matched, and though we never saw or heard of his deeds in the pit, we know some of his offspring, of somewhat lighter weights, to win much praise; and have since bred the strain to a greater or less extent. It is in many respects like the Strychnine, and almost if not quite equally serviceable for pit purposes.

THE BARKER BLUE REDS.

A pretty and rich colored strain, with pure blue breasts, light red hackles, turkey-red saddle feathers, very dark blue tail, and yellow legs. It must be called a blue red, but well approaches the general blue color. The cocks run in weight from five to six and a half pounds. The origin is Irish.—Good for all purposes.

THE BARKER DUCK-WING GRAYS.

A handsome strain with lively colors and glossy feathers—as most duck-wings have. The breast was shining black, the hackles gray, with turkey colored and red feathers on the back, and light gray saddle feathers. The strain shows some very large fowls, known to have reached eight pounds, the average being six. The station was good, head medium sized, carriage proud. They are the result of a cross from English duck-wings, and are thorough game.

THE PETER DRUM STRAINS.

We have already informed the reader of Drum's connection with Barker. He was a very careful breeder, deriving his profit from mains and matches, and seldom selling fowls. We have repeatedly exchanged with him, the confidence being mutual between Judge Cook, Barker, Drum, and ourself, and all of us more or less intimate with Wilson, Graves, McClellan, Dorsey, Gad and other prominent cockers. The following is descriptive of the more prominent strains and breeds shown by Drum in the mains of thirty and fifty years ago, some of the stock being still in good hands:—

THE DUSTY MILLERS.

Why so-called we were never fully informed, though always presumed it was because of their color, which was a peculiar pile, with white specks in all parts of the body, as though sprinkled with flour or meal. They maintained a good popularity East and West from 1825 to 1835, and were greatly desired but rarely obtained. As we have intimated they were in color a dusty white or yellow, with yellow and green legs. The hackle and saddle feathers showed both white and muddy yellow feathers, the tail white, or blue and black, the body showing more or less white all over it. In weight they average about five pounds. They have long maintained a high reputation among the cockers of Kentucky, and by some of the older stock are yet greatly valued, but difficult to procure. It is yet a question with us whether Drum was indebted to Kentucky or Kentucky to Drum for these fowls. They were equally popular in Ohio and West Virginia. A match was made a few years since against the Dusty Millers, the opposite party showing our Strychnines, loaned by Dr. Greenfield. The Strychnines won the main, and were in most respects superior fighters, but all on the other side showed full gameness and retained the confidence of their friends. We would, if called upon, pronounce the Dusty Millers a cross between game piles and some still lighter game breed, though pretend to no absolute knowledge of the origin.

THE DRUM BLUE REDS.

A rusty blue in color, not prepossessing in appearance, but game-like and good for pit purposes. They were never favorites even in their own locality—the admiration being mainly confined to Drum, who won some good fights with them. In size they run from four to five and a half pounds. The hens were small, with little life in their general blue colors. The strain ran out with Drum's ceasing to use it.

THE DRUM PILES.

This variety showed the best fighters in the possession of Drum, and it was by him more generally propagated than any other. The pile colors were very pretty, the legs being dark; the size of the cocks varied from four and a half to six pounds, were easily matched, and when in the pit showed both skill and pluck in fighting. They came from imported Piles, and were of pure and good blood. We never heard of one, in the hands of Drum or Barker, showing the white feather; and they maintain their gameness to this day, some of them now being in our possession.

THE DRUM BLUES.

This strain varied somewhat in its blue shades from light to intermediate and dark. Some of them had blue-black hackles, with red on the tips o the wing; others light blue hackles with brass colored saddle feathers, and yet others almost entirely blue. They had yellow and green, and a chance one white legs. They ran from five to six and a half pounds, and were generally well and prettily feathered. They owed their origin to Ireland, and are in certain places yet valued as one of the best Irish strains in this country. Drum valued them highly, and frequently used them in matches.

THE DRUM GRAYS.

This was a large steel gray strain, resultant from a cross between Barker's black gray and an Irish gray hen, both of good size. The progeny showed fine, well-stationed, large and muscular stags which excelled in many qualities the originals. The breast was pure black, iron-gray hackles, and saddle feathers a shade lighter in gray. The tail was black and flowing, and the general conformation of both stag and pullet very good. They were in frequent use during the life of their breeder, and were always well liked.

THE DRUM DUCK-WING GRAYS.

The reader has noticed before this that many of the fowls of Judge Cook, Barker and Drum ran pretty well together in color. Such was the fact, and as all of them imported and exchanged, we can only presume that these met the popular taste at that time both in England, Ireland, or America, or that the parties exchanged their imported stock after use, and crossed it with their own strains. Either presumption may be correct. The Drum Duck-Wing Grays were produced by a cross between the Barker imported duck-wings and a gray Irish hen, imported by Drum. The mark of the duck-wing was well retained, and by this cross Drum succeeded in winning several friendly matches from Barker—for it was the practice of these parties to fight single matches against each other, in test of their stock. Drum's taste ran toward mixed colors, and we never knew him to breed pure reds, or pure black or brown breasted reds.

THE KENTUCKY GAMES.

A fine trio of the strain known by this name was a few years ago presented to the author by Dr. Van Meter, of Bowling Green, Ky. The cock weighed nine pounds, had single comb, and was in color a black red with green legs. He was a magnificent bird, stood well upon his pins, had a broad black breast, was wide across the shoulders, and well tapered to the base of the tail, where he was quite narrow for such a large fowl. His hackles were of a deep red, his back of a deep turkey red, wings long, and a long and full black tail. He was very smart upon his feet, good at sparring, and was in every way fitted for a noble contest in the pit. Accompanying him was a large deep blue hen, with rose comb, she being in weight nearly six pounds; also a large brown hen with single comb of nearly equal weight with the blue. From this trio we obtained some remarkably fine stags and pullets, the stags turning out first-class, and acquitting themselves well wherever heard from.— One, sent to New York State, yet stands unconquered after several battles, and the owner thinks there is not his equal in that State.

Accompanying the fowls was a written pedigree, which has been misplaced. The strain, however, was traced back to the cock-fighting days of General Jackson, and owes part of its origin to some of his stock. It has been carefully preserved by mingling with it some of the best blood of Tennessee and Kentucky, and for a number of years has been in the hands of Dr. Van Meter—a gentlemen who takes great pride in pure game blood, raises no other, and is thoroughly conversant with all the approved modes of breeding. He "cultivates" games for his own pleasure, and has done so all of his adult life. We are indebted to him for many favors, not the least of which are some of his contributions to this book.

THE LaRUE GAMES.

The brothers LaRue are large land proprietors in the Shenandoah Valley, Virginia, "the garden spot of America," and a region famed for the production of good games. They are wealthy Virginia gentlemen, and in common with others of their class suffered much by the raids of the two armies, especially in live stock. They however, in the fastnesses of the mountains skirting the Valley, managed to preserve much of their game stock, and since the war have carefully renewed its propagation. They count many personal friends in different States of the Union, and to these they frequently present their surplus stock, and occasionally exchange with others.

VIRGINIA BLACK-BREASTED REDS.

Col. LaRue (we believe the younger brother, neither of them having reached middle life) presented the writer with a fine game cock of the Virginia Black Breasted Red strain, noted in the Shenandoah for good fighting qualities. The strain was produced by crossing Goss' Rose Comb Counterfeits with a Georgia Dominic, the two throwing a black breasted red, instead of a brown red, the Counterfeits generally showing a blending of the colors. They have golden yellow legs, a peculiarity taken from the Dominic, but show the rose comb of the Counterfeit. They are small, but well stationed and very pretty fowls, easily matched, and apparently well designed for the pit. We have not yet tested any of the stock, but where it comes so thoroughly recommended, we have no doubt of its purity.— The strains from which the cross was made have already received favorable notice in this work, and their progeny must be good. Goss (of Baltimore) Counterfeits have long been known to the Shenandoah Valley, and are very justly prized there, as well by the LaRue's as other gentlemen.

LARUE WHITES.

This breed of fowls was imported, and crossed the ocean with the celebrated race horse Prior, being owned by the same parties. The horse and fowls were taken to Richmond, Va., and while one increased his celebrity on the turf, the other added to its laurels on the tan, and both became favorites in Virginia. One cock of this strain was noted for having won five fights before the gaffles were taken from him. They are now called the LaRue Whites, because of their somewhat extensive propagation by these gentlemen. They are not, however, pure white fowls, and never show any such. The cocks have clean white breasts, with hackles of beautiful silver gray, and saddle feathers a mixture of gray and black, or iron gray. The legs are of slate color or light blue, and the eye is marked by a black margin around the rim. There is a general and almost prevailing light mahogany tinge on the wings, with their thighs a light blue. They are a light colored fowl throughout, and are probably miscalled whites. The cocks are of fine station, and are quick and active in battle, showing weights from four to five and a half pounds. Their reputation extends throughout Virginia, where they have many admirers, and seem to be worthy of all the admiration bestowed upon them.

LARUE MARSH REDS.

This strain of games takes its name from a stream of water in the Shenandoah Valley, the fowls being bred and raised upon its banks by the Messrs. LaRue. The Colonel pronounces them among the most rapid fighters of the world. He sent the writer some of them, and when the stag was tested he fully came up to his recommendation. The cocks are small reds, very round in body, rather low set, and of different shades of red. They show skillful crossing among small fowls, the design being to make them hardy and quick of motion.

To Col. LaRue we are indebted for the Marsh and the Black-

Breasted Reds; to John LaRue, Esq., we are indebted for the Whites, Georgia Dominics and Stone Fence and White Leg Derby varieties. They also propagate Sut and Muff games.— To both of them we owe thanks for a steady and generous correspondence, from which we have gathered much reliable information.

THE SILVER GRAYS.

This breed of games is in appearance very much like the Lord Derby Silver grays in color; but they are better stationed and much larger fowls, and of stronger bone and muscle. They have light blue legs. They are of imported stock, and well maintain the silver gray characteristic. All of the cocks are quick and industrious fighters, the only objection being that they are not as long-winded as some American strains.

THE SPANGLE GRAYS.

These are the result of a cross between the Silver Grays and Twaddle's English hen, the progeny showing what may well be called Spangle Grays—that is, a rich yellow and red being intermingled with the silver gray hackles and saddle feathers. The breast is of black ground, dotted here and there with white spots. They are singular and very pretty fowl, are good game and fine fighters.

A somewhat similar cross made between the LaRue Silver Grays and English red hens, shows spangle grays with more of the black colors intermingled. They are very pretty, of good carriage and action.

THE SHIELDS STEEL GRAYS.

This strain was bred by John Shields, Esq., and presented the writer by his brother Benjamin. The cock was about six and a half pounds in weight, with beautiful steel gray hackle and saddle feathers and black breast. His tail was black, long, wide and flowing, with two principal sickle feathers which almost touched the ground. He was of excellent station, being high-headed, broad-chested, with short and broad back, showing a gentle taper. His legs were blue in color, strong and well made, and when in hand was close-fisted and wirey. The progeny show some very fine and large stags and pullets.— Many of the hens have the habit of crowing, particularly after a battle which they witness. The strain is thorough game and reliable every way.

JOHN BARD GAMES.

John Bard and Frederick Bard, Esqs,, were for a long time noted cockers and game fanciers in Pensylvania, and we believe are yet living. Both of them have bred mainly for pit purposes, and care less for name of breed than substantial breeding and fighting qualities. Per consequence they can each show a variety of games, most of which are healthy and strong, and many of which have won fair names.

JOHN BARD BLUE REDS.

A strain both sides of which were originally imported from England and Ireland. The blue appears to be the ground work, with the red intervening. They are mostly tasselled games, with long feathers back of the comb and covering part of the hackle. The cocks vary from five to seven and a half pounds, are muscular, well boned, and good for pit purposes. Some of them show smooth or untasseled heads.

JOHN BARD GINGER REDS.

Very much like the blue reds, save in the ginger color.— Some are smooth and some tasseled in the head-feather. In leg they show a variety of colors, and throughout denote mixed blood. The cocks are strong and active, and vary from four and a half to seven pounds. They have won some celebrity in the pit, in Lancaster, Harrisburg, Marrietta, &c.

FRED BARD BLACK REDS.

A beautiful strain, of fine and full plumage, with hackle almost shawl-like, long and flowing tails, all the stags being of remarkably fine station. We received, two years ago (1867) through Benjamin Shields, a very fine seven pound cock—a model in his way. He well displayed all the points of gameness, being a beautiful and glossy black red, with black breast, broad and full-blue legs, strong and boney. His eye was savage and keen, head small and devoid of any tassel feathers. In battle he was quick and savage, good winded, and almost constantly forced the fighting.

The stock well displayed all of the leading characteristics of the original, and are now greatly valued by us.

FRED BARD BROWN REDS.

A handsome strain, carrying the brown red to perfection—of good station, fair plumage, and fine general bearing. Some have black, some dark gray, and others firey red eyes. All have either green or blue legs. Like the fowls bred by his brother, some of this strain show in a modified degree the tasselated head, while others are smooth. They are reliably game, full of action, close-fisted, quick and savage.

FRED BARD GRAYS.

We take it that this strain was produced by a mixture of the Mexican and the Irish grays, for it well shows some of the characteristics of both. They show small, smooth and snake-like heads, with short, plump bodies, and strong legs and thighs. We have often seen them tested, and never knew one to show the white feather. They show weights from four and a half to six pounds.

FRED BARD BRASS BACKS.

These fowls are mainly black, with yellow and black hackles and saddle feathers. Nearly all of them are tassel-headed, showing the cross with John Bard's stock—doubtless made to increase the size, for some of the weights run as high as seven pounds. They are of full plumage but not very rich in color, and in this respect inferior to many brass back varieties. They are however good and strong fighters, and make good shake bags.

FRED BARD BLUE REDS.

These show mixed red colors with blue back ground, giving them a rusty and not a pretty appearance. Here, too, is shown the tasselated head, and a variety of color in legs. They are good for pit purposes, and as we have said, were bred for no other object. Many of the stags are hard and rapid fighters, and all of them have given good accounts of themselves. Two year old cocks show weights running from five to as high as seven and a half pounds.

BARD COUNTERFEITS.

These are bred by both the Bard brothers, the originals having been obtained from Goss of Baltimore. They still retain the old name, with the addition of that of the men who have bred them perhaps as extensively as any other game raisers in Pennsylvania. The Bards have crosssed the Counterfeit stock with their own, and they show single and rose comb reds, with occasionally tasselated heads. The strain is large and has been well kept up, the cocks running from five and a half to six and a half pounds, and occasionally to seven. The Bard Counterfeits show well the utility of breeding for the pit, for the Counterfeit strain, in single hands could not have been kept so large and strong by any other means.

BARD BLACK REPUBLICANS.

This strain was so named by Fred. Bard, who holds it in high estimation, and pronounces it his favorite. This is the second strain within our knowledge, named probably because of political bias, the other being the Copperheads, owned and raised by Dr. Van Meter, of Kentucky. If the two were to meet in open contest, more than local interest would attach to the main, for political feeling and pride would have full play.

The Black Republicans are black fowls, some almost purely black, others with brass colored feathers on the butt of the wing, and yet others with the back and saddle feathers well sprinkled with brass ; legs a dead green or blue.

The cocks are powerfully built, round in body, broad chested short back with the proper taper to the tail, and with heavy thighs and good boned legs. They are not pretty, but of very game-like appearance, and handle well. The cocks show weights running from five to seven and a half pounds ; the hens are large, and some of them dark colored, many black.

The strain has been known since 1858, about eleven years, and has been in our own possession much of that time. We have carefully bred some of them together and have crossed others.

The best cross we succeeded in making was an Eslin cock with Black Republican hens. The result shows more gray and spangled feathers, but fowls if anything improved in size, strength, activity and general fighting qualities. The plumage is to our taste also somewhat improved. The station of these stags is all that could be desired, and we highly esteem them for both pit and breeding purposes.

BOWMAN WHITE LEGS.

A black breasted red strain with white leg and beak, the largest of the kind known to us. They were evidently bred by Bowman with a view to retain the white peculiarity, and at the same time gradually improve the size of the stock. This plan was persisted in until the cocks, some of them, reached as high as seven pounds—their muscular proportion being equal to their weight. A fancier of breeds would immediately pronounce them pure Derbys, but one better posted could only see the manifestations of a careful course of crossing.

The strain won its first honors in a main between Lancaster and Marietta, Bowman backing the former, which had lost most of the fights, and had the odds against it on the main.— To regain failing fortunes Bowman showed a seven pound white leg, which was pitted against a cock of equal weight. The first blow made the Marietto cock turn a somersault, the white leg following his advantage, taking his hold, and ending the fight by quick and hard boxing.

This cock was for a time classed as the champion of Lancaster county, and elicited general admiration. Several have since bred from the stock, ourself among the number, but it yet remains scarce, for all have not succeeded in retaining the peculiarity of the white leg and beak.

KESSINGER TOP-KNOTS.

A strain the celebrity of which is mainly confined to Lancaster and adjoining counties in Pennsylvania. The cocks run as high as six pounds, are reds, with black breasts and blue legs, and all have a small red top-knot behind the comb.

We had a cock of this strain running in our yard at the time of Mr. Cheek's visit, and after some persuasion we allowed him to take the fowl to Tennessee. He subsequently appeared in the main between Alabama and Tennessee, and after a long and remarkably rapid contest won his match, and won also the general admiration of all who saw his action.

There are but few of these fowls in the country. They differ from the Baltimore Top-Knots in being of lower stature and more rounded form, and run from four and a half to five pounds in weight. The hens all show the small red top-knot back of the comb;—it comprises only three or four feathers apparently loose and longer than the other hackle feathers.

THE WELSH GAMES.

Albertus Welsh has long been a game raiser of York county, Penn'a., his style of breeding showing pit fowls.

WELSH BLACK REDS.

The Welsh black-reds are truly named, as they show all the color marks coming under that general head. "Black Reds" are known by black breast, with back of a dark mahogany color, with saddle feathers one or two shades of red, black tail, and black down feathers at the base of the tail. When cut out they show black under-hackle feathers—the surface being a deep red.

The Welsh black reds show different colored legs, the yellow best suiting the general fancy; but the color of the leg does not in any way interfere with the correctness of describing a fowl as black red, a minute description of which we have given above.

But a month ago we sent a Welsh black red with willow colored legs to Mr. Peck of Woonsocket, R. I., and when some of his club looked at the stag they said he was not a black red in color. Many of these gentlemen were poultry fanciers, and sticklers for a feather, but we think they showed lamentable ignorance in disputing color in this case. A black red, in a general poultry fancier's notion, is a handsome red fowl with jet and glossy black breast, and with the wings to about half their extent of a brick or tan color; the back, saddle, and hackle feathers a bright and rich red. Such a fowl we pronounce a *black red*, and not a *black breasted red*, and any old cocker in the land will bear us out. It has always been their habit to recognize these distinctions between black breasted and black reds, and it is not for amateurs to step in and change a description of characteristics acknowledged to be correct since the settlement of our country, and everywhere else employed as extensively as here.

Many of these younger fanciers give their fancy a freedom incompatible with good judgment upon game qualities. They are pat in all the leading characteristics of Spanish, Partridge, Cochins, Shanghæs, Silver Spangles, Hamburgs, Malacas, Dorkings, La Fleches, Silver-laced Bantams, Brahams, Indians, Silver Polish, Frizzled and other fowls, and thereby display a general knowledge of poultry admirable in its way—but that way is never admired by the old and experienced cocker, and the opinion has obtained among this class that a knowledge of these things does not add to one's knowledge of either game qualities, characteristics or descriptions. We have read many poultry books in our day, and have found this fact always apparent—that where much was known and given of all varieties of poultry, little was given, and less known, of the game. But we shall better illustrate this further on, if we have space for a general criticism upon the game descriptions of poultry authors. The Welsh cock sent Mr. Peck was a black red, the opinion of all Rhode Island to the contrary notwithstanding, and the description will be recognized as correct by all old game raisers.

The Welsh black reds generally well answer the description. They are good and hardy fowls, wirey, active, tight-fisted, and excellent for either breeding or pit purposes. The hens are black reds—that is, the ground-work of their plumage is black, with red hackle and occasional red breast feathers. The cocks run from four and a half to seven pounds in weight. We have long bred them and find them hardy and in every way reliable.

WELSH BLACK BREASTED REDS.

A fine and pretty strain of fowls, of rich and full plumage.—The cocks have shining black breasts, bright red hackles, with two shades of red saddle feathers, and long flowing and rich black sickle feathers. They have short, broad back, assuming a wedge-shape as it tapers to the tail. They are in a measure duck-wings, being of glossy green and light mahogany in color. The hens are reds. The cocks occasionally show good weights, are all compactly made, wirey, active and good fighters. We have long bred them, some seasons in large numbers, and esteem them equal to any English black breasted reds.

WELSH BROWN REDS.

A large strain of brown reds, some of the cocks weighing as high as eight pounds. They are not of any separate breed of brown reds, and show the fact at first glance—some of them having blue, green and willow colored legs, and black, gray, dun and red eyes. The general colors are not rich, but the plumage is good. The strain is good for pit purposes, and was so designed.

WELSH BLUE REDS.

A pretty strain, handsome plumage, and of good general bearing. The breast feathers of the cock are sky blue, the hackles of light lead, the saddle of deep red, the tail of dark blue, and the legs mostly of rich golden yellow. Many of the hens show general blue colors, and are very pretty. Many of the cocks are of good size, and vary from four and a half to seven pounds.

We have long propagated the stock, and value it very highly, both for fancy and pit purposes. When Welsh bred these games, he had several kinds of blue reds, being different in their shades of blue, and of different colored legs.

WELSH STEEL GRAYS.

Years ago we obtained a cock of this variety, which weighed seven pounds and fourteen ounces, the hens being of proportionate size. He was a pure steel gray in color—breast, back, saddle and wing all gray, the tail only being fully black;—

legs were blue in color, well boned and strong, his thighs showing good muscles. His breast was unusually high and full, and his general appearance all that a cocker would wish, there being no awkward motion about him. His head was very small for so large a fowl, his countenance dark and savage—his eyes of a deep gray, with a well-defined black margin around the lids.

We bred from him as long as he was properly able to serve his hens, and when old refused $25 for him. The stock showed fowls which show the marks of their parentage, and are in all respects first-class. We have acquired the habit of calling them "Gray Eagles," that name seeming to answer their general description, and especially their dark-rimmed eyes and small heads, better than any other. We have sent the stock to many parts of the Union, and good accounts have always been returned and satisfaction confessed.

WELSH PILES.

A rather large and fine Pile strain, showing cocks running from five to six pounds. They are reds with white ground, and red and white stripes in the hackles; the saddle feathers are of a dark red, the breast interspersed with white feathers. They show mixed game blood in having yellow, blue, willow, green, and even white legs. They are good pit fowls, but in some respects not equal to other Piles described in this work.

WELSH DOMINICS.

A large Dominic variety, with no marked peculiarity other than size—some of the cocks weighing eight and some of the hens six pounds. They are of rather pretty dominic colors, with yellow legs. We have long bred them, and always found them of pure game blood, and generally of good action in battle.

GOSS GAMES.

We have already spoken of Goss, of Batimore county, Md., as the gentleman having the credit of originating the Baltimore Top Knots. He also, by his game creative genius, reproduced the Counterfeit strain, and did it so well that the progeny retained all the leading characteristics of the originals, and won a general reputation as good in the pit. Their celebrity was co-extensive with many of the Southern States, and reached Pennsylvania, Ohio and New York. We once procured from him twenty hens, of different varieties of games, and some stags. Many of them showed rose combs, thus attesting the fact that he had crossed nearly all of his strains with his favorite Counterfeits. When we last communicated with him he was an old gentleman, and probably by this time has lost much of his activity with and fondness for games. He long enjoyed the reputation of breeding good fowls, and we know of no game-raiser in Maryland who equalled him in general reputation.— Beside the Counterfeits, he for a time kept black-breasted reds. Mexican Grays, Dominics and Baltimore Top-Knots—all good when they came from his hands.

CONKEY GAMES.

Mr. Conkey lived, or yet lives, somewhere in the interior of Pennsylvania. We never enjoyed his acquaintance, and knew him only through the representations of Lancaster cockers and fanciers, among them the Messrs. Shields and Jonathan Dorwart, and from these parties we from time to time procured Conkey fowls, all of which turned out well, and some of which are described in this work. He, too, apparently bred with a view to the cultivation of qualities suited for the pit, and because of this his fowls soon acquired reputation.

THE GWINN GAMES.

Some fifty years ago a blind man named Gwinn lived in Cumberland county, Md., where at one time Barker also resided.—He propagated games with remarkable success, notwithstanding his infirmity, and in his day they were perhaps as much noted as any games in America. He was assiduous and careful, and seemed to tell all the points of a game by handling, and could do this with his hand much better than many amateurs could with their eyes. He could feed with fair skill, and was at all times aware of the condition and numbers of his stock. These things attracted the attention of cockers and fanciers, and Gwinn was himself as much a matter of curiosity as were his fowls. We always suspected Barker of procuring some of his more valuable strains from Gwinn, and once asked the question of him, receiving only an evasive answer, which somewhat confirmed our belief. Gwinn rarely parted with his fowls, keeping them for his own investments. He would select his walks among connections of his family, in whom he could place confidence. One of our brothers (then living in Westmoreland, Pa.,) procured a trio through a brother-in law of Gwinn's, with shining black breast, yellow legs, and a rather large rose comb. His weight was six pounds. The hens were yellow, rather small, with yellow legs, and a thin drooping comb—the lot being represented as the same blood. While it was true that they were of Gwinn stock, it was apparent that the cocks and hens were not of the same blood, and were doubtless each the product of some cross made by Gwinn. However, we bred the fowls, and afterwards had the cock tested, and then again the progeny of the cock and hens, and all proved to be dead game. Ten or twelve years afterwards we had occasion to travel through Cumberland county, and in the vicinity of Gwinn's residence many of the farms were stocked with beautiful games, all of them being styled "Gwinn Games," and perhaps truthfully so. Gwinn was then dead, and the stock had been taken up by those who knew it best, and valued it highly.

The Gwinn Black Grays were a large and beautiful variety, with prominent black eyes, dark legs. The ground-work of their coloring was black, with gray hackles and saddle feathers. Cocks run from five to six and a half pounds.* They were greatly admired throughout Cumberland county, and their reputation extended through Maryland and the States bordering it, as indeed did all of the old blind man's stock.

His duck-wings were large and well stationed fowls, had beautiful black and shining breasts, light gray hackles, red saddle and black tail feathers, with red eyes and green legs. These showed all the marks of having been well bred to the feather, and were doubtless imported.

The Gwinn Piles appeared, as nearly as we can remember, to run from five to six and a quarter pounds—then considered a good size for this variety. They had no other peculiarity, unless we except the tail, which in both cock and hens, showed more than an ordinary mixture of light feathers.

The Brown Reds were a variety somewhat extensively grown by Gwinn, were at that day considered large, and were of fine station and plumage.

His blue reds were especially handsome, rich in color, and with full blue tail, red eyes, yellow legs, the cocks running from five to six and a half pounds.

The White Games were somewhat popular in that section of country fifty years ago. Gwinn grew a white variety, very large, the cocks weighing from six to seven and a half pounds. In general color they were white, with yellow saddle feathers.— Nearly all of them had white legs.

The Gwinn Shad-Foot Game acquired much local celebrity, and for a time was the subject of close watching and study on our part. What was then known as the National Turnpike ran through a part of Cumberland county, in Maryland, and fifty miles west passed the hotel kept by Gad of Fayette county, before described as a game raiser and cocker. In passing along this pike, and while in Cumberland, we were attracted by a large game cock, of fine station, plumage, and good weight and muscle. We were surprised at his close resemblance to our then pet fowl, the Prince Charles. Only the women of the household were at home, and no satisfactory information could be gained from them. We therefore stopped at the nearest hotel, and here fell in with a gentleman fond of fast horses and games. He said that the fowl in question was known in that neighborhood as the Shad-Foot, and that it ranked in the estimation of the citizens with any games known to them, that it sprang from the Gwinn stock, if not directly raised by Gwinn —the blind cocker being then but recently deceased. My informant was Squire Hunter, who was throughout gentlemanly and courteous and showed me his own games, which were of the Tartar and the Gwinn varieties. We observed to Mr. Hunter that "that section of country seemed to be overrun with game fowls, and mostly of good varieties, if appearances were to be trusted." His answer confirmed the truth of the observation, and he said that many there, particularly land-holders, refused to raise any other than pure games, that this was to a greater or less extent true of all the section of country beginning east at Harper's Ferry, in Virginia, and running northwest to Brownsville, Fayette county, Pa.,—taking in Hagerstown Frederick City, Martinsburg, and Gettysburg. That the Gwinn varieties were much sought after, but could only be fairly reached after his death. That while living some of them had been stolen by teamsters and others emigrating by way of the pike. This explanation only aided the suspicion previously formed with regard to the connection between the Prince Charles and Gwinn's best variety, and we could easily account for the presence of the Prince Charles stock in Fayette and Westmoreland counties after acquiring this information.

It was said of Gwinn when living, that he was the most remarkable, as he was one of the most successful cock fighters of the country—that he would take as much interest in a main, and get as greatly excited during the fights, as any man in the pit, and seemed to know just how each battle progressed. He confidently staked his money on results after handling fowls, and at all times on his own. He almost every year imported games from Ireland, and had an agent there to select him the best.

Earl Derby and Lord Sefton, in their day, justly boasted of high station, scholastic attainments, and success in cock fighting and game fowl breeding, but if the reputation of Gwinn did not greatly belie him, we believe he was entitled to equal praise, and from what we know and have seen of his fowls, we believe they could, in the days of fifty years ago, have beaten in the pit any produced by these noblemen, or any bearing their names.

Gwinn's thoughts seemed to be constantly wrapped up in game fowls; they seemed to be his "chattering grand-children" by day, and the companions of his dreams by night. If one of his fowls happened to be stolen, he would mount a trusty mare, and search carefully the country all around about, listening at every barn-yard to hear the cocks crow. It was said that he knew the crow of every fowl he had; it is perhaps true that he knew the peculiarity in the crow of every strain he possessed, and could thus readily distinguish them from others. In this way he found many stolen fowls, and added not a little to his reputation for good judgment. He was a high-hearted cocker of "Auld Lang Syne," and ranks in our estimation above any we ever knew or heard of.

DR. BUTLER'S GAMES.

Dr. Butler was noted in Western Maryland and Pennsylvania as a successful game raiser and cocker, and often joined in the mains of Mathew Wilson, Graves, Dr. Dorsie and others. He was given credit for excellent judgment and management, and frequently did his own heeling and handling. In 1836 we saw some of his fine strains in Chambersburg, Pa., then being raised by a relative. They comprised Black Grays, Blue Grays, and Reds. Twelve years ago the old Doctor was yet alive, and wrote us a letter describing some of his varieties. He had then a few fine fowls, but had given the care of most of them to his son, who was then propagating a number of fine strains. The war made sad havoc with games in this section of country extending North by way of the Cumberland valley into Pennsylvania, and South for miles beyond Harper's Ferry—the soldiers of both armies having little respect for blood when very hungry. Occasionally a soldier, conversant with and fond of games would come into possession of one, and would then frequently take more pains to keep it in the line of march than he would of his own knapsack. The fact was well illustrated at the grand review in Washington after the war, where many pure game cocks were seen mounted upon mules and horses. These were captured in the Gulf States of the South by Sherman's bummer's, while Sheridan's raiders had not a few gathered from the valleys of the Shenandoah and Cumberland. A gentleman from Shepherdstown, Va., wrote us a sero-comic letter saying that the 16th Pennsylvania Cavalry had taken every game fowl he had in the world, and he asked an exemplification of friendliness on our part to the extent of inflicting direct personal chastisement on any members of this regiment living in our vicinity—a task not very congenial at the age of sixty-five, and small and light in proportion!

Similar losses were common to Southern and Western sportsmen, especially in all the Border States; but these are gradually renewing their stock, and in many cases improving on the old by gathering fresher and purer blood.

CROSSING GAME FOWLS.

A judicious system of crossing is, and should be, a matter of study, among all fanciers of poultry, of whatever kind; but to those who attend alone to the propagation of games, whether from mere taste, or for the purpose of using them in the pit, it should claim a share of their attention commensurate to the gain that can be acquired by putting it into practice.

Many oppose crossing *in toto*, and declare that they can get no benefit from it. Why? Is it because such have made an intelligent effort and failed? We fancy not. Is it not rather because they ascribe the origin of the innumerable tribe of Dunghills to it? But no one can truthfully say that such are the result of a judicious system of crossing, nor of the crossing of any truly game blood.

While we admire and yearly put in practice the only true plans, we are by no means the advocate of *indiscriminate* crossing. It is as greatly productive of evil as the other is of good. The failure of that which is false, forms no sufficient reason for discarding that which is good.

The arguments in favor of careful crossing are abundant; indeed, we will venture to assert that there is not a single reader of this book, but what daily observes the wasting, decaying effects of constantly breeding in-and-in; the small, weak, and consumptive bodies of fowls, whose owners, because of a superstition worthy only of the dark ages, and in defiance of every law of nature, imagine that the purity of fowls cannot be maintained unless the brothers are mated with their sisters, the fathers with their daughters, and the sons with their mothers. Indeed, the whole object with such is to make relatives breed with relatives—to thus breed in every conceivable way, in utter contempt of all reasonable opinions to the contrary.— Anatomy and Physiology, as well as all the laws of health, have not taught us the nature of the fowl to the extent they have of the human kind, but cannot we *venture* to be governed by the latter, until our experience confirms the truth?

Go to any poultry yard, where game fowls have for a long train of years been bred in-and-in, and you will see a stock, which if not robbed of its gameness, possesses few if any of those qualities which cause the species to be so widely admired. They have not the vigor, plumpness, size, health, nor at all times the plumage of such as have been judiciously crossed.— This is the result of a life-long experience in raising games, and we fear no opposition to our plan after it has been thoroughly tested.

CROSSING FOR PIT PURPOSES.

When sportsmen wish to breed fowls for the pit, they should in the main discard color, and look to strength, endurance, activity, and the best fighting qualties generally. Thus, having a single object in view, it is more readily accomplished, and the task is plainer. They must not breed in-and-in, and ought to avoid any prejudice in favor of a certain color of feather, as they are apt to be led from the object. Common sense shows the danger of keeping fowls closely related too long together, as rapid degeneration of progeny is produced; and attempts to breed to a feather often lead to the same error, because of the likelihood of one, in order to secure his favorite color, breeding fowls connected, especially when his stock is small.

First, take good, strong, healthy, and truly courageous fowls, and cross some of them every year. A variety of colors may follow—some beautiful, others approaching ugliness—but bear in mind that the object is not color: that it is health, strength, endurance and courage combined.

It is not advisable to place more than four hens with a cock; indeed, two is a better number (unless the cock is very attentive), and will be more likely to breed strong chickens. Too many hens to a cock engenders weakness, not only in the cock

himself, but in his young, and should be carefully avoided.—
However, four can hardly be called too many, and three is a
very common number.

Say that you are compelled, or wish to purchase fowls: procure a good cock and two hens, or four hens, of any fighting breed, (the best known preferable, of course) such as are not related to each other. Breed from these one year, or you may venture as high as three years—but then change, with stock equally as good, *better if possible*, and completely cross the old ones with those newly obtained. Or, if you have already good stock of one breed, of your own, there is no actual necessity for getting more than one lot within three years, unless you desire a variety of breeds. Place the purchased cock, with your own hens, and your stags with the purchased hens or pullets; thus completely crossing them; unless you wish to maintain some of a particular strain, which you can do by keeping such together, or with cocks or stags to suit. If you have fowls of your own, not nearly related, they will do very well.

CROSSING TO A FEATHER.

We have remarked, that when breeding solely for the pit, it is better to discard color and look alone to propagating strength, health, and fighting qualities, because, having a single object in view, the cocker would be more sure of realizing his anticipations; but there is another class of men, who would prefer applying the system of crossing to additional purposes. We allude to those who are both cockers and fanciers—by far the more numerous. Men *will* fancy certain colors, and these wish to adhere to the feather, if it can safely be done. There is but one danger to apprehend, one which we have frequently spoken of, but which can be avoided, if care is used. If you have a sufficient number of fowls, or can procure them, suited in colors, yet bearing no close relation to each other, you may safely breed colors and marks suited to your taste. You must cross, and cross carefully, else, while you may continue color, you may gradually lose the best characteristics of your fowls. The system of crossing is not to be applied indiscriminately, nor are you to select any fowls suited in marks, because they bear no relation to each other. Careful judgment is to be used in the qualities as well as colors of the fowls you select for crossing, if you would have good as well as pretty offspring. Our plan is, to select a cock (first learning his history, in order to be safe,) and if he has been raised from stock which has been bred in-and-in for *no more* than three years, I am satisfied to take him, provided he is right in all other respects, and has maintained his color. We then get hens suited in color, and such as, in our judgment, will aid in breeding the color we want, being equally careful that they are not related to the cock. We then breed one season from these, and get the desired offspring. Then, during the following Spring, change about, as it were, and put the old cock with the young pullets, and the young stags with the old hens, and get their respective and separate offsprings, being careful to keep to the color.— This is done in order to keep up the strength of the fowls.— At this stage of the process, the pullets are three-quarters— that is, the second year's pullets. We then put the orginal old cock with the last bred pullets, being the commencement of the third year, and the offspring will be nearly as full-blooded as the original stock, and will not be weakened by the process. This system will enable any one to maintain a particular strain, preserving the colors and marks suited to his fancy. It can be continued for any length of time, by procuring new fowls, of the same breed and color, to cross with at the end of every three years.

The plan has not only the advantage of keeping to the color, but will maintain the purity of any particular strain. By it we have been enabled to preserve the great Tartar breed for upwards of thirty years, and, therefore, know that the system is sound in all respects, and infinitely preferable to regular in-and-in-breeding. In breeding our Tartars, we did not endeavor to breed to the feather closely, as our fancy did not run in that way; we had in view the preservation of those qualities for which the breed was justly noted.

APPROVED CROSSES.

We will here enumerate and describe several very successful crosses we have made, exclusively for pit purposes, commencing with that which is now highly esteemed in Europe, through its introduction by "Censor," a gentleman already spoken of, viz:

THE CLIPPER AND TARTAR.

You cannot, of course, make a failure of a cross, where you mate two noted and trustworthy strains or breeds. If one be generally large, strong and active, with heavy limbs, and perfect in physical organization, while the other does not possess all these advantages, but is unrivalled in quickness, courage and skill in battle, the cross must necessarily be of the first-class. This was true of our Tartars and Clippers, and we determined to apply the system so consonant with nature. It is not for a moment to be supposed, that immediately on receipt of the two trios from "Censor," we placed them helter skelter with a lot of Tartars. Our plan was to take the young "Censor Cock," as we called him (i. e. the brown breasted red,) and place him with four of our own hens, each of a separate and approved breed. Our choice was a Tartar, Prince Charles, Strychnine and Top Knot hen. But our immediate subject is that of the Clippers and Tartars, and of these we will speak. The progeny of the cross are black reds, brown reds, and not unfrequently blue reds; some with willow colored or green legs, others with yellow or blue; eyes black, red and dun colored.— The weights of the cocks will run from 4 lb. 12 oz., smallest, to 6 lb. 8 oz., largest—at least such is the smallest and largest we have yet seen produced, though we have known some Tartar cocks to weigh over 7 1-2 lbs. The Tartars are unusually savage and strong, the Clippers all that games of their size can be, the two combined possess all the fighting qualities that any one can desire or hope for. We have known stags of this cross to fight to the bitter end at a very early age, though such a trait cannot be general, as it depends most upon the raising of such stags, reaping advantages at other's losses—or, in other words, fortunate enough to keep boss of his comrades in the innumerable fights they have from chirping chicks to crowing stags. The hens of the Tartar and Clipper cross will breed black, black red, blue red, with legs, eyes, &c., similar to the cocks. We find the hens remarkable layers, and better mothers than even the pure Clippers. In all our experience in raising games, we have yet to learn any better mothers than pure Tartar hens; they are savage and deadly in their contests with any inter-meddler, and tender and solicitous of the welfare of their young. Clipper hens are more noted for their laying than raising qualities, seeming not to have that desire so usual with other hens to set at the end of every usual quota of eggs.— Therefore the cross, with the hens at least, gains an advantage considered not unworthy by all raisers of poultry.

We could here give long lists of recommendations, for this cross, from those who have obtained them, but choose not to do it, for obvious reasons. That they are well liked throughout and have as yet never failed to give satisfaction, it is proper for us to say.

CLIPPERS AND PRINCE CHARLES.

This cross has many of the characteristics of that between the Clippers and Tartars, and produces fowls rarely surpassed for pit purposes. Their colors, however, are sometimes more mixed, with the exception of the legs, which vary as do the first mentioned cross. White feathers can frequently be observed at the lower part of the wing, a peculiarity, however, liable to any fowls not bred to a feather. The smallest weight of the cocks is 5 lbs., the largest 7 lbs. They are frequently very beautiful, stand up well, with fine, heavy points, broad shoulders, strong pins, heavy wings, and are physically perfect.—They are fully able to "hoe their own row," and can compete with any pure breed known to us.

CLIPPERS AND BALTIMORE TOP-KNOPS.

The Top-Knots, generally speaking, are larger than the Clippers, but not proportionately so plump in body, nor so finely made. Being tall, they seem to have over-grown in one respect, slightly, and lost in another. Therefore, crossing them with the Clippers could not make them less plump, and would better to a slight extent, the use of their heels, already, however very good. The experiment was tried, and our best anticipations realized. The cross now has the billing advantages of the Top-Knots, and the skill of the Clippers, rendering them very formidable in contest. Their colors are almost universally admired—reds with black breasts, brown reds, and reds with blue breasts; have green, yellow and blue legs; eyes red, black and hazle, plumage fine, and many of the cocks with small top-knots back of the comb, while a majority of the hens have the same, only somewhat longer. All will see that the top-knot cannot always exist, even if bred together, as the Clippers, have no such ornament, and there is a likelihood of breeding back. The weight of the cocks is from 4 lbs. 12 oz., to 6 lbs., but rarely over. They are tall, stand well, are reasonably plump in body, have good legs, and look very active.—They are good for pit purposes, and can be relied upon.

CLIPPERS AND STRYCHNINES.

The pure Strychnines are birds of no ordinary celebrity, as has already been shown. They possess substantial fighting qualities, and it was therefore desirable to cross them with the Clippers. This was effected in the Spring of 1859. The result of the cross was greyish cocks, with blue or black breasts, and green or blue legs. The color of course is generally somewhat mixed. In the pullets the marks of the Strychnine can nearly always be observed, the color being different from that of the body, and tending strongly to gray. The cocks weigh 4 lb. 6 oz. to 6 lbs. They appear to have good fighting qualities, and can safely be ranked among first class fowls, and will not prove unworthy the regard of any fancier or cocker in the land.

CLIPPERS AND RATTLERS.

The reader has already been informed that the Rattler strain is the result of a cross, which, whilst it produced small fowls, seemed to unite in their small bodies all the good qualities that nature could pack in so small a bulk. The Clippers could increase their size somewhat, and would not change their color and general characteristics. It was therefore deemed advisable not to stop with the foregoing crosses, but attempt one between the breed and strain heading this item. The cross has produced wirey, active and bold cocks, always reliable as small weights, and fit to cope in any main or single battle.— Both sexes are beautiful, and stand as proudly as though they were the lords of all the feathered tribe. They are reds generally, though the mixed colors from the Rattler side not unfrequently show itself. The weights of the cocks range from 3 lb. 12 oz. to 5 lb. 4 ounces, and is seldom beyond the latter figure.

Since the benefits of crossing have been discovered, and widely promulgated, small fowls are in less demand; yet frequently their services are required, either for fancy or battle, and to those desiring them we could recommend no better than the Rattlers, or some of their crosses.

TARTARS, AND YELLOW-LEGGED BLACK-BREASTED DERBYS.

Did you ever hear of a yellow-legged, black-breasted Derby

fowl? Do not some think that white legs are the only pure ones? We answer that white-legged were Lord Derby's favorites, yet he did not confine himself to one strain of fowls, and his breeders did much at crossing with Seftons, &c., and maintaining the charactetistics of their crosses by breeding to a feather. Further, it is the general practice to call all fowls from this source Derbys, and as a matter of course, the varieties are not few. Well, I have a good strain of fowls called Derbys, which breed black-breasted red cocks with yellow legs, hardy, savage, and quick in their actions. In beauty of plumage they outstrip any other variety of Derbys; their breasts are glossy, the red of their hackles, &c., very brilliant eyes, red or dun color, with a truly graceful carriage. We, last spring, selected four red, or rather yellowish hens of this strain and placed with them a 6 1-4 Tartar cock, with shining black breast, yellow legs, dun eyes, and, in fact, all the characteristics of the stags of this branch of Derbys. Our reasons for doing this were, we wished to preserve the marks of the Derby, and, at the same time, keep them healthy by not breeding in-and-in, and we wished to add some to their size and strength. The result satisfies us in every particular, and the young stags "keep to their colors," and promise to be of good size, some as high as 6 lbs. The Tartar breeding cock, after having obtained sufficient chicks from him, we sent to a member of the well-known Rhett family, in South Carolina, who pronounced him, after a sufficient acquaintance, "a model cock."

DUCK WING DERBY GRAYS AND STRYCHNINE.

There are many admirers of the gray color in games, and a man's stock is not complete unless he has some. There are Irish, Mexican and Derby grays, the latter duck-wing. Having a fine imported duck-wing Derby cock, we were determined to make good use of him, and therefore placed him with some of our finest Strychnine or Mexican gray hens. This cross with any of the gray species we believe to be second only to the Tartar and Strychnine.

TARTARS AND PRINCE CHARLES.

These will breed cocks in weight from 5 1-2 lb. to 7 lb. 8 oz., have good feathers, though of various colors. The Prince Charles are generally noted for their size and strength, and the breed, united with the Tartars, will make both savage and strong fighters, eminently calculated for the pit. They are unsurpassed in courage, and are characterized by a dogged perseverance, that is sure to "win or die." Their eyes are hazle, black and red; have large, heavy wings and legs, with, generally, unusually large and plump bodies.

✓ RATTLERS AND TARTARS.

The Rattlers are a small breed of games, and seldom weigh over 5 lb. 10 oz. The correspondent who wrote the item relative to the gallant cock-fight in Louisville, in which one of our half Rattlers and Tartars conquered the old champion of that city, mentioned that the cock weighed 6 lb. 4 oz. It should have been 4 lb. 6 oz., just the reverse—an error, doubtless, caused by his hurry in writing, but which has misled many as to the weight of this cross. True, the size of the Rattlers is improved by the cross with the Tartars, yet seldom gets over the figure I have placed them at, while many are only four pounds. They breed reds with black breasts, reds with brown breasts, blue reds, black reds, and occasionally colors more mixed; have black, green, and hazel eyes, fine plumage, are hardy and plump in body. They are noted for their extraordinary quickness. I have frequently, in sparring stags, seen them fly three or four feet in the air, meet, and strike a dozen blows before they touched the ground. For small weight, I believe they have no equals, and where such sizes are desired, they are the kind to obtain.

CLIPPERS AND PRINCE CHARLES.

This cross will produce cocks from 5 lb. 8 oz. to 7 lb., of mix--

ed colors, yet very beautiful; legs green, yellow, and blue. They stand up well, with fine heavy fronts, and chiefly because of their strength and fierceness, will prove excellent for the pit.

TARTARS AND WHITE-LEGGED DERBYS.

This cross we rank among the best. You know our preference and unbounded confidence in the Tartars, and we assure you that we have a very high opinion of all pure Derbys, the white-legged included. It is said, and I believe truly, that this breed is possessed of the original blood, and was the favorite of Lord Derby and his gamekeepers, (though these noted game-raisers were always fond of crossing.) A pure white-legged Derby cock is a round-shaped bird, with white-striped bill; fiery dun eyes, full and strong neck, close-feathered hackle; short, stiff, and close-feathered back; tail long and sickled; wings round, and good protectors of the thighs; belly small, thighs short and thick, legs long and white, and general carriage excellent. The hens differ from this in about the same proportion that hens of other breeds differ from cocks. With a cock of the above description, direct from the yard of the Derby game-keeper, we have placed some of our finest and largest Tartar hens. The only drawback in this cross is the change in the Derby's legs, which are converted to either willow, green, yellow, or blue, the pure white being lost easier than these colors. But in all other respects, it is just the thing. We have some black-breasted reds, some brown, dark reds, and occasionally blue reds—colors which suit most men, and are always attractive. The two breeds average nearly the same weight, the Tartar having somewhat the advantage; but the mere fact of crossing, of breeding from fowls in no way related, increases the size and strength, and, therefore, the progeny are of good size. For pit purposes they will be a stout rival of any breed or strain known to the country.

SEFTONS AND TARTARS.

It is very difficult to get pure Lord Sefton fowls, though we believe we have them. We are breeding some pure, and have placed others with Tartars. One of the Sefton cocks weighs 6 1-2 lb., a black-breasted red, and quick and savage fighter.— We have placed him with very dark red Tartar hens, and consequently all his chicks will be black or brown reds, of good size, and excellent fighters. We have been using this cross for several years, have sent many away, all of which seemed to give great satisfaction. They are beautiful fowls, and as good as they look.

EARL DERBYS AND BALTIMORE TOP-KNOTS.

You are aware that there are other fowls of Derby breeds than the White-legs; indeed, the strains are so numerous that we could give you a list of thirty names, including as many different colors, produced, doubtless, by liberal crossing. Well we have taken a fine plump, brown-breasted Derby cock, and placed him with some Top-Knot hens. The main result will be plumpness of body in the progeny (the thing most needed with Top-Knots), inherited from the Derby, while all will have to a great extent the carriage, height, and billing properties of the Top-Knots. Some will have top-knots, some will not.

TARTAR AND AMERICAN.

We have already given the cross between the Tartar and Mexican Grey or Strychnine Games. The Tartar and American springs from a large dark gray Virginia cock, as pretty and as fine a bird as we ever saw, and full Tartar hens. The weight of the cock was six and a half pounds, his eyes were black, legs turkey colored, with fine large black tail, and long gray hackle and feathers. His station was lofty and proud. We frequently refused twenty-five dollars for him, and only parted with him after we had an abundance of his stock to start with. The Tartar hens were selected with a view to fine, large and muscular build. The result was a progeny of stags and pullets fine enough to grace any cocker's yard. They showed dark grays, grays with blue breasts, blue, and blue reds. It is a good rule that when two first-class breeds or strains are bred together, nothing is lost by the process in pit qualities. We rank the Tartar and American cross among the finest we have ever made, in its show of fighting qualities.

CONKEY AND BAKER CROSS.

Produced by putting a Conkey cock with two of Baker's choice Pile hens—the cock a brother to the one which made the gallant fight in Wilmington, Del., elsewhere mentioned. The hens were sisters of the gallant Pile cock sent to Dr. Greenfield of Tennessee. The result shows some reds and some piles, of good bone and muscle, wirey and active. The piles excel many of the color in strength and endurance—the only object sought.

BRENIMAN DARK REDS.

A cross from a fair sized Rattler cock with large brown Breniman hens, the object being to increase the activity of the Brenimans. The progeny shows black reds, brown reds, and occasionally blue reds; the cocks running from four and three-quarters to six and a-half pounds in weight. The object sought was well attained.

CONKEY AND BOB MACE.

Obtained by placing one of Bob Mace's largest shuffler cocks with a brown Conkey hen. This was a good "hit," the stags showing a determined and rapid style of fighting which wins universal admiration. They show reds with black breasts, blue reds and brown reds, and run from five to six and a-half pounds in weight—very good match sizes. They mature early, and we have seen some of them cut down at seven months old.

CONKEY AND MCCLELLAN.

These combine all the good qualities of the Conkey and Mace cross, with increase in bone, body and muscle—some of them weighing as much as eight pounds. They are good stationed, not over-long in leg, fair plumage, and show light red and pile colors.

CONKEY AND ESLIN.

If anything exceeding in weight the Conkey and McClellan cross, and showing better red colors. They run from six and a half to eight and a-half pounds, and breed beautiful black breasted reds and brown reds. The hens are large and plump, with fine and close feathers. The cocks conduct themselves admirably in battle, and are excellent for all pit purposes. At the same time they are not to be despised for fancy.

TARTAR AND CONKEY.

The reader has by this time properly enough reached the conclusion that the Conkey strain has been one of our favorites; and of the Conkey crosses our favorite is that with the Tartar, for it shows, in an eminent degree, the mingling of good qualities, and the dark red colors are well maintained. A young Tartar cock, a black breasted red, was placed with full sized brown red Conkey hens. These were the originals, some of them afterwards bred with somewhat lighter colored Tartars, so that now we can produce, black reds, black breasted reds, brown reds, blue reds, and occasionally a brass back. Nearly all of them are of good weight, and some suitable for shake-bags. They show well the savageness of the Tartar, are vigorous, strong and healthy.

THE BLOOD REDS.

These are the result of a partial feather cross, long continued. Good and bright red fowls of the Tartar, Clipper and other approved breeds were selected, the blood being kept fresh and the color improved. The reward of patience and industry is what might be called blood red cocks and red hens. The cocks show weights from five to seven pounds, are beautifully feathered, with long and rich red hackles and saddle feathers. They have generally firey red eyes, with fine black margin on the lids—the hens showing the same peculiarity, as a rule.— They well meet the fancy for reds, and combine many good pit qualities. They are the subject of much pride in us, as they well attest the fact that equal results can be produced by breeding fresh blood to a feather, as by breeding relatives.

GREEN LEG BLUE REDS.

A strain produced by a cross with a Twaddell blue red shuffling cock, and a dark blue McClellan hen—both noble game specimens. The colors are very pretty and rich, the station good—the whole fowl built for strength, with round body, and heavy set and muscular thighs and legs. They have shown themselves to be winning games, having thus far been very successful. Many of them mature early. They are in color simply blue reds, showing several shades of blue and red, but all of them have green legs.

BROWN REDS RED EYES.

A cross of a counterfeit brown red cock, with red eyes, and a fine, red-eyed brown English hen, the blood of both being good. The mother had previously been known to throw very hard fighting stags, and the Counterfeit cock had made a reputation of his own, having won two battles, by quickness and perseverance, in a single day. Their build is round and plump, leg of medium length, and blue or dark green in color; the cocks show weights varying from four and a-half to six pounds, the object of the cross being to produce cocks as quick and as energetic in battle as the Rattlers, and the effect was in the main successful. Some of these stags seem to force the fighting at all stages, and strike with or without a hold. Many of them are exceedingly savage in action, but are withal intelligent, and seldom peck or strike other than their own kind. The cross is an admirable one in all respects—the red eye being a peculiarity which if anything adds to their beauty.

√ BLACK-BREASTED REDS WITH YELLOW LEGS.

The peculiarities indicated in the above heading, strike our fancy above any others, and we have always made it a point to breed black-breasted red games with yellow legs, combining with these colors useful game traits. Such a fowl, strong and well proportioned, we have always looked upon as a model.— For a number of years we have propagated a handsome strain of this character, a cross between English black-breasted reds and Tartars of the same color—both having yellow legs. We have occasionally changed the blood by mingling unrelated fowls, thus keeping up and adding to the size and strength.— We have now cocks of this variety running from six pounds to eight, and occasionally beyond that mark; all well built, and most of them of excellent plumage. The eye is red, the head a pretty size and well shaped, the hackle blood red, the back turkey red, the saddle feathers long and brilliant, and the sickle feathers long and beautiful. The breasts are full, broad and shining black, the legs and beaks of a yellow golden color.—They are as good at fighting as they are in looks, and in our judgment surpass any purely English black-breasted reds we have ever seen. We confess that we have had very many cockers decry our fancy for these fowls, and we have argued with some of them long and fruitlessly. It *is*, after all, only a fancy, but each man claims the right to have one—and so long as his mark is within the limits of pure gameness, it cannot be properly denied. These are within that limit, and so acknowledged everywhere. Some of our favorite yellow-legged black breasted reds have won a name wherever sent, and the number of their admirers is daily on the increase. They are first-class pit fowls, are long-winded, active, and so industrious in battle that it is rarely one is counted out.

BLUE LEGGED BLUE REDS.

A cross springing from a large Bowman hen and a blue McClellan cock, which weighed seven pounds while on his walk.— We afterwards sent him to a Philadelphia main, where a six pound four ounce fowl was wanted, the party agreeing to reduce this cock to that weight. He did this by physic and exercise, after being warned of its weakening effect. The result was partial physical prostration, and a crippling of the powers of the cock. He fought one hour and fifteen minutes, loosing the battle, but won the admiration of all who knew the circumstances. His powers of endurance were remarkable, and if fought at his proper weight—for he had little or no waste flesh —the fowl against which he contended, could have won the battle only by chance. One of the strain was used in the Long Island, New York main, and won one of its hardest battles by his superior endurance. The progeny show various colored blue reds, all with blue legs, are well feathered, very large boned, and solid and strong. They well combine all the good qualities of the original stock, the cocks running from six to as high as eight pounds. The color is one that will not meet general approbation, and will find more patrons among Irish sportsmen than those of any other nation ; but the pit qualities will everywhere win respect, and the fowl, when once tried, always be propagated by cockers. They produce a large number of shake bags, and in general show good sized hens and cocks. The one we are now breeding from is a blinker, seven and a-half pounds in weight, and the winner of several fights.

RATTLING TOP-KNOTS.

A cross convenient in size for matches, the weight of the cocks being from four to five and a-half pounds. They show various colors, black-breasted reds, brown reds, ginger reds, and in some cases pile colors. They are of course the result of a mixture of the blood of well selected Rattlers and Baltimore Top-Knots—both strains valuable. They pick and show fight as long as life is in them, and when sound fight with a speed that seems marvelous. We have long bred and used them, always with confidence, and have found them to give satisfaction wherever sent. They show good, heavy bones and thighs for small fowls, are plump and muscular, and while they are not objectionable to the fancy, are quite popular among cockers.

WELSH AND ESLIN GRAYS.

One of the originals of this strain Mr. Welsh got from old Mr. Eslin, of the District of Columbia. He was described to us as a very pretty fowl, a black breasted gray, with yellowish gray hackle, red saddle feathers, black tail, and green legs.— He was bred to some of Welsh's own gray hens, we obtaining part of the progeny some years ago. They are fine fowls, well made, and vary in size from five to six and a-half pounds.

The Welsh duck-wing grays, a very fine cross by the way, was obtained by breeding a gray Strychnine with duck-wing hens.

BROWN REDS.

So called because they answer this discription, and are of no separate and distinct blood. They were produced, in our hands, by a cross of the Bowman and Bailey brown reds, the first of large size and bone. As already shown, the originals had won fair names, and the best of these varieties were selected in order to increase the size, retain the color, and commingle the pit qualities. The result shows brown reds equal if not superior to most of the pure English brown reds, They are hardier, of fresher blood, and stronger, Their plumage is fine, station good, and in bearing they are equal to any. The cocks vary in weight from five to six and a-half pounds. The breeds of both Bowman and Bailey are already familiar to the reader, and the characteristics of the cross need no detailed description.

DUSTY MILLER GRAYS.

Obtained by crossing the Cook Silver Grays with Cook brown red hens, so like in appearance to the old Dusty Miller fowls that they have taken that name. They would look much like Piles, only their light colors prevail with yellow and gray. They are rather pretty, improve to the eye on acquaintance, and are good pit games.

BLACK GRAYS.

These are the result of a cross between a large black game cock sent us by Jack McClellan, and pure gray Strychnine hens, of good size. They throw very dark grays, or what we choose to call black grays. Breasts, tails and backs a glossy black, with iron gray hackles, and saddle feathers. The Strychnine side of the strain is well known throughout the entire country, and the McClellan, though less known, was almost equally as good. The black cock was as pretty a fowl of that color as we ever remember having seen, and as game "as they make them." We have since sent the progeny to many parts of the Union, and it has thus far won universal admiration, and given a good account of itself in the pit. They have a gray, savage eye, sombre countenance, and show at a glance a determined and savage disposition.

GREEN LEG PILES.

A strain we believe to be entirely American, produced by the breeding of a McClellan white cock with a Goss Counterfeit hen. The result is a beautiful pile, strong, of good bone, and throughout well made, and are quick and hard fighters. The cocks run in weight from five up to six and a-half pounds—a convenient size for general pit purposes. They have always given satisfaction.

YELLOW LEG PILES.

Crossed from a McClellan pile cock and a Baltimore Top-Knot hen, showing pile colors, and occasionally a very small top-knot, consisting of loose feathers back of the comb. The cocks show weights from four to six pounds, are strong, active, and far more healthy and enduring than most pile fowls.

BLUE LEG PILE.

Produced by breeding a large McClellan pile cock with full Clipper hens, all of them throwing blue legs. The legs of the

Clipper hens were a deep blue, those of the pile cock a light yellow—all of the progeny being blue legged—a fact which would argue well for the strength of the Clipper characteristics, if the color of feather were not mostly taken from the cock.— He was a light pile, and threw in this cross somewhat darker piles. They are fine stationed, plump in body, of pretty good leg, and are quick and persistent fighters. We have sent many of this cross to New York State, where they have many times been placed on local exhibition. Some are breeding on Long Island, where they are greatly admired. Pile colors were always greatly favored by the Yorkers both in city and country, and many of the men who there make a business of breeding poultry have purchased fowls from our yard and afterwards honored (?) them with their own names. We prefer that they should do this, for games, inter-mixed, or in close proximity with all kinds of poultry, never long retain their game blood, and when this is lost we prefer the blame being saddled just where it belongs.

RED MCCLELLANS.

Of the several cocks obtained from McClellan, none were a pure red, and we determined to make the stock show this color. After a few years' breeding we succeeded, the first cross being with red Eslin hens, the next with the Bailey English brown reds. We then succeeded in getting a brown red stag, in weight nearly seven pounds, by selecting pullets having the best red colors, we next got some brown red and some black breasted red stags, and can now show both colors to perfection —most of the blood used being fresh and unrelated. As a consequence the fowls are large and strong, and little, if any less worthy of admiration than the originals.

REMARKS ON BREEDING AND CROSSING.

We have thus given the approved crosses made by ourself in a forty years' course of breeding, or made by parties with whom we are entirely familiar. The system is one which should be *individually* pursued, wherever the party has opportunities for breeding fowls. If he desires fowls to meet an emergency, or for immediate use in the pit, then the only rule which applies is that which directs him to get the best that can be procured, and to procure these only from parties in whom he can place implicit confidence, or of those who have a fair reputation for honest dealing, and who breed *games only*. It is akin to madness for a man to trust games in the vicinity of fowls of common blood, for the mixture of one will destroy confidence in all.— For pit purposes the crosses are often preferred to the breeds, because they are of fresher and frequently of more vigorous blood, and can better stand long journeys and rough usage.— These are considerations not to be despised where hundreds of dollars depend upon a single advantage.

But for breeding, cockers and fanciers prefer carrying on the process under their own observation.—It is part of their daily pleasure, and to these men pleasure is profit. But these must not hang too much affection upon a *breed*, else they will suffer from their want of discretion. Fowls of a given breed are of course all more or less related, no matter from whence or whom obtained, and the chances are about even that you will get them too closely related. In any event, you cannot add to size, and muscle, and endurance, by breeding them with their like in your own yards; you *can* freshen the blood, renew life and vigor and health, and measurably add to their value. The choice is with the individual, and it will in most cases depend upon the object in view. The one practice is beneficial and probably safe—the other is assured. A *strain*, good in game blood, is worthy of as much pride as a *breed*, whether in the hands of the cocker or the fancier. We distinguish the two by our limited knowledge of each, and that which some of us now in pride call a breed, may after all be but a strain with peculiarities trained in the hands of early and skillful breeders.

We have already shown the possibility of this, and if we were disposed we could trace it so minutely that a doubt would possess the minds of even the most skeptical. Suffice it to say that the majority in America trace their knowledge of cock fighting and game raising back to England, Ireland, Scotland and Wales—the more remote the individual origin, the greater the presumption to a general knowledge of the subject—a position that will not bear very close inspection. But only a limited knowledge of history will show us that in the days long gone the lords of manors in all these countries, took more or less pride in exclusiveness, in differing with their neighbors, and personal and clanish feuds everywhere prevailed. The same was true in the matter of sports, the opposition being only partially hidden behind the courtesies of the gentleman.—Games were bred, just as were horses, of the purest attainable blood, and when breeds could not be obtained, strains were sought, and the result was a cross, which, long bred in single hands, finally won consideration as a breed, and was thereafter so classed. Clans of Scots bred games different from other clans, counties of Celts different from those of neighboring counties—just as did lords those differing from other noblemen, but it is not probable that one fourth of the blood thus obtained was that from separate and distinct breeds, and if such were the fact, it could not remain so to this day, and above all could not be applied to this country, where individuals have in many cases imported at haphazzard, and where, among the actual and persistent cock-fighters, the system of crossing has prevailed for at least fifty years.

It is true that in England the game-keepers of the several lords noted in the game fowl line, bred to a feather, and well retained odd marks of distinction, and herein is the justification of the term breed, as applied to all of these fowls. But it is equally true that men as skillful as they could have produced the same marks by at first crossing, and afterward selecting fowls with given peculiarities, and breeding them together for a series of years. And some such plan must have been pursued, if not at the beginning, at some stage of the breeding, else the reputation of the fowls in the pit could never have been retained; for fowls bred in-and-in for ten or twenty years are weak and worthless. The same would be true of fowls bred for a century by mingling those most distantly related, the question being one of time, the latter mode having the preference of the former, of course. There are few game fanciers or cockers but have seen Earl Derbys and Lord Seftons which have been bred in-and-in, perhaps in this country, for ten and twelve years. They have remarked their small size, thin and ricketty limbs, and general physical deterioration—retaining nothing in fullness save the feather, which ought, in the providence of nature, to be more protective on weak and sickly fowls than on those strong and hardy. All the marks of game blood are there, and the gameness of the fowl can never be successfully disputed—for this is a quality at once so innate and natural that nothing but an admixture of common blood can weaken its attribute of courage. But the efficiency and health of such fowls stand questioned to any and every observing eye, and the faith that places them in the pit against hardier fowls of their kind is sure to have a fall.

A skillful course of breeding can make Earl Derbys into Lord Seftons, and *vice versa*; that is, all the peculiar marks of each can be shown and can be perpetuated, and there is no fraud in that which is better than the original, unless a false representation accompanies the transaction. It can be done in this way:—Take a white leg Derby cock and place him with three yellow or willow legged Sefton hens; all throwing black breasts. The progeny will show some of white and some of willow colored legs;—select the pullets with white legs, the darker the color of feathers the better, and breed them to a fresh white leg Derby cock or stag. These will throw a yet clearer white leg; select the clearest and breed again in like manner, and you will throw all or nearly all white legs. The sixth generation will thus tell a complete story, and if the fowls are unrelated, the vigor, muscle, bone and size will all be relatively increased. Parties will say that this is *breeding back*, and that the same process would restore all of the original blood. If the fowls were related, this assertion would approximate the truth; if not, the blood of the breed desired would be measurably restored. This is not a distinction without a difference, *for the commingling of unrelated blood is not breeding in-and-in*; if it is commingled in a cross for too long a time it is almost equally as injurious as if commingled in a separate breed. The one plan is returning to a feather or known peculiarity, the other is knitting relationship at the expense of all the concomitants of such a course of debility, deformity and loss of vitality. The one is justified to one's self, and is only wrong when misrepresentation is made to deceive others—the deceit bolstering a pride that we may have no sympathy for, but yet have no right to tamper with, especially at the expense of our own honesty.

So that, where men admire the peculiarity of white legs, or any other distinguishing mark, we advise them, if they wish to preserve it and at the same time preserve the strength and efficiency of their fowls—and especially where they have not the means or facilities to import—to cross their games with given colors, and to breed back to a peculiarity of feather, or leg or head, and to rest satisfied with *pure game blood*.

This thing called breeding back to the original is impracticable, especially in game fowls—we mean in breeding back to the pure original blood. For instance: Take a white leg Derby cock, a black breasted red, and breed him to a gray Strychnine, both fowls almost wholly unlike. The first progeny will be half of each; put a Derby to this progeny, and the result will be three-quarters; the next similar process will show one-eighth, the next one-sixteenth, the next one-thirty-second, and so on up. It would require years upon years to wholly obliterate the blood of the Strychnine, if it ever could be reached—but the feather and all the leading characteristics would be merged and submerged in the Derby at a comparatively very early stage. The result would be a benefit to the Derby in more ways than one; the proper name would be a Derby *strain*, and not a Derby breed.

We have already in this work disputed the theory that Derby games *must* be black breasted reds with white legs, and we have established the fact in newspaper contests against those who contended for the one peculiarity. The following, quoted from an article sent by us to the "*Old Spirit*" better defines the position than anything elsewhere said in this work:—

"It is a matter of no little difficulty to be definite in enumerating all which have been deemed worthy of a name, because in many cases the distinctions are so slight, arising, doubtless, from the system of *inter*-crossing, so highly valued by the former Derby game keepers. It was the practice of Lord Derby to keep a register of all his crossing with fowls from Sefton, Stanley, and others, in many cases changing only slightly the color, yet sufficient for a name. The *first* strain of Derby's were known as having *white* legs, a strain greatly admired, and carefully preserved to this day. In the States of Georgia, South Carolina, and Alabama, they are known by the name of Claibornes, and are among the best fowls in those States. Still, I am not prepared to say they are the best of the Derby's; I consider the black-breasted, yellow-legged ones, equal in point of courage and general fighting qualities to any. I have seen a cross between this and my own Tartars, in which the color has been preserved, but strength, bigness of bone, and eagerness greatly increased. But I am quitting the original. Thos. Roscoe, who had the superintendence of the strain, thus describes the white-legged Derbys:

"The cock is a fine, round shaped bird, with white striped bill, dun eyes and fiery, round and strong neck, fine round close-feathered hackle, feathered points to shoulders, short, stiff, broad back, close feathered and hard; tail long and sickled, tufted at root; wings round, and well prolonged, so as to protect the thighs; breast-broad, belly small, and tight in the pinions; thighs short and thick, well set in the body; legs long and white; the comb of a stag is large and red, before being cut; weight, about five pounds.

Subjoined is a list of names attached to the various strains of Derbys, which proves a remark I made in reply to "Game Fowl," that the white legged was not the only variety. But to the names:—

Black-breasted birchen duckwings.   Smoky duns.
Brown-breasted, or ginger.   Whites.

Silver black-breast duckwing greys.
Clear mealy greys.
Red duns.
Black duns.
Blotch-breasted red.
Turkey-breasted greys.
Large marble-breasted greys.
Brassy wings.
The Polecats.
Copper Wings.
Piles.

Red whites.
Dun piles.
Cuckoos.
Pheasant-breasted reds.
Large spot-breasted reds.
Shady-breasted and birchen duck.
Marble breasted birchen duck.
Muffs.
Tassels.
Spangles.
Wavy Birchens.

The above, including white and yellow legs, number thirty-two varieties, some of which are of course deemed better than others. The various strains have white, yellow, green, willow, olive, blue, and dark legs. Their bills and legs frequently correspond in color. Their eyes are red, pale yellow, dawe, dark-brown or black. The following are generally considered as the best: Black-breasted, yellow-legged reds; do. white legs, dark black-breasted birchen ducks, dark black-breasted berry-birchens, silver black-breasted duckwing greys, clear mealy greys, piles, dark black-breasted greys, and red duns.

Above I purposely omitted the *blue* duns, noted for their familiarity, impudence, and pugnacity. They are impetuous and courageous, and good in a fight. The breast of this strain is of a rich, dark slate color; the feathers having a broad margin and a darker hue; the saddle of a deep blood color, and the hackles of the neck and tail of a dark red, gradually shading to a beautiful golden tint; the tail black and flowing with a brilliant green shade. The hen is marked in the same manner, all over the back and body, with the hackle of the same golden color.

Have I not said and quoted enough of the Derbys? Or is it neccessary for me to show authority to prove all these strains? If "Game Fowl" wishes it, I can do so. It is not necessary for me to review minutely their fighting qualities as almost every cocker and fancier in the land is acquainted with them. 'Nuf sed.

Yours truly,
GAME FANCIER.

No one will pretend that Lords Derby, Sefton or Stanley, with all their wealth and facilities for getting games, had original blood for all the numerous varieties properly bearing their names, nor will any now say the same of Cobden, Heathcote and Caldwell—the last named being "Censor," one of the best posted sporting gentlemen known on this or the other side of the Atlantic. He procured the Clippers from the hands of Cobden, and he had so bred them that they won celebrity in most of the pits of England. We do not claim that they are a distinct *breed*, nor would we value them higher if we knew them to be so. Censor did not thus describe them, but in effect confessed that they were a cross, as will be seen by the following, taken from *Porter's Spirit*, and in part repeated under the head of "Clipper Games:"—

"DEAR SIR:—Allow me to thank you most cordially for your kind and handsome present of game fowls. They reached me in perfect safety, in a few hours after I had put a notice in Porter's Spirit saying they had not arrived. I am sending you, by Saturday's steamer, two trios of as good birds as ever flew—the cock on the left (that is to say, on the left of the other when both are looking through the bars) has won two fights, and is slightly lame. You will find him a nice bird to handle, and very tame. He was bred by Mr. Cobden, in Sussex—within three miles of Goodwood Race-Course. Whenever a main is fought in the South of England, his birds are sought for, and odds are sure to be laid on the party in alliance with Cobden. This bird would, I fancy, make an excellent cross with the Tartar hens. The two hens with him were got by a brown-red Nottingham cock, out of hens of our late celebrated jockey, Frank Butler, of the black-breasted red sort. He had an immense number in all parts of England, and won an enormous quantity of mains. The other cock was bred at Epsom, by Mr. Heathcote, part owner of our famed Epsom Race-Course, who is a thorough sportsman; he keeps a pack of stag-hounds, and breeds none but the best game fowls he can procure. I liked him better than a stag I thought of sending, brothers of the hens in this pen—they of the Staffordshire stock, where more cocking takes place at present, than in all the rest of England put together. You will, if they reach you in safety, have two sets of hens, no relation to either cock, and no relation to each other, excepting that the pairs of hens are sisters.

"The Baltimore Top-Knots are nice birds; but I infinitely prefer the Tartar hens, and shall *next* year cross them with a Staffordshire black-breasted red; that must be a good cross I think. Allow me to remain, dear sir, very faithfully yours, CENSOR."

Here we find the names of several noted game raisers mentioned, and we venture the assertion that confidence was engendered by these names to an extent equal to the known purity of the blood of the Clippers.

The brief quotation well establishes another fact, even more pertinent to this part of our subject. That fact is, the acknowledgment by implication at least, that the successful game raisers and cockers of England, of the present day, pursue the system of crossing, or of mixing the blood of breeds, and to this they owe their success. So that it is no longer truthful to represent the English, when at home, as yet in the main adhering to the practice of breeding in-and-in. We never believed the practice to be universal in that country, and always credited the success of the most noted cockers to other means—chief of which was the replenishing of pure stock with fresher blood. We trace the prevailing error to the known fondness of these men for breeding to a *feather*, and we claim and insist upon a distinction being made between this and breeding *in-and-in*. That once comprehended and recognized will pave the way for rationally, accounting for a success so greatly envied.

We have classed our description of fowls under breeds, strains and approved crosses—in the latter case, approving only those with which we are perfectly familiar. Some so-called, may not be breeds, but they are generally accepted as such, and we preferred not to change a habit which can show many good reasons for its continuance. Strains are those known to have originated in a cross, more or less remote, but subsequently bred together, not in-and in, but with like crosses. These may or may not be bred to a feather; there is absolute safety in either plan, provided the fowls are unrelated. Crosses are those either recently made or constantly continued. They are continued in this way, and the freshness of the crossed blood must be apparent to all. Tartar and Strychnine spring from Tartar cocks and Strychnine hens (*or vice versa,*) and the progeny for two or three generations can be safely called a cross; then the original plan is renewed, and sometimes the progeny of the second originals is bred with the progeny of the first, provided these originals were not closely related. The same plan can be pursued with all strains and breeds of fowls, the raiser being always careful not to breed too long with the same crossed fowls, else he will be breeding in-and-in to almost as great an extent as would the man propagating fowls of a known and single breed. It would not take many years to make the danger equally as great, and sub-crosses would eventually run out, just as breeds have been known to do.

BREEDING IN-AND-IN.

Men, not fully conversant with their own natures, cannot be expected to comprehend fully the nature of fowls ; but it is a good rule to acknowledge to be true in the nature of fowls that which we acknowledge to be true in our own natures, in other words, that the law of nature is uniform with all living kind, and seeks exceptions in no tribe or species. An intelligent man will not now defend inter-marriage in the human race, and where this is effected in the present day, there is generally some immediate motive stronger than one's respect for the truths of physiology. The result is apparent in ten thousand households—decrepitude, deformity, weakness, hereditary disease, liability to disease and insanity. Such examples show themselves in almost every family where first cousins have inter-married, and in many where second and third cousins are blessed or cursed with offspring. The human race is countless and long lived. There is every facility for avoiding inter-marriage, and with "well regulated minds" it is avoided, and the world is better for it. Game fowls have never been so plenty, and while they remain game, never can be, notwithstanding they breed rapidly, and have an ordinary poultry longevity.— Their nature makes them destructive of each other, no matter how closely related, and, beyond given ages, they have no veneration for parentage or offspring. Such as are not killed in administering to man's pleasures and appetites, have the "fatality" of getting killed in some way or other, the usual death not being a natural one, unless in true sporting faith we call it natural to die fighting. The stock has never been known to be super-abundant in any country or clime, and will never be, even if in the approaching poultry millenniem a pure and simple poultry peace society should be organized. The game would be the first to break the covenant, under the plea that he was only at peace when fighting, and no fowl, however wise,

could confute the argument by any course of moral suasion.—
To attempt anything else would be fatal, for the game would
appeal to the spur and rely upon blood to settle all disputes.

Games die from all causes, natural and unnatural, for they
are the poultry world's adventurers, but no cause is calculated
to so rapidly decimate them in any locality or nation, as the
system of breeding relative blood in-and-in, to foster a pride
which would fail in argument even if evil consequences were
not direct and inevitable. Men are frequently led to covet
peculiarities in games because these peculiarities more nearly
attach their own names to that of the games, and personal
ambition is subserved. To this we do not object, for a man
succeeding in propagating good breeds and strains has a right
to claim property in them, and to force a courteous acknowledgment from others ; but we do object to the means employed
to carry out the plan, when others are at hand in all respects
preferable and better, and which would be employed if it were
not for a prejudice which had its foundation in ignorance—in
a false deduction made from presumed English practices.

The minds of men in both Europe and America have of late
years been well directed to the study of breeding stock of all
kinds—the horse, the cow, the pig, the dog, and every variety
of poultry—and all who give the subject their attention are
uniting in the view that the breeding together of relative blood
will not perpetuate but rather diminish the good qualities of
the originals. The question has latterly been thoroughly discussed in some of the leading agricultural journals as applied
to horses and cows, and the same conclusions are being reached.
Full blooded Alderneys are for practical purposes not more
valued now than the cross of the Devon or Alderney, and a
fraction of the blood of each is in many cases more valued than
the thorough breds. All intelligent farmers know this, and
stock raisers, who breed for practical personal use, recognize
the fact. We cannot better illustrate the fact we are contending for than by quoting the following article on the production
of trotting horses, copied from the "*Galaxy*" of April, 1869 :—

AMONG THE HORSE GROWERS.

The Newburg Farm—How Thoroughbreds are Reared—The American Road Horse.

About two miles west of Newburg is the Newburg Stud Farm, in a broad, open valley, packed by broken hills, with a swift stream running through it. Comfortable houses and good stables indicate a well-considered expenditure, and with reference to profit rather than show.

On this great farm are to be seen, running loose on the snow-covered fields, herds of yearlings and two year olds, rough, unlicked, long haired. It is not easy for the uninitiated to believe that some of these unkempt creatures are worth more than a thousand dollars as they stand. But, with singular confidence, they come up to you, they put their noses into your hand, they wish to nip at your coat, they have no other idea than that you are their friend.

Then you begin to see that they have broad faces, great, intelligent eyes, quick, flexible ear, and confidence. You are pointed to the depth of chest, which indicates lung-power and large hearts. You see that they are even now strongly developed behind, where the great propelling power of the trotter lies. You see, too, that the stifles are wide, and that the muscles creep well down toward the hock-joint, which is low on the leg.

Very soon you begin to believe that these uncombed, wild-looking, but gentle colts are indeed worth money, and that they are the stock from which is to be developed the gentleman's road horse of eastern America in the coming time. You go into the open yard and find, in groups of five or six, the blood mares, as rough looking, as unpromising as their children; but you learn that most of them have racing blood in their veins—are descendants of Mambrino, or Abdallah, or Clay, or Star, or some other of the noted horses; and nearly all have made their mark, have done their mile in 2.50, 2.40, or 2.30, and so have won their places as mothers of noted offspring.

Now, your first impression may be that these colts are hardly treated; that they do not have the shelter or the cleaning they ought. But you will be assured that this open-air treatment insures a hardy and enduring horse, and is infinitely superior to blanketing and sheltering, and you will believe it. If you feel of the skin you will find it loose and the hair very thick and close, more like fur than hair; and you will understand that, with room for exercise, the colt will not be likely to suffer from cold.

Possibly you will be taken into a small yard, inclosed by a high fence, in one corner of which is an open shed. Out of this will rush at you a young three-year old stallion. He will snort and lash his tail, stand on his hind legs and paw the air, and you may fancy you are going to be devoured; but the manager holds up his hands or his whip and speaks to him, and then you see he is entirely under control. And this is one of the peculiarities at all these great farms—the horses are intelligent and tractable; they know their masters, and *like them ;* they hurt no one, and rarely hurt one another.

I asked the manager at the Newburg farm, "How many do you lose by accident or injury."

"Not one in fifty, perhaps not one in a hundred." And this I found the answer at all the farms.

"Do you practice high feeding—forcing the colts?" we asked of the manager.

"We give a little grain when they are about three months old—enough to get them accustomed to it, and when we wean them we give some four to six quarts a day throughout the year while they are running in the fields.— We lessen this the second year to about four quarts, because then the colts are kept up more; do not have so much exercise. We want to give feed enough to keep the colts growing without check."

'How much do you keep them out in the air?"

"All the day except in stormy weather. The more air and sunlight the better they do, the healthier and stronger they grow."

I come now to a curious and still open question,—Whence comes this tremendous trotting action as shown in the American road horse?

Racing men assert that the natural *fast* gait of the horse is the run, and that no high-bred horse trots fast *naturally*—therefore that the thoroughbred *must be* crossed with the "dunghill" or "cold-blooded" mare to secure a fast trot. We introduced the subject to Mr. Goldsmith.

"I will show you a little of the *natural* fast gait."

Then were brought in succession three young horses, three-year olds.— They were turned loose on the open field and went trotting away at a great stride, head and tail erect. Then they were scared along by running at them; the dog went at them, and still they trotted fast; if they broke into a run they came down almost instantly; it was evident they had a fast trot, which was the gait they preferred.

"What is your explanation of this matter?"

"I will tell you. There have stood in this country the following stallions, all except Bellfounder and Abdallah thoroughbreds, and they nearly so— Messenger, about 1795; Barouet, about 1795; Seagull, about 1820; Bellfounder, about 1831-2; American Star, about 1840; Abdallah, about 1848-50, and some others. Of these Messenger, Bellfounder, American Star, and Abdallah were natural trotters, and it is asserted that Messenger has come in at the end of a running race on a fast trot. Out of these natural thoroughbred trotters have come our great road horses."

For the first time we non-professional men got what seemed a reasonable explanation of a great fact. The great road horse is not a mere accident.

England has produced or perfected the race-horse, America the road-horse.. England, by great care, great skill, and vast expenditures of money, has perfected the race-horse wonderfully fine and altogether useless: America, by great care, skill, and considerable expenditure of money, has produced the trotter, altogether valuable—that is the difference.

This quality—the swift trot—has been, in a sense, created by man, and is now transmitted and perpetuated. How?

By breeding from such horses as showed such a tendency, and by training the progeny so as to create increased speed when increased speed has been transmitted and intensified. It has now reached a single mile in 2m. 17 1-4s. and twenty miles within the hour. What more can be done? No man can tell.

Early training all experts seem to deprecate, but not early handling.— High feeding and early training have filled the English racing stables with weedy colts which come to nothing. A few trotters have made fast time at three years, but it is considered dangerous for a horse which is meant to do his best and to last, to urge him so early.

Woodruff, admitted to be an authority upon this point, strongly deprecates early training, and states that the best horses have not been so trained. But early handling—gentling—is of the first importance.

"What," I asked of a great and most intelligent grower, "do you consider of most importance, next to blood?"

"Handling, gentling, so that the colt knows you as his friend. He must never be frightened. Once frightened, it is impossible for him to do his best. He must have perfect confidence in man."

We may as well make up our minds that the day of cheap, or rather low priced, horses has ended. A good road horse cannot now be sold for less than $400 and that upward. The cost of a good four year old is not less than that amount, and may be more. Whoever, therefore, buys a horse for less than this, may be sure that he is not getting a good horse. And there is better economy, too, in buying this class of horses than low priced ones, they are really cheaper. A horse that has the blood and training which will insure him to be good at the age of twenty, is cheap at anything under one thousand dollars.

Here is a confessed system of crossing, carried on in precisely the same way that we have for years carried on the system of crossing game fowls, and of pursuing other plans calculated to prevent the too close commingling of related blood. Instead of breeding in-and-in, if we wish to or must preserve the peculiarity of feather or leg, we do it as described under the head of crossing, always taking care that we mingle equally strong and if possible better fowls. We struggle for intelligent and compensating results, and combine with peculiarities such *qualities* as we desire. Thus, having weak fowls of known game blood, we place with them unrelated and stronger fowls of equally known blood; if too small in limb, we breed only from the larger limbed, or commingle with them unrelated fowls of larger limb; if wanting in speed, we breed from the most rapid, placing these with other rapid fowls, and frequently making a radical change in blood. We constantly seek the attainment of that which is better, and we strive never to let any stock seriously deteriorate. It *will* deteriorate if bred too long together, if bred too closely to *breed*—unless facilities are ample for freshening the stock. One can with comparative safety breed Derbys in this country, by avoiding related blood, and he does this by purchasing approved stock not of his own neighborhood, or by directly importing it from England. Importation makes each fowl bring, as it were, his weight in silver, unless large quantities are imported, and where this cannot be afforded the next best thing to do is to purchase from some dealer of approved reputation who raises no other than game fowls. Fancy dealers, who keep all kinds of poultry, seldom long hold pure game blood.

After all that has been said in this and other works, and in the leading sporting and agricultural journals, against the directly injurious effects of in-and-in breeding, we hope that cockers and fanciers will everywhere discard it. It is a plan which ought to be obsolete and effete, for it is not in keeping with the spirit of this age, and, if the truth were known, we believe was never *successfully* practiced in the ages gone.

THE PLEASURE IN RAISING GAMES.

Poultry raising is, in the object of many, only a source of profit; to others, the question of profit is a matter of secondary importance; to yet others, the question is solely one of *pleasure*, and here is the proper place of the gentleman cocker and game fancier. For ourselves, we know of nothing around a country, suburban or town residence, so pleasurable as the presence of pretty game fowls. They are objects of interest not alone to all the household but to every passer by. Every lady has an innate admiration for the courtesy and attention of the game, and for the motherly affection and care of the hen. The one teaches man his duty to shield and protect, if need be at the cost of his own life; the other confirms the affections and the warmer impulses of the woman, and on the contrary to making true affection the subject of a shamed display, teaches its sublimity and importance.

No words can portray all the sensations of the cocker and fancier on witnessing or coming into the possession of a favorite game. The sight of one, no matter how often repeated, is to him pleasure intensified. Those only can realize who have felt. Listen to the heart-words of "Privateer," one of the old "*Porter Spirit's*" most gifted correspondents :

"SPIRIT, I do love the woods immense, the fields extending spacious, and the wild waters! And now to proper *moutons*, the sports—for what's a world without sport? I am glad that the ancient and gallant sport of Cocking is coming into vogue again. Some call it cruel; but this is the mistake of ignorance. The armed heel renders the contest the most rapid, gallant, and deadly that can be engaged in. Cocks fighting without heels punish each other far more painfully. Not for nothing, I wiss, was this very essence and concentration of the game principle implanted in this species of the cock. He is gallant, he is fierce, he is beautiful exceedingly! Like the horse of Scripture, he smelleth the battle afar off; he claps his wings at the crows of his adversaries, and sayeth, among their trumpets, ha! ha! Well did the Grecian general of old point to the valor and game of two cocks fighting, as an example for the imitation of his troops. Who has not heard of the game cock, on board of the British ship, that flew upon the stump of the mainmast, when his coop was shattered by a round shot and crowed out loud and long during the balance of the terrible engagement? I like the game cock! I do rejoice in a fine black-breasted red; I dote upon a black brass-wing; freely I bet upon a gallant gray; upon a white pile, I will put my pile; and upon a duck-wing, I will put my " pot." I raised game-cocks in England, SPIRIT, when quite a boy, and raspers, too. One of them won a Welsh main, sixteen battles in the main, for a trotting pony. Since then I have fought bye battles with the Malays of the Eastern Archipelago, when on a voyage to the Spice Islands. A notable cocker is your copper-colored Malay. He has good birds, handles them well, and backs them freely. Joining battle in Batavia harbor, under the main-deck awning, with a Malay boatman, whose proa rode astern with sugar for our ship, a black, muffed cock, of the Lancashire breed I had with me, killed three of the Indian varieties straight on. I won all the Malay's money; and the last battle was for twenty-five rupees staked against his heavy gold ear-rings. I swapped that cock afterwards, to the same Malay, for a "cus" of a Sumatra monkey, that was fool enough to jump overboard between the Cape and St. Helena.

Cocking, in a philosophical point of view, was ably treated by that rare wit and ripe scholar, the late Dr. Maginn. I think I can remember the verses, though it is twenty years, or thereabout, since I read the novel, "John Manesty, or the Liverpool Merchant," in which they are. The scene is in Lancashire; the place, Bullock Smithy, a country hamlet; the name has been changed, by some sentimentalizer, to "Rosedale." The *dramatis persona*, a young lord, a sporting baronet, a tippling parson, who is waiting for the old rector of Everton cum Tof'y to die, that he may succeed to the benefice—a sporting character who once fought Jack Broughton, and rejoices in the cognomen of "Broken-nosed Bob," and other worthies—have been exhibiting a main of cocks; becoming convivial afterwards, the tippling parson obliges the company with a song.

> "The main is fought and passed,
>   And the pit is empty now—
> Some Cocks have crowed their last,
>   While some more loudly crow,
>   From the shock!
> In the world, the same we see,
> Where'er our wanderings be,
>   So here's a health to thee, jolly cock!
>
> "When once you're stricken down,
>   And the spur is in your throat,
> You are surely over-crown
>   By the world's insulting note,
>   Fierce in mock!
> However game you be,
>   In the day of thought and glee,
>   So here's a health to thee, jolly cock!
>
> "Then with eyes and feathers right,
>   And with spurs sharp and prime,
> In condition for the fight,
>   And sure to come to time
>   As a clock!
> We will crow out bold and free,
> With no care for what may be,
>   So here's a health to thee, jolly cock!"

That just fits the spirit of the cocker and the amateur, and will be recognized by both as standard authority. Now to the fancier, whose taste has been supported in all ages and by all peoples. Hon. Erastus Brooks, proved to be the fancier's representative oracle, when he closed an eloquent address before the New York Agricultural Society in March, 1869, and, we are happy to add, at the same time confirmed the theory of this work in relation to the origin of game and other fowls. We quote the closing paragraphs :—

"The domestic fowl has a most respectable as well as aged ancestry. "Man shall rise up at the voice of the bird," spoken of in Ecclesiastes, means, of course, at the crowing of the cock. Though the home-bred fowl is not directly named in the Old Testament, it is included in what are spoken of as among the clean birds which could be eaten. The common fowl was well known among the domestic birds of Palestine ; was abundant in Persia before Darius ; is seen stamped upon the most ancient coins ; upon the Etruscan tombs, and on the marbles of Asia Minor. They were dedicated to Mars, Apollo, Mercury and Æsculapius. The courage of the Rhodian, Persian, Medean and Chalcian fowls was well known, as was their superiority for endurance in fight, and the delicacy of their flesh. They were as familiar to Aristole and Pliny as to us, and obviously of long cultivation. The ancient Britons had them in abundance when Julius Cæsar invaded their territory, though it was not lawful to eat them then. Cock fighting, also, was as common among the ancient Greeks as among the Malays, or a class of English, French, and Americans, who delight in such kind of sporting, which I confess I do not.

"It is more interesting to us, perhaps, to know of the first appearance of American fowls ; but of this and of the origin of the ancient domestic birds, books and study give us little or no satisfactory explanation. In truth, we know, if possible, less of the latter than the former. No domestic fowls were found by the discoverers of the country, upon the adjacent Atlantic Islands, nor upon the so called Fortunate Islands known as the Canaries ; but as we know really so very little of the earliest discoverers of America, who probably had a lodgment here over 1,000 years since, instead of with Columbus, we need not be much astonished over our small attainments in the knowledge of the poultry yard. In the gloomy forests of Guiana, 75 years since, the domestic cock was heard at day-dawn, crowing in similar though in feebler voice than our own birds. So at Cayenne, in the far up country, wild fowls were discovered of the same gait, form, combs, with brown plumage, but hardly larger than the American pigeon.— At the Society Islands, per contra, they are of prodigious size, while in the tropical islands of the South Sea the cock and hen are about the only tame birds. Captain Cook found them on Islands never before trodden by civilized man.

"Next to woman, the hen is the most devoted of mothers, while the cock more than man is the most gallant of attendants. If well bred, indeed, he will see his hens provided with the choicest morsels before making any provision for himself, and it is only when he is cowed or demoralized that he becomes really ungallant and selfish. His great satisfaction is, as with many men, that he is "cock of the walk," and as such he struts upon the stage in all the pride of place and pomp of plumage, and in all this, too, he is very human. It is also noticeable that fowls are perhaps the most constant attendants of man's migration and civilization. They have followed him with the dog to unknown lands, and are found everywhere, except in the highest latitudes, and not there probably because not profitable. It is but fair to suppose, though stated without knowledge of the fact that all the domestic fowls of the world are but an improvement secured from time to time from the wild fowl. Trace them up to the game cock, and in no class of animals are there finer traits of character. The game bird is better than his reputation. While he is not aggressive nor revengeful, and does not provoke assaults, he will suffer no intrusion and submit to no injury. He is brave in combat, patient in pain, and like Barnaby Rudge's raven, his motto is, "never say die." When death comes, no martial warrior ever yielded up his life with more grace and courage, and murder is rarely upon his garments, unless provoked.

If he suffers no intrusion upon his domain, it is as much because he is liked as because he is master of the barn-yard, and the dames he protects are as fond of his courage and attentions as he is proud of his skill and address. If the fairest maid likes the epaulets of a general more than the plain clothes of a civilian, why should we quarrel with a game cock, clothed in red, gold, or imperial gray, with his breast of a black, his eyes large and active, his neck marked with a circle of scarlet, and a beak that denotes as much character as one of Napoleon's generals, most of whom were selected for the quality of their beaks. They are human too, in this, that "might makes right,"—but not worse again in their treatment of inferiors,—only meaning the inferiority of weakness,—than men and women unused to the cultivation of the best affections.

" The game hen is not a whit inferior to her lord and master. They are not only model mothers, but model nurses. No young mother, indeed, was ever more careful of her first child than the hen of her first clutch of chickens, and woe to those who assail the little ones. The second and third clutch, like a second and third child, also receives a grateful care, but they are brought up by one who acts as a more experienced woman.— The story is beautifully illustrated for real life in those words of our Saviour:

'Oh, Jerusalem, Jerusalem, thou that killest the prophets, and stonest them that are sent unto thee, how often would I have gathered thy children together as a hen doth gather her brood under her wings, and ye would not.'

" Hens and their masters are also human in this. Where there are numerous fowls, each cock selects his own feminine family, each has his own train, society, coterie and haunts, and any new intruder of the male sex must win his mastery by fight, or play second fiddle as a defeated champion—but the cock is as necessary to a well regulated and orderly household as a man is to the domestic home. Indeed the domestic household perhaps could get on without the man, but not the hens without a strict and determined master."

We could yet further, by argument and quotation, show the pleasure in keeping games; but their superiority is so generally recognized among those whose nature it is to admire them, that the task is superfluous.

DUBBING GAME FOWLS.

The practice of dubbing games has for a long time, and perhaps always will be in vogue. It is supported by obvious necessity. In early times the wings of game cocks were so trimmed that they would endanger the eyesight of the opponent, a practice not commendable ; but the operation of dubbing was performed to prevent either cock catching the other's comb or wattles. A good hold at either place would give great force and effect to a blow. It will be said that here the chances are mutual, and all cockers will agree on this, but the practice of dubbing has little or no immediate use in the pit. Game fowls are placed on walks, and when preparing for the pit, or after a battle, have their spurs sawed off. They are at all times liable to meet other cocks, and if the one met should be a game, he is in all probability trimmed in much the same way, and the contest which ensues is comparatively equal. At least, time is often afforded for separation. If the cock met be a dung-hill, he is pretty sure to have about him all that nature originally gave, and the game should have the advantage of keeping him from inflicting fatal wounds before his cowardice takes shape in the length of leg. With blunted spurs he can rarely kill in a short time, whilst with long and sharp spurs even on a dung-hill cock there is always some danger of untimely death. The owner of the game is the greater loser from an accident, for his fowl is worth ten times over the market price of the other, and perhaps cannot be replaced. So that the game raiser is always justified in preserving his stock by whatever means he possesses. After all, the pecuniary protection is with the owner of common poultry, for if the game added to his advantage in blood, strength and boxing, long and sharp spurs, the dung-hill would very probably be killed before he had time to get away—or, pursued and caught, be cut up piecemeal. Game cocks, with full natural spurs, have been.

known even to kill foxes at the first fly, and in defense of their hens, they will fight an enemy no matter in what shape he may appear. Dubbing is justified as an ordinary and practical means of protection, not alone to the game raiser, for it shows the utmost consideration to the raiser of other kinds of poultry. We have no sympathy with that cant which says that "all fowls should appear as nature formed them." Humanity might possibly be wasted on a fowl whose nature it is to covet pain, and the practice of dubbing is less cruel than a constant subjection to pecking.

The practice has existed for many years, and has prevailed in England and America probably from the inception of cock fighting. It is said that in India and on the Islands of the Mediterranean it is not resorted to; but it is true of these places that they fight cocks without regard to full or pure gameness, fight them with their naked heels, and frequently have them to run at that. The qualities of the Bantam would be valued there, and indeed would show more pluck than many of the varieties from thence imported. We do not deny the presence of games there, but we believe them to be there the exception, just as they are the exception here.

The plea of humanity against dubbing game cocks will not hold water, for the practice of cutting combs and gills and spurs preserve life both in the dung-hill and the game, and furnishes chances for escape which could not otherwise be reached. Cockers will always practice it, and as a rule will give little attention to that false spirit of kindness which has no other support than that of misdirection.

RULES FOR GAFTING.

Let your fowl be held by a competent person; let him be held so that the inside of the leg is perfectly level, then take your thumb and fore finger, and work the back toe of the fowl; while doing this you will see the leader of the leg rise and fall at the upper joint. You will set the right gaft on a line with the outside of the leader at the upper joint of the leg, and the left gaft you will set on a line with the inside of the leader at the upper joint. Be careful not to set the gaft too far in, as it would cause the cock to cut himself. As a general rule for a young beginner, he had better set the right gaft on a line with the outside of the leg opposite to the upper joint; and the left gaft on a line with the outside of the leader at the upper joint. The young beginner can heel in this way until he becomes competent to work according to the first mentioned plan. For if a gaft be set a sixteenth of an inch inside of the line of the leader, the fowl would probably kill himself; and hence the utmost care should be used in placing the gafts properly. This rule for gafting we practiced for 30 years, and always conquered with a few exceptions, which were not the fault of the gafting. We have never known fowls to fight thirty blows when gafted according to this rule without one or the other being killed. This thing of fowls fighting for a great length of time without either being killed or cut down, certainly shows bad heeling.

When you are preparing your fowls for the pit, and before you put them into the coop for feeding, have their spurs sawed off. Not too short, but long enough to come a little through the socket of the gaft, so that the latter can be attached firmly. You will then cover the spur with a piece of damp paper or very soft buck skin, so as to get the socket of the gaft to fit tightly, and to prevent its turning or shifting. When you have the gaft arranged properly, tie it with good wax-ends, but not so tight as to cramp the legs or toes of the fowls. The kind of gaft to be used is generally arranged by the parties before the fight. Their length and kind should be so near alike as to make it difficult to distinguish them apart. It is the duty of the judges to see to this by examining the gafts after the usual preliminaries are settled. They must also attend to the weighing. While your fowl is being weighed, slip a sack, made for the purpose, over his head, in order to prevent him from struggling, and allow you to get his precise weight. All being ready, fight according to the rules of your section, or those laid down in this book.

Many are perhaps unacquainted with the various kinds of gafts, fair and foul, a description of which we will here give.

The fair gaft is round with nearly round socket, and its appearance familiar. Those known as drop-sockets, are unfair, and their use should be guarded against. In these the socket is long, and the lower side is filled up with leather so that it will fit the spur, and being cushoned on the lower side, will drop the gaft near to the toes of the fowl; the blade of the gaft also drops in its bend near the socket, thus almost throwing the gaft down to the foot. Slashers can be made either from a fair or drop-socket; the blade is generally sword shape, though we have seen them with three edges. All gafts made different from the round sockets and round blades, are considered unfair. Heelers and pitters of cocks, as well as the judges, should keep an eye to the matter.

BREEDING COCKS.

Breeding cocks should be in perfect health, with feather close, chest compact and firm, full of girth, of lofty and elastic gait, large and firm thigh, and with beak short and thick at its insertion. Neither select a cock that is too old nor one that is too young; let the age be from nine months to three years.— Some cocks retain their vigor until they are seven years old, but it is never safe to calculate upon this. If you can, secure a young and vigorous bird, just at his prime. Steer equally clear of premature and often deceptive developments, and of incipient age and decrepitude. Avoid every extreme. It is generally best to breed stags to hens, and cocks to pullets.— Good fowls can be obtained by having the cocks and hens of equal age, provided all are in their prime, but youth to age is the safer plan, especially where not fully acquainted with the ages of your fowls.

The breeding cock should have the natural attribute of cleanliness, careful of the appearance of his plumage, and if this is the case he will be frequently observed pruning and dressing his feather with his bill. Dr. Bennett says, "that while he may not have the ambition of the nightingale, nor of the thrush in excelling by his notes, it may be inferred that he is particularly jealous of proving his voice to be loud, shrill and powerful."— We in part dissent from the correctness of this view, and it will strike every cocker as not filling the measure of his desire. We prefer the short, quick and savage crow—the cock cutting it off like pie-crust, as though greedy for a contest;—the crow that displays an anger too long pent up, savageness chained, and as it were, indignant at the impotency of a crow in comparison with the power of the bill and heel. Bennett continues the description of his model crow by saying:—"hence, when he has crowed in his strongest manner, he always listens to know whether he may be answered by any rival or neighbor, and if so, he answers by a strain if possible louder and bolder than the first." This may be Bennett's experience with games; our study has led us to be more exacting in the style of the crow, and the manner of repeating it. We prefer having the game cock issue his as a challenge, a challenge not to crow, but to fight, and to test blood with blood. There is no patient waiting for a response, and no effort at making a longer or a louder crow for the crow's sake; it is if possible shorter and more savage, as much as to say, "we've already had enough of this petty by-play, now to work!" Only dung-hills, or mingled dung-hill blood willingly enter a crowing contest, and find replete satisfaction in it. It is the nature of cocks to crow, but it is also the nature of the best games to cut this business as short as possible, in the near presence of an enemy. We would feel very much like dedicating to the pot a fowl which would stand and crow in the presence of any enemy, and thus await an assault. That plan is too much like one boy inviting another, to "knock a chip off of his hat."

When cockers and fanciers have the opportunity, they ought carefully to study all the prominent characteristics of breeding cocks and stags—a study that will be both a source of pleasure and practical use.

BREEDING HENS.

When you want to breed games expressly for fighting, you should not put more than three or at most four hens to one cock. If you wish to preserve a certain color, it is best to have the hens the same color as the cock, but not of the same or of related blood. Absolute crosses are generally best for the pit, provided the breed you cross with is equally good in fighting qualities as the one you wish to have crossed. If you have an approved breed and wish to preserve it, there are two ways in which it can be done. The more simple plan is to procure unrelated fowls of the same breed, and breed them with your own

—hens being mostly used in this way, as they are more easily and cheaply procured. The other is, to procure either a cock or pullets, and breed in-and-in for three years, putting an old cock with your own pullets, and a young cock with your hens. At the end of the three years, reserve some of the best stags and put them on good running walks for further use. You will now mingle the breed with the next best of the same variety you can get, breed in this way for three years, and after this you can for a time commingle the reserved breeders with the newer progeny without material injury. Breeds can thus be preserved for any length of time, and instead of becoming inferior, they will be constantly improving.

Breeding hens and pullets should be selected with the same care exercised in the selection of stags and cocks. If you want to add to the size and strength of your stock, select large pullets and hens, solid and plump, with good bills, legs and feathers.

HATCHING.

The length of time required for hatching, as a rule is twenty-one days; if the eggs are fresh, the nest good, and the hen sets well, twenty days will tell the story under the ordinary heat of the hen. Nests should be so prepared that they will secure all the needed warmth. This can be done by making them of clean, soft straw or hay; not too much of either, but just enough to form a nest, so that portions of it will come up to the body of the hen for a short distance. Beneath the straw place a handful or two of guano; this will keep lice from the nest and its vicinity, and the hen can set without being subject to this usual annoyance. When the eggs are not fresh it will frequently require twenty-three days for hatching, and the nests should never be destroyed short of this time. The number of eggs should be determined by the size of the hen, say eleven to small, thirteen to common sized, and fifteen to large hens.

FEED FOR THE CHICKS.

Select a dry place, where the chicks can have the warmth of the sun; sprinkle the ground where you feed with dry hickory, or other wood ashes, so placed that the rain cannot get at and weaken the ashes. Let the food be crumbs of bread for the first few days; after this boil Indian meal, let it dry as much as possible, cut it into slices, then feed. As soon as they can eat cracked corn or wheat, let them have it. Keep them as far away from the house as possible, so that they will have no opportunity to drink the stagnant water or soap suds, usual to gutters. If you have no pure water running near by, then have vessels well supplied with fresh water, and in each vessel put a small lump of gum camphor. Do not let the chickens out of their coops too early in the morning or whilst the dew is on the ground, and do not at any time suffer them to run in wet grass. This is a very common cause of disease and death, when not guarded against. Shelter them, while yet young, against sudden and unfavorable changes of the weather, more particularly if attended with rain or snow. Most of the diseases of chickens arise from cold moisture. At the expiration of four or five weeks the hen may be allowed to rove with her chickens, when she will soon leave them and commence laying again.

FEATHERING CHICKS.

The most trying time with chickens is when they begin to feather. This is particularly true of the game varieties, as they feather much faster than most other species. Chicks which feather too rapidly when very young, are always weak, however healthy in other respects, from the fact that the food goes to sustain the feather rather than the body; and where this is the case, many frequently languish and die. Such cases are most frequent in small bodied games, probably in part at least due to breeding in-and-in, the vigor of the blood having thus been expended. This is a potent reason against continuing the propagation of small strains. Large fowls generally feather slowly, and hence larger varieties of the game more safely pass the period of chickdom than small ones. The food and blood in early life is mainly demanded by the body, until they become old enough to sustain the shock of feathering.— Chicks which feather rapidly must be kept perfectly dry and warm in changeable weather.

SELECTING EGGS FOR SETTING.

Take fresh eggs, of the average size laid by the hen, as these are most apt to prove productive ; reject the first and the last egg of the cluck, for reasons already discussed in this work.— If you place an egg between your eye and a candle or the sunlight, you will be able to discern the position of the vacancy or vacuum caused by the little air bag at the blunt end of the shell. If this be in the centre, the egg will produce a cock ; if at one side a hen. Some select the pointed eggs with rough swells on the tip of the egg shell—these being presumed to be male eggs. Mark your eggs so that you may know if any has been laid since setting ; also the day of the month you set them.

There is no difficulty whatever in testing eggs; they are mostly examined by a candle. Another way to tell good eggs is to put them in a pail of water, and if they are good they will lay on their sides, always: if bad, they will stand on their small end, the large end uppermost, unless they have been shaken considerably, when they will stand either end up. Therefore, a bad egg can be told by the way it rests in the water—always end up, never on its side. Any egg that lies flat is good to eat, and can be depended upon. An ordinary mode is to take them into a room moderately dark, any hold them between the eye and a candle or lamp. If the egg be good—that is, if the albumen is still unaffected—a light will shine through a reddish glow; while, if affected, it will be opaque or dark.

HOW TO PRESERVE EGGS.

However compact and close the shell of an egg may appear, it is notwithstanding perforated with myriads of small pores, which cannot be seen without the assistance of a microscope. The effect of this is evident, for by this means the daily decrease of the moisture of the egg takes place through evaporation, and the vacuum is supplied by air from the time of its being laid. When the egg is quite full, a fluid is constantly passing through these perforations in the shell, which is the occasion of decay, and this is accomplished more rapidly in warm weather than in cold. An egg quite fresh is proverbially full, but in all stale eggs there is some vacancy, which is in proportion to the loss they sustain through evaporation. If the end of a fresh egg be applied to the tongue it feels cold, but that of a stale egg feels warm, because the white of the former being in contact with the shell abstracts the heat from the tongue more rapidly than the air of the latter. The cutting off of the access of air to the embryo in the egg does not kill or prevent its being hatched, but on the contrary preserves it alive for a much longer period than if otherwise treated.—By covering the egg with a spirit varnish we have produced chickens from eggs of two years' keeping. The following is the recipe:—Dissolve some gum Shalac in a sufficient quantity of alcohol to make a thin varnish; give each egg a coat, and after they become thoroughly dry pack them closely in bran sawdust, with their points downward in such a manner that they cannot shift about. After you have kept them as long as you desire, wash the varnish carefully off with alcohol, and they will be in the same state as they where before packing, ready either for eating or hatching. This is beyond doubt the best and safest method known and has been amply tested.

POULTRY HOUSES.

EXTRACT FROM DR. BENNETT'S WORK ON POULTRY.

The Doctor truly says, "It is indispensable that poultry houses should be properly lodged, and that such conveniences should be provided for them as will secure them comfort and health. Every collection of poultry requires some place to be provided for them to secure these advantages. Often they are left to take care of themselves, and roaming about the farm or about smaller premises they become at last burdensome to themselves, unprofitable to the owner, and a nuisance to the neighborhood. A certain degree of confinement is therefore neccessary for fowls. Close confinement, however, will in a degree prevent from laying and destroy their health. A yard or walk connected with a place for shelter and roosting is what is required. Care should be taken in fixing upon a situation for these accommodations; a south or south-east exposure is the most proper place to be chosen, and a building of brick or stone is preferable to one built of wood. The extent of the place should be proportioned to the number kept, and if any error is to be tolerated it might better be on the side of small buildings. It is said in good authority that infectious diseases are not to be feared even in the case of confined accommodations, and laying in the winter season is rather promoted than otherwise when fowls are thus situated. A medium course should be adopted as at once the wisest and most economical. If fowls are not sufficienlly defended from the cold of winter, they become torpid; if exposed to intense heat in summer they are enfeebled. To avoid the numerous diseases which are induced by dampness, care should be taken that the poultry-house should be in a dry situation and properly defended from the effects of rain. A due regard to ventilation is indispensable to guard against an infected atmosphere, and suitable facilities should be afforded for the necessary exercise which all kinds of poultry daily demands. Arrangements for securing an ample supply of water must never be overlooked, and it is advisable to have receptacles of ashes or dry sand within the enclosure, in which the fowls may enjoy the luxury of rolling themselves.

In order to secure freedom from vermin and amusement for themselves, when poultry are kept on a large scale, a yard is set apart for their use, enclosed either by a wall or by a fence of pailing of sufficient height to prevent any escape. This yard should be well drained, but if a stream of water can be made to flow through it, it is an important advantage. A part of the yard should be floored or flagged, to feed the fowls upon. A part should be covered with sand or gravel for them to wallow in. A part should be laid down in grass, or planted with such plants as furnish them proper feed, and somewhere there should be a deposit of dry mortar or broken oyster shells, so prepared that the fowls may pick and scratch amongst it. The house, as already stated, is preferable if built of brick or stone; but whatever the material, it is of the first consequence that it should be so constructed that the access and harboring of all vermin may be prevented. The floor should be raised from the ground sufficiently to allow of its being kept scrupulously clean. The entrance should be large enough for convenience and strong enough for security, and a hole at some distance from the ground may be made to allow the poultry to go in to roost. To reach this a ladder may be constructed by making a slanting board with strips of wood nailed across, by which the fowls may ascend on the outside, and a similar one to allow them to descend within. All fowls like to roost high, and they should have some rails fixed for them near the roof, so arranged that the fowls on the lower rails may not be exposed to the droppings from those above. The rails are frequently only branches, or the trunks of young trees, but if made of timber they should be nearly square, with only the corners rounded off, as the feet of fowls are not made for clasping smooth round poles; and there may be boxes or baskets against the walls for the fowls to lay in. The floors of the roost-houses should be kept sanded, and in fine weather the doors should be left open to give access to fresh air. In the erection of poultry houses considerations of fancy or economy will furnish the rule in fixing upon a plan. A sufficiently good and in every respect suitable poultry-house may be built very readily and at an insignificant cost.

There should always be a door or opening to allow of the cleaning out once a week, at least of the poultry-house; a process too often neglected, but very essential to health in the poultry. They never will thrive long amid uncleanness, and even with the utmost care a place where poultry have been long kept becomes what the housewives call tainted, and there they will thrive no longer. The surface of the ground becomes saturated with their manure, and is therefore no longer healthy. To avoid this effect some poulterers in the country frequently change the sites of their poultry houses to obtain fresh ground, and to guard against the same misfortune farmers who cannot change their hen-houses and yards purify the houses by fumigations of blazing pitch, by washing with hot lime water, and by strewing large quantities of pure sand, both within and without the poultry house. Washing the floor of the house every week is necessary, for which purpose it is of advantage that it be paved either with stones, bricks or tiles. But as these modes are expensive, a good flooring, which is cheaper, may be formed by using a composition composed of lime and ashes together; these having been all finely broken must be mixed together with water, and put on the floor with a mason's trowel, and nicely smoothed on the surface. If this is put on a floor which is in a tolerably dry situation and allowed to harden before being used, it will become nearly as solid and compact as stone, and is almost as durable. The inside of the laying boxes requires washing with hot lime water to free them from vermin which greatly torments the setting hens. For the same purpose, poultry should always have a heap of dry sand or fine ashes laid under some covered place, near their yard, for them to dust themselves in; this being their resource for getting rid of the vermin with which they are annoyed. In every establishment for poultry raising there ought to be some separate crib or cribs into which to remove fowls when laboring under disease, for not only are some of the diseases highly contagious, but the sick birds are also regarded with dislike by such as are in health, and the latter will generally attack and maltreat them, thus at the very least aggravating the sufferings of the afflicted fowls, even if they do not actually deprive them of life. The moment, therefore, that a bird is percieved to droop or appear pining, it should be removed to one of these infirmaries. The office of keeping and managing domestic fowls should be performed by some individual whom the hens know, as the voice and presence of a stranger scare the fowls and disturb the operations of the hen-house. To distribute food and drink at regular hours, to visit the nests, to remove eggs as soon as laid and carry them to a cool place, to examine by candle-light what eggs are fecundated and to place these under the hen and mark the time they are set, are among the daily duties performed by the keeper."

The above plan of Dr. Bennett's, well answers all the ends required in erecting suitable houses for poultry, and his mode of cleaning is well adapted to the purpose and conducive to the health of the fowl; but there is one all-essential method for destroying chicken lice, which should be employed in every case.

In each and every hen-house, or in any apartment where chickens are kept, have a square box made of inch boards, large enough to hold three bushels; fasten it on the ground floor about the centre of the house; in this box place three bushels of pure Guano—leave the box uncovered, and when the Guano becomes heated, as it will by its own properties and weight, there will be a chemical operation constantly going on, which will throw off fumes of *ammoniacal gas*. This will constantly issue forth night and day. *This gas destroys all the lice in the building, and in fact all on the fowls that roost within it.*

We know this to be true from actual experiment, have tested it for the past four or five years, and never yet knew it to fail, in any particular. And it is reasonable that it should be true. Wild pigeons are migratory birds, and yet they have roosts in given localities, and these they almost invariably visit. They do this not alone because they wish to be secure from man, but because instinct points the way to get rid of the annoyance of vermin. Either this is true, or the provision of nature is there, with its cause and effect, each resulting to the benefit of the bird. The same is true of many of the sea and island birds.— These, by having roosts in given localities, deposit offal,—by chemical process the offal becomes Guano, and the escape of ammoniacal gas from Guano destroys the lice of all those roosting above it.

We have already said that we have tested this plan, and found it to be successful in every case. We have at times purchased the guano, at others allowed it to form. In our stable we have a roost where the droppings of the fowls will fall directly into a large open trough, and when sufficient of these were deposited, to form a natural heat through their own weight and bulk, the fumes of the ammoniacal gas ascended, and from that time lice disappeared. We first discovered this fact in this way:—We had in use this trough beneath the roost, made at the suggestion of some neighbors, so that we could give them the droppings for garden manure. When the bulk was there no lice annoyed the fowls, when it was given for the neighbors' use, lice returned, and continued until there was another large and solid deposit, sufficient to eject the chemical gas. The lice would thus return, notwithstanding absolute cleanliness, the premises well limed and whitewashed.

We now so roost our fowls that their droppings will be deposited well together, and refuse to allow any removal of the manure. We can now safely defy any man to discover a single hen louse about that stable. The purchase of pure guano, in good bulk, is the quicker way to reach the evil, as it would take a deposit, with a small number of fowls, of two or three years, to give back sufficient to form natural heat, and its concomitant, ammoniacal gas sufficient for the purpose.

We will complete the subject of constructing poultry houses by quoting the following admirable plan, detailed by a writer in the *Country Gentleman*, and worthy of any poulterer's endorsement:—

MESSRS. EDITORS—In the *Country Gentleman*, vol. 11, p. 45, and also in *The Cultivator* for 1851, is an ar'icle on the "Construction of Poultry Houses," by your correspondent H. of Maryland, which is the best I have ever seen. My own experience leads me to discard all permanent fixtures. The nests should be separate boxes, placed on movable slats, so as to be easily taken out to be cleaned, when they should be thoroughly scalded and then whitewashed, and every bit of the straw and dirt burnt or buried.

The inside of the hen-house should be so plain and accessible to the *white wash brush*, as never to deter from undertaking that *often* necessary job.

I have used coal ashes as a deodorizer, sifting freely over the roosts, nests and floor; it keeps the house perfectly sweet, assists to expel vermin, and is the very best article to compost with the droppings, containing as it does, a large proportion of allumina.

I send you directions for building a neat, substantial, and *roomy* poultry house, in the *very cheapest* manner—any man can build it without assistance, with a saw and hammer—it can be made two feet wider by using 14 feet instead of 12 feet boards, and any desired length; mine is of the size indicated, and is abundantly large for me; I keep from 12 to 16 fowls over, and raise about 50 chickens; I think it will accommodate double this number.

I took the hint from the July number of the Cultivator for the year 1854.

Procure one 4 by 3 inch—one 4 by 2 inch—one 6 by 3 inch joist, each 20 feet long—two 4 by 3 inch 8 feet long—two 4 by 2 inch 6 feet long—two 4 by 2 inch eight feet long—one 4 by 2 inch 18 feet long—260 feet of inch boards 12 feet long—250 feet do. 16 feet long—two strips 1 1-2 inch board, 2 1-2 inches wide, grooved on one edge, and two of the same grooved on both edges, (same as for matching) and 10 feet long—mark off the ends of the 6 by 3 inch joist down and draw a ma·k diagonally accross, then strike a line from these points along the top and under side, and split with a splitting saw, (if you cannot get it done at the mill.) This will give you a *sill* for the front side, with the right bevel for the slope, 3 inches on the top and 4 1-2 inches wide on the bottom. The smaller strip is the *plate* for the rear, for which the 4 by 3 inch will be the *sill*—lay *that* on the ground where you want it should stand; lay the plate to the right and parallel with it, 5 feet 5 inches from outside to outside, so that the ends are perpendicular—lay on the 12 feet boards, nail and saw them off even with the plate—mark the boards as they are sawed off, and put them aside for the roof. The broadest or beveled side of the plate is the side to be nailed to, bringing the narrow edge uppermost, with a bevel very near that of the slope of the roof—raise it up to its place, and secure it with braces in the rear—lay the 4 by 2 inch joist broadside down in front, parallel with and one foot from the rear—place the sill with its beveled side up, in its place in front, saw off a few boards 8 feet long, and tack them on even with the sill and plate. Now raise it up and secure it so that it shall be 6 feet wide on the ground, and 6 feet on the slope of the roof—nail the 6 feet joist on to the ends of the plates, (which should be shortened the thickness of these joist—spike the 9 feet 4 by 3 inch joist across the ends, on to the sills,

17

even with the ends—(they should be halved in)—cant in, and nail the two 8 feet 4 by 2 joist 5 feet from each, into the plate sill, so as to be level with them, the narrow edge out, and 10 feet apart—place the 12 feet 2 by 4 joist horizontally across them, projecting 1 foot beyond them, cut out the joists so as to receive it level, and nail in, 3 feet and 4 inches from the bottom of the sill—draw a line through the middle, cut off some boards 3 feet 6 inches long, bring them to the line, and nail them to the joist and sill between the two perpendicular joists, and lapping 1 1-2 on to them—fill out the front to the joists, (lapping half an inch on to them) to the ends— nail into the joists, and secure the projecting ends of the horizontal joist to the boarding, with wrought nails well clinched, as the weight of the sash will rest principally on it. Board up the ends, leaving two boards of suitable width at one end loose, to be fitted for a door.

Place the boards on the roof in the order in which they were cut off, and nail on. Now take one of the single grooved strips and fit into the opening in front, nailing it on to the horizontal joist, covering the ends of the short boards—make two gauges 1-10th of an inch longer than your glass—take one of the double grooved strips, place it above the first, resting on three gauges, (in the grooves,) screw to the joist 2 1-2 inch screws, (one in each end.) Now unscrew one end of the second strip, raise it slightly and slide in the glass, beginning at the fast end and putting the edges together without lapping; fill out to the end and screw up as before—proceed in the same manner until you have filled up the sash—then put an additional screw into each end, and you have a window *sufficiently* tight, answering all the purposes of a glazed sash, at a trifling expense. In the summer the sash can be removed, and a *blind* improvised as cheaply, viz, procure 13 strips of boards 5-8 or 6-4 inch thick and 10 feet long—cut off two strips and fit them into the sides of the opening, and screw into the joist—saw off two squares, cut them to the right slope, and nail them on to the bottom of the strips—place on to them one of the long strips and nail—cut off two more blocks, nail them to the strips resting on to the first slat, and proceed in the same manner until you have filled up the opening.

The joints of the roof should be covered with battens not less than 4 inches wide—the sides and ends may be battened on the inside with sawed laths, or on the outside with 3 inch board battens; they should be nailed only on one edge until the boards are done shrinking. Fit up the inside as suggested by H., placing the front, and one foot from the ground. I have a moveable partition with a door in mine, which enables me to separate my breeding hens, (always the choicest,) from the others in breeding time, which to me, as I am experimenting on Dorkings with a view to improvement, is important.

It would be impossible to build such a house in a cheaper manner, there being no waste either of material or labor. It might, however be an improvement to cover the sides with boards of uniform width, (or nearly so, and not over 12 inches) at equal distance apart, nailing in the space between, a strip of equal thickness on to the plate and sill, and covering these spaces with other boards, lapping at least one inch over and on to the under boards—each board secured by one nail only in the centre, driven into the sill and plate, with a narrow strip nailed over all at the top and bottom, and nailed also through the centre of the boards to the sill and plate—the boarding then will neither split or warp in shrinking. The builder can consult his own taste as to the widths of the boards, and if the boards can be selected at the yards, without additional sawing, the expense will be no greater, than the first plan, if that is battened on the outside, and will present a much neater appearance, and be more substantial and tight. W. E. C. *Cleveland, O.*

FEEDING IN GENERAL.

Most persons are doubtless aware that fowls swallow food without mastication. That process is rendered unnecessary by the provision of a crop—an organ which is somewhat similar to the first stomach of the cow, and in which the food from the gullet is masticated and partly dissolved by secreted fluids from the crop. The food passes downward into a second small cavity, where it is partly acted on by a digestive juice, and finally it is transferred to the gizzard or last stomach, which is furnished with muscular and cartilaginous linings of very great strength ; in the gizzard the partially softened food is triturated and converted into a thin paste fit to be received into the chyle gut, and finally absorbed into the circulation. Such is the power of the gizzard in almost all kinds of poultry, that hollow globes of glass are reduced in it to fine powder in a few hours. The most rough and jagged bodies do no injury to the coats of the gizzard. Spallanzani even introduced a ball of lead, with twelve strong needles so fixed in it that their points projected a fourth of an inch from the surface, and the result was that all the needles with the exception of one or two were ground down in a short time to the surface of the ball, while those left were reduced to mere stumps. It is remarkable that to add to the triturating powers of the gizzard fowls are gifted with the instinct of swallowing stones with their food. Fowls when left to roam at large pick up all sorts of seeds, grains, worms, larvæ of insects, or any other edible substance they can discover, either on the surface of the ground or by scraping. They also pick a little grass as a stomachic. The more that hens can be allowed to roam about and pick up their own food, the better for their own health and the pockets of their keeper. The very pleasure of ranging and scraping seems advantageous to the fowls. If kept in a yard or a pen, and requiring altogether artificial feeding, their natural tastes should be consulted as far as conveniently practicable. They should be fed regularly and with a miscellaneous kind of diet, allowed at all times access to clean water for drinking, and have earth, sand or dust to scrape at pleasure and roll themselves in. A certain quantity of chalk or lime should also be scattered about for them to pick up, as that material is required by them in the production of eggs. If you mixed with their food a sufficient quantity of egg-shell or chalk, which they eat greedily, they will lay, other things being equal, twice or thrice as many eggs. A well-fed fowl is disposed to lay a vast number of eggs, but cannot do so without the materials for the shell, however nourishing in other respects her food may be ; indeed, a fowl fed on food and water free from carbonate of lime, and not finding any in the soil or in the shape of mortar, which they often eat off the walls, would lay no eggs at all with the best will in the world. In a state of domestication the hard food of which fowls seem most fond are peas and barley, (oats they, do not like,) and besides a proportion of these they may be given crumbs of bread, lumps of boiled potatoes, not too cold, or any other food. They are much pleased to pick a bone ; the pickings warm them and excite their laying propensities. If they can be supplied with caterpillars, worms and maggots, the same end will be served. Any species of animal food, however, should be administered sparingly, and the staple articles of diet must always be of a vegetable nature, corn, barley, and wheat; the latter is 100 per cent. the best.

LAYING.

The ordinary productiveness of the hen is truly astonishing, as it usually lays in the course of the year two hundred eggs, provided it be allowed to go at liberty, is well fed, and has a plentiful supply of water. Many instances have been known of hens laying three hundred in a year. This is a singular provision of nature, and it would appear to have been intended peculiarly for the use of man, as the hen usually incubates only once in a year, although she will occasionally bring out two broods. Few hens are capable of hatching more than from twelve to fifteen eggs. In the depth of winter, under ordinary circumstances, hens very rarely lay eggs, though by artificial means they can be made to do so, if the temperature of the place be kept warm.

The fowls of the Irish peasantry, which are usually kept in the cabins of the owners, lay often in winter in consequence of the warmth of their quarters, and there can be no doubt that warmth affords the most effective means of procuring new laid eggs in winter, though stimulating food may aid in producing the same result.

The fecundity of hens varies considerably; some may lay once in three days, others every second day, and others every day. In order to induce laying each hen should have its own nest made with soft straw, and furnished with a piece of chalk as a decoy. The signs which indicate when a hen is about to lay are well known. She cackles frequently, walks restlessly about, and shows a brighter redness in her comb and wattle.— After the process of laying is over, she utters a loud and peculiar note, to which the other fowls usually respond. Shortly after the egg is laid, it should be removed, for the heat of the hen soon corrupts it. When the eggs are taken away by the keeper they should be immediately laid in a cool and dry place. If allowed to absorb damp, they soon spoil. Indeed, one drop of water upon the shell quickly taints the whole egg. If the eggs are intended for setting, they should be turned by the dry hand once a day, or once every other day at least; this process will secure a better formed chick. If the egg is suffered to lay any length of time in the same position, the egg will congeal, as it were, on that side, hence deformity in both eggs and chickens.

BREEDING FOR BREEDERS.

When you want a stock of choice stags and pullets, and desire to keep them for breeding purposes alone, select a tested cock from a well known and well tested strain—a quick and vigorous fighter. The hen should be a choice one, known to throw good and sound fowls. Put the cock and hen in an enclosure built for the purpose, the house to be about ten feet high and twelve feet square, with ground floor, and the slats so fixed that they will at the same time prevent escape and freely admit the rays of the sun, both from the east in the morning and from the west in the afternoon. Keep no more than one pair in one enclosure. Destroy the first and last eggs of the cluck, and set none but perfectly formed eggs. When chickens are hatched, remove old and youug alike to a place where they will have plenty of range, and access to pure running water. When the stags are four months old, trim them of their combs and wattles, and place a private mark on both stags and the pullets—the mark on all of the cluck being alike. This will aid you in any after selection of breeders or for any other purpose.

PACKING EGGS.

How to properly pack eggs is at this writing the subject of much discussion, and various are the plans proposed. Some pack them in bran just as they are laid; others by wraping each egg in paper and then placing in bran; yet others by using pasteboard boxes, so divided that each egg has a single apartment, in which it is placed after being wrapped in paper or cotton,—bran or sawdust being also used. Other plans, even more ingenious are suggested, and for some years we had faith in one plan which we practiced. Almost any plan which gives ordinary protection to the egg, will do for packing, provided the journey is not a long one, and some of them will hatch, while others will not, no matter how fresh they may have been when started. But never yet have we known of a plan whereby eggs could be safely sent, and the faithful trial of the most approved ones has forced this belief. The shaking by the cars will addle the eggs no matter in what shape they may be placed, for the motion of every parcel in the car is simultaneous, and the movement would extend to the centre of a box just as easily as anywhere else. It is this movement which mixes the eggs, the white with the yellow, and the generative power is destroyed, however good it may be for eating purposes. So that we are completely skeptical on the shipment of eggs intended for long distances, and we wish we could warn all game raisers against making any attempt to secure games by this means. We have of late refused to dispose of eggs for these reasons, and have only shipped them to parties who would not be convinced, and who voluntarily assumed all risks.

WORTHLESS GAMES.

A few years ago the popular passion for game fowls forced many worthless varieties upon the market, which were disposed of at exorbitant prices by fancy dealers. Cock fighting was traced to India and the Mediterranean Islands, as well to parts of Asia and South America. The simon-pure original game cock was said to have hailed from India, to have been bred in the jungles, in the fancy of some from the wild pheasants, in the direct interest of others from something else. Poultry books gave plausibility to these lies, and for a time humbug was the order of the day. In showing the origin and history of game fowls, we exposed with tolerable clearness the little faith we have in pheasant, Java, Malacca and other games, and we shall now treat only of some of the most noted "frauds."

The so-called Wild Indian, Spanish and Sumatra games are of

good appearance, and bear many of the marks of game fowls, but so far as known in this country they are utterly worthless for fighting in the pit. Most of them will stand the natural spur with a fair show of courage, just as will the Bantam. The desire for the Sumatra's was created by the publication of Dr. Bennett's work on poultry, wherein the hens of this variety were said to have mastered English and Irish game cocks. Some were credulous enough to swallow this stuff, and the Sumatra and Indian games soon entered every State in the Union, and were almost as soon everywhere condemned. We will not burden these pages with a minute description of the Indian or Sumatra games. They are familiar to all, and fancied only where *game* qualities are neither understood or desired.

The Malay fowls are of somewhat more recent importation, and are described as of game blood. In a recent general poultry work issued by Simeon M. Saunders, the breed is thus spoken of:—

"This is another of the Asiatic breed, supposed to come from the islands of Sumatra or Java, and, though formerly much fancied and sought after, has of late years been suffered to decline. It has fallen before the spirit of utility; it was not useful, and it has lost ground. It is a long rather than a large bird, standing remarkably upright, falling in an almost uninterrupted slope from the head to the insertion of the tail, which is small and drooping, having very beautiful but short sickle-feathers. It has a hard, cruel expression of face: a bold eye, pearled around the edge of the lids, a hard, small comb, scarcely so long as the head, having much the appearance of a double comb trimmed very small and then flattened; a red, skinny face, very strong curved beak, and the space for an inch below it on the throat destitute of feathers. It has long yellow legs, quite clean; it is remarkable for very hard plumage, and the hinderparts of the cock look like those of a game-cock trimmed for fighting. The hen is of course smaller than the cock. She has the same expression of face, the same curious comb; and in both sexes the plumage should be so hard that when handled it should feel as though one feather covered the body. From this cause the wings of the hen are more prominent than in other fowls, projecting something like those of a carrier-pigeon, though in a less degree. It is a beauty in the breeds if the projection or knobs of flesh at the crop, on the end wing joint, and at the top of the breast are naked and red. They are good layers and sitters ; their eggs have a dark shell, and are said to be superior in flavor to any other. The chickens feather slowly, on which account no brood should be hatched after July ; otherwise the cold and variable weather of autumn comes upon them before they are half grown, and the increase of their bodies has so far outstripped them of their feathers, that they are half naked about the neck and shoulders, which renders them extremely susceptible to wet and cold. The chickens are not difficult to rear ; but are gawky, long-legged creatures until they have attained their full growth, and then fill out. The original colors were cocks of a bright rich red with black breast ; and hens of a bright chocolate or cinnamon color, generally one entire shade; but in some instances the hackles were darker than the rest of the pumage. Some beautiful white specimens have lately been introduced, and a few years ago there was a handsome breed of them colored like pied games. The Malays have one great virtue ; they will live anywhere ; they will inhabit a back yard of small dimensions, they will scratch in the dust-pit and roost in a coalhole, and yet lay well and show in good condition when requisite. The Malays are inveterate fighters (?) and this is the quality for which they are chiefly prized in their native country (?) where cock-fighting is carried to the extent of excessive gambling. Men and boys may be frequently met, each carrying his favorite bird under his arm, ready to set to work the moment the opportunity shall offer. The general character of these birds is vindictive, cruel, and tyrannical."

No doubt Mr. Saunders believes the Malays are what he represents them to be ; but they share the objection common to the Indian and Sumatra—*they are not of pure game blood*, and while they will stand well with native heels, they will flee before the steel. We know this by actual test.

The following description of a pair of Java fowls we take from Dr. Bennett's work on poultry :—

"These, like all other pure Java fowls, are of a black or dark auburn color, with very large black legs, single comb and wattles. They are good layers, and their eggs are very large and well flavored. Their gait is slow and majestic. They are, in fact, amongst the most valuable fowls in the country, and are frequently described in the books as "Spanish fowls," than which nothing is more erroneous. They are as distinctly an original breed as the pure-blooded Great Malay, and possess about the same qualities as to excellence, but falling rather short of them as to beauty. This, however, is a matter of taste, and some consider the pure Java superior to all other large fowls, so far as beauty is concerned. Their plumage is decidedly rich."

Mr. C. N. Bennet, a distinguished breeder, and writer on the subject of poultry, says of this fowl:

"This is a singular breed, which partakes of the common fowl and the India fowl, peculiar to the island of Java, where they are seldom reared but for fighting; and are said to be so furious, that they sometimes fight together till death in one or the other separates them. According to Willoughby, it carries its tail nearly like the turkey. The Sieur Feurnier, informs us, that one of this species was kept in Paris; it has, according to him, neither comb nor wattles; the head is smooth, like that of a pheasant. This fowl is very high on its legs; its tail is long and pointed, and the feathers of unequal length; and, in general, the color of the feathers is auburn, like the vulture. It is generally supposed the English game cock originated, or is a cross of, this variety."

The above quotation is a description of the wild Indian game, and not of the Java, except in color. Courage with native heels will be shown by both varieties, but neither will stand any approved test.

We will classify what are, in our opinion, bad breeds of games, as follows:—

Sumatra Pheasant	Game.	Wild Indian Mountain	Game.
Malacca,	"	Java Pheasant,	"
Wild Sumatra,	"	Wild Indian,	"
Simple Sumatra,	"	Chinese Albin,	"
Sumatra Ebon,	"	Hen Tail Mexican,	"

CHICKEN TALK.

Barring Saunders opinions of the gameness of the Malays, we pronounce his work one of the best on general poultry extant, notwithstanding its brevity. All of it that is valuable to the reader of this, embraces his discription of games, their colors, points, &c., which we quote, with parenthetic differences in opinion:—

"The game cock is of bold carriage; his comb is single, (not always) bright red, and upright; and wattle of a beautiful red color; the expression of countenance fearless, but without the cruelty of the Malay; the eye very full and bright, the beak strong, curved, well fixed in the head, and very stout at the roots. The breast should be full, perfectly straight; the body round in hand, broad between the shoulders, tapering to the tail, having the shape of a flat-iron, or approaching heart-shaped; the thigh hard, short and round; the leg stout; the foot flat and strong, and the spur not high on the leg. The wings are so placed on the body as to be available for sudden and rapid springs. The feathers should be hard, very strong in quills, and like the Malay it should seem as though all their feathers were glued together till they feel like one. A game-cock shoud be what fanciers call "clever," every proportion should be in perfect harmony; and the bird, placed on his breast in the palm of the hand, should exactly balance.

"This is another breed of fowls where deviation from perfection is fatal. It has been well said, "a perfect one is not too good, and therefore an imperfect one is not good enough." Abundant plumage, long soft hackles and saddles, too much tail or a tail carried squirrel-fashion over the back, the least deviation from straightness of the breast-bone, long thighs, in-knees, weak beaks, or coarse heads, are all faults, and should be avoided.

"These birds are generally "dubbed" before they are shown at fairs or exhibitions. This should be neatly performed; every superfluous piece of skin and flesh being removed, so that the head should stand out of the hackle as though it was shaven. The plumage should also be so scanty that the shape of the bird, especially the tapering of the back and the roundness of the body, may be seen. Every feather should feel as if made of whalebone, and, if raised with the finger, should fall into its original place. It should be almost impossible to ruffle the plumage of a game. The tail should be rather small than otherwise, and be carried somewhat drooping. The plumage of these birds is trimmed before they fight. This is called "cutting out," and the less there is to remove in the way of feather the better for the bird. They are in every respect fighting birds, and every one who sees a set-to between two of them must look on with pleasure, if it occurs as they pass through a yard. The hens should be like the cocks allowing for difference of sex, the necks and heads fine, legs taper, plumage hard, and combs small, upright and serrated, (when not double combed.) Hens should not be chosen with large or loose combs, and they should handle as hard as the cocks. A word or two may not be out of place as to the table-properties of this beautiful breed. It is true they are in no way fit for the fattening-coop; they cannot bear the extra food without excitement, and that is not favorable to obesity. Nevertheless, they have their merits. If they are allowed to run semi-wild in the woods, to frequent sunny banks and dry ditches, they will grow full of meat, though with little fat. They must be eaten young, and a game pullet four or five months old, caught up wild in this way and killed two days before she is eaten, is, perhaps, the most delicious chicken there is in point of flavor. The classes into which the game fowls are divided are: black-breasted red, brown-red, duck wings, and brassy winged, and shawl-necks, or what are sometimes called Irish grays, which are of the largest class. Among all the varieties of the game-fowls, the precedence must be given to that variety known as Lord Derby's breed, which have been kept and bred with great care for upwards of one hundred years. The following is a description of the cock of that breed:—He is of a good round shape well put together; has a fine long head; long and strong neck; wings large and well quilled; back short; belly round and black, tail black and sickled, being well tufted at the root; legs rather long, with white feet and nails; plumage deep, rich red and maroon; and breast and thighs black. The Derby red hens possess little of their consort's brilliancy of feather; their body is brown, each feather-shaft being light; the breast and hackle being also light. The Duckwings are among the most beautiful of all game-fowls. The cocks vary in the color of their hackle, saddle and breast feathers; the hackle-feather of some strains being nearly white, in others yellow; while with some again, the breasts are black, with some streaky, and with some gray. To breed fancy, streak-breasted brown red cockerals, mate a streaky-breasted hen to a black-red cock; nine times out of ten the cockerals will resemble the hen in color. To breed pullets to match, the cock must be streaky-breasted, and the hen black-breasted red; these will be brown-breasted reds. To obtain Duckwings, breed from a light gray-back and winged hen, with silver hackle and salmon breast, and a black-breasted red cock; the hen should not have the slightest shade of red on the wing; this is fatal. To obtain similar pullets, the cock must be Duckwing and the hen black-red. Pieds are bred from a white cock and black-red hen. The color of the eggs of the game-hen varies from a dull white to a fawn. They are good layers, as many as twenty-four eggs being constantly laid by them, before they manifest a desire to sit. As sitters, game hens have no superiors. Quiet on eggs, regular in the hours of coming off and returning to their charge, and confident, from their fearless disposition, of repressing the incursions of any intruder, they rarely fail to bring all good broods. Hatching accomplished, their merits appear in a still more conspicuous light. Ever on their guard, not even the shadow of a bird overhead, or the approach of man or beast, but finds them ready to do battle for their offspring; and instances have been known where rats and other vermin have thus fallen before them."

[We will have to pick several flaws in the above description. He better meets the views of fanciers than cockers, in his divisions of color, and his description of their varieties. He gives ten, there being at least fifty, and entirely ignores the cocker's standard or model color—known as the black red. This was fifty years ago handed down to us a proper model, by cockers who were then as old as we now are, and if age and long wear gives authority, the black red is entitled to it. It was the old habit to support this view by several reasons. I. The black red is thought the most game looking. II. He is of strong constitution, and very hardy. III. Less liable to early sickness. IV. A greater number of them are more perfect in form and station than any other known color. Frankly, if we wished to breed and rear a model cock, we would not confine ourself to any known breed. We would select as a breeding cock one six and a-half pounds in weight, a black red in color—with black breast, hackle feathers a dark mahogany, a dark turkey-red saddle but one shade darker than the hackle, the tail black, long and of full sickle feathers, carrying it with a slight slope downwards, but not near so low as that of the Sumatra cock. His head should be well shaped, neither too long, nor too stumpy or thick; his eye a light gray or fiery red; his bill strong and well set and shaped, with a hook or curve at the point. Our fancy would also take in a rich yellow leg, but the color of that is not important, as yellow, green, white or blue almost equally become a black red cock. His stature should be erect, his carriage bold and defiant; broad across the shoulders, broad flat breast, and from his shoulders a gradual taper until the base of the the tail is reached, at which point he should be narrow. His wings should be long and well quilled, and should go so far back at their point as to come within an inch of touching. The back or saddle should be slightly raised, as this indicates strength; his thighs should be long and stout, hard muscled; his leg of medium length and good thickness; his feet and toes large and long, the spur a regular or symmetical distance above the toes. When in hand he should be wirey and full of motion—fond of talking and chatting, all the time having his toes tightly drawn and his legs kept close to the body, as though ready for any emergency.]

Saunders talks very sensibly when he says :—

"Fowls, like human beings, are subject to atmospherical influence ; and if healthy fowls seem suddenly attacked with illness that cannot be explained, a copious meal of bread steeped in ale will often prove a speedy and effectual remedy.

For adults, nothing will restore strength sooner than eggs boiled hard, and chopped. If these remedies are not successful, then the constitution is at fault, and good healthy cocks must be bought to replace those whose progeny is faulty. "Prevention is better than cure." The cause of many diseases is to be found in enfeebled and bad constitutions ; and these are the consequences of in-and-in breeding. (*Right, Saunders! go ahead!*) The introduction of fresh blood is absolutely necessary every second year, and even every year is better. Many fanciers who breed for feather fear to do so lest false colors should appear, but they should recollect that one of the first symptoms of degeneracy is a foul feather ; for instance, the Sebright bantam loses lacing, and becomes patched ; the Spanish fowls throw white feathers, and pigeons practice numberless freaks. An experiment was once once tried which will illustrate this. A pair of black pigeons was put in a large loft, and allowed to breed without any introduction of fresh blood. They were well, carefully fed. At the end of two years an account of them was taken. They had greatly multiplied, but only one third of the number were black, and the others had become spotted with white, then patched, and then quite white; while the latter had not only lost the characteristics of the breed from which they descended, but were weak and deformed in every possible way. The introduction of fresh blood prevents all this ; and the breeder for prices, or whoever wishes to have the best of the sort he keeps, should never let a fowl escape him if it possesses the qualities he seeks. Such are not always to be had when wanted, and the best strains we have, of every sort, have been got up by this plan."

[All of which we pronounce correct, and we are glad that our views are sustained by at least one modern writer. Mr. Saunders is connected with the Massachusetts poultry association, and wrote his little work after visiting France, and inspecting the henneries there.]

One of our correspondents has suggested to us the propriety of reviewing the opinions of all the prominent poultry writers in regard to games, and stating wherein we differ; but this pursued at length, would be a work of supererogation after so freely ventilating our own and the views of others in various parts of this work. All fanciers and cockers have marks peculiar to the taste of the individual, and always will have. We have neither the power or wish to change any preconceived notions in others unless they run counter to pure game qualities, and this is rarely the case.

DISEASES.

ROUP.

Among all the diseases of fowls nothing has heretofore been more fatal than that known as the rope. The first symptom is a peculiarity in the breathing, the skin attached to the wattle being seen to rise and fall at every breath. When this occurs the fowl should be immediately removed to a warm place, and put under treatment. There is no doubt but cold, damp and windy weather, operating upon fowls of feeble constitutions, frequently produces the disease; strong and vigorous fowls are seldom attacked, and when attacked are more readily cured.— We believe it proves more fatal to white and dominic games than to any other varieties. Where fowls are well fed and well sheltered the disease is less fatal.

Symptoms.—Rising and falling of the wattle at each breath, a whooping sound in the throat, fetid discharge from the nose; in some the head and eyes will swell, then the swollen parts are feverish, and if not soon attended to, a yellow matter will form in the eyes, which, if not regularly dressed, will destroy that member. All localities are subject to the disease, but it is more common and fatal in low and damp situations.

The disease is in its nature very contagious, and for many years has troubled some of the most experienced poultry raisers, and in later years we have given the disease much attention, and have been so successful in its treatment that we seldom lose a game from this cause.

Treatment.—As soon as a fowl shows any symptoms of rupe, separate it from the other fowls, put it in a warm box or barrel with straw or hay in the bottom ; then bathe the head and throat with warm salted water, after which, with the thumb and fore-finger open the eye, and with the end of a rag saturated with the salted warm water, wash it well. Give a pill made of equal parts of Cayenne pepper and prepared chalk. Follow this treatment every morning, and if there should be any rattling in the throat, give a teaspoonful of cod liver oil every night. When the fowl appears to be considerably improved, which is usually the case after the third or fourth day's treatment, you can tie it by the leg, and let it out of the box so as to expose it to the sun, but every night it must be returned to its warm box. Put in clean straw or hay once each day.

This treatment faithfully followed, will cure the Rupe in forty-nine out of every fifty cases.

CHOLERA.

This is a disease of recent introduction, and from letters received, we find that it has prevailed in every State of the Union, and in some localities it has swept away both chickens and turkeys. Its first symptom is a drooping of the wings, a sticky slime in the mouth and throat. In some instances the diseased fowl dies in less than one hour after the attack. Upon dissection the liver is found to be very much enlarged, and a slimy, sticky substance covers its whole surface. This slime appears to everywhere pervade the mucous membrane, and clogging up the airipassages, produces death. In our own experience, it made its appearance for the first time in the summer of 1868. When feeding one afternoon in the yard adjoining our dwelling, the fowls appeared to be as usual well, and in one hour thereafter we found one of the hens with her wings drooping, her bill partly open, with slime attached to the tongue and inner part of the bill. She failed in attempting to fly up to an object about three feet high. We thought of the cholera, having carefully studied it in the agricultural prints, and immediately gave her a pill the size of an ordinany marble, placed her in a box, and kept water from her until the next morning, when we expected to find her dead. To our astonishment we found her looking tolerably well, and that day she laid an egg. While in the yard, we heard a breeding cock making an unusual noise, and going to his box we found the hen mated with him apparently in the agonies of death. We put her under similar treatment, and the next day she was well. We have since used the same pill with invariable success, and have recommended it to the use of many farmers in our own vicinity, who have successfully employed it both as a preventative and a remedy. The following is the prescription:

Cayenne pepper two parts, prepared chalk two parts, pulverized Gentian one part, pulverized charcoal one part—all by measurement and not by weight. Mix all well together and form a paste with either lard or sheep-suet, and for a fowl already diseased give a pill the size of a common marble once a day, and keep in a warm and dry place forty-eight hours, when a cure will be effected. As a preventive make a paste of Cayenne pepper one part, prepared chalk one part, pulverized Gentian two parts, pulverized charcoal two parts, all measurement, mixed with lard or sheep-suet. If the disease is known to be in your neighborhood, give, once a week, all of your grown fowls an ordinary sized pill.

PIP, OR GAPES.

This is a very common disorder among young fowls, and is most prevalent in the hotter months. It is not only troublesome, but frequently fatal. It is caused by dirty food, muddy water, dung and water, cold damp places, drinking rain water, &c. What constitutes Gapes are worms in the windpipe.— The membrane of the tongue is thickened, particularly toward the windpipe. The breathing is impeded, and the bill is frequently held open, as if gasping for breath.

Treatment,—Cut off the tip end of the tongue, give a small pill once a day, made of equal parts of prepared chalk and ground black pepper, form a paste by mixing with lard or sheep suet. After the paste is made, add a few drops of Oil of Wormseed, and mix and incorporate it well in the body of the paste. Give a pill as large as a pea once a day. Pills of all kinds must be forced down the throat. This treatment destroys the worms, the remedy being taken up in the circulation of the blood, and permeating the entire system; the mucus membrane is relieved by the wormseed oil. The life of the worm is destroyed with no injury to the fowl, and there is less danger than in the plan of dipping the end of a quill in spirits of turpentine, putting it down the chick's throat, and turning it round before drawing it out; or by introducing a twisted hair and pulling the worms out. The horse-hair plan is well described by a gentleman from Radnor, Delaware County, Pa., as follows:—

"For performing the operation, take three hairs from the tail of a horse; you can perform with one, but three will do the work much more effectually. Take each hair and twist it singly, and double it;—after having done so place them all together and tie a knot on the loose ends, leaving them about seven or eight inches long. Be careful and have them all about the same length from the knot. In performing the operation hold the chicken fast between the knees by the feet, with the fingers open the bill and catch the tongue, pulling it out a little—and hold it firmly against the lower portion of the bill with the thumb nail of the left hand; catch the hairs thus prepared near the lower end of the opposite one from the knot, and pull the neck out straight. The chicken in breathing will open the windpipe; with some trouble, perhaps, at first, you can then insert the hairs as far as they will go —perhaps four or five inches—or in proportion to the size of the chicken. After having the hairs inserted in the windpipe, twist them round between the thumb and forefinger of the right hand a number of times, still holding the chicken in the same position,—carefully withdraw the hairs, slowly twisting them round as you do so. You will very often find some of the worms or portions of them sticking to the hairs when thus removed, though not always—looking like coagulated blood. Repeat the same operation several times. In closing it, with the feet of the chicken still fast between the knees, insert the hair again and turn the head of the chicken downward, —twisting the hair round in that position, you will see the chicken throw out the worms, all cut up by the twisting of the hair in the windpipe, and looking very much like clotted blood. At first you will find some difficulty in inserting the hair into the windpipe, but after operating on a few you will accomplish it readily. The hair thus prepared you can use the whole season, and after being used a few times works much better from sticking together."

Diseases.

RHEUMATISM OR LIFTS.

Fowls with this disorder are stiff in their limbs and joints.— Some will lift up their feet and walk as though they were going to the tune of the Dead March, lifting their feet high, slow, and painfully; while others jerk by starts. This affection is witnessed in fowls in mid-summer, after much wet, and is not unfrequently caused by plunging them in water for the hatching fever. After much exposure in very damp and wet weather this disease is very likely to exhibit itself.

Treatment—Bathe the upper joint of the thigh with liquor or alcohol, dry it in well, then make an ointment of fish-worms, simmer them down in butter, then strain and grease the whole leg and thigh every day until you have given the remedy a fair test. A few applications could not be expected to perform a cure. If the cock is a valuable breeder, it will pay to go to a considerable trouble in order to perform a cure. We had once cut the spurs off a fine cock to place gafts on him; he bled profusely, to stop which we singed his spurs with a red hot iron. He was immediately attacked with the lifts.

GOUT.

This disease is almost invariably confined to old fowls. It is known by swelling of the joints, and is treated the same as the rheumatism.

CLUB FOOT.

This ailing generally manifests itself in large fowls, and is caused by flying off of high roosts—the weight of the body causing too severe a jar.

Treatment—Scarify the limb with a sharp knife or a scalpel, cut just through the skin, begin on the outside of the lump and let all the cuts run to the centre. Then scrape out all the coagulated blood that the tumor contains, and, well cleaned out, bring all the flaps to the centre; then double a strip of muslin four or five times; have it large enough to cover all the sole of the foot; place this over the flaps when brought together, then tie with narrow strips of muslin or broad tape; bring it through the toes, so as to have it well tied or sewed fast above, which is better. Secure it so that it can not come off; let it remain so for one or two weeks, then take it off and you will find the foot nearly well. All that will remain is a tender foot for a few days, until the air has time to harden the skin.

INFLAMMATION OF THE EYE.

When this occurs, small abcesses are formed on the coma, which are filled with a white colored pus. The whole of the eye becomes inflamed, the eye-lids swell to a great extent, and a coagulable matter like the white of an egg accumulates beneath the swelling, and if no treatment is given will become a yellow and tough substance, and will destroy the eye of the fowl; also produce death. It originates by exposure to cold and moist weather, attended with easterly winds.

Treatment—Bathe the head well with water as hot as the fowl can bear without burning him, water that a good portion of salt has been dissolved in; when the head and outer part of his throat has been well bathed, remove any pus that has accumulated in the eye, after this is done, wash the eye out by holding the eye lids open, and put in fine table salt, fill the eye up with this salt. Repeat this treatment once a day, keeping the fowl in a warm dry place. Give him inwardly half teaspoonful of fine black pepper; open his mouth and pour it down his throat in a dry state; place the fowl in the sun for a few hours daily. This treatment, if carried out faithfully, will cure every fowl and save the eyes.

INDIGESTION.

Treatment—Lessen the quality of food, give the fowl a good walk, and once a day for several days give him a large pill prepared for preventing the Cholera and mentioned under that head. Bake a cake of corn meal, crumbs of bread, and egg; soak the cake in good ale before feeding.

COSTIVENESS.

The existence of this disease will become apparant by observing the unsuccessful attempts of the fowl to relieve itself. The cause is dry diet, without access to green vegetables; fowls should always be furnished with vegetables of some sort. The chickens if penned or confined in a yard where there is no access to vegetables, should be furnished with green cabbage, chick weed, green and tender grass, &c. If a physic should be required give as much pulv. rhubarb as will lay on a two penny piece, to open the bowels.

DIARRHŒA OR SCOURING.

This resembles the yoke of a stale egg sticking to the feathers near the vent. Of late years this disorder is in some cases the fore-runner of the Cholera and will terminate fatally if not attended to. Physic with pulverized rhubarb, as much as will lay on a two-penny copper, or silver quarter dollar.— Then give daily the following pill: Prepared chalk three parts, Cayenne pepper one part, pulverized Gentian one part, charcoal pulverized one part, all by measurement, mix in lard, butter or sheep-suet; give a pill the size of a common marble, once a day for several days; the fowl may run at large after a few days, confinement in a warm place.

OBSTRUCTIONS OF THE NOSTRIL.

The nostril is an important portion of the breathing apparatus, and when obstructed disease supervenes. It is sometimes produced by wounds in fighting. When this is the case it forms a hard crust; wash the head with wine, afterwards grease with sweet oil. This will cure. Canker and ulceration of the nostrils is not infrequent, and a catarrhal affection sometimes produces this disorder. The fowl gaps and pants for breath.

Canker—The mouth and inside of the bill has a very fetid smell ; the canker substance is of a yellow color. This should be all scraped off with a small stick made to suit the purpose; be careful to get it all off, no matter how much the fowl bleeds, as this bleeding will do no injury. Then take fine table salt on the thumb or fore finger and give the diseased parts a good scouring with dry salt. Every day repeat the process. Give half a teaspoonful of dry cayenne pepper inwardly every day until a cure is effected.

ASTHMA.

A complaint common among fowls, and caused by obstruction of the air-cells and an accumulation of phlegm which interferes with the exercise of their function, and causes them to labor for breath.

Treatment :—Give a physic Pulv. Rhubarb, bathe the head with warm salt water, give one teaspoonful of vinegar every morning, and at night give half a teaspoonful of fine black pepper.

MELANCHOLY AND MOPING.

The symptoms are a want of appetite, drooping, and other effects of indigestion.

Treatment.—Give a physic of Pulv, Rhubarb, after this give the pill every day recommended for cholera, and occasionally half a teaspoonful of vinegar inwardly.

Diet.—Mix in meal a little fennel-seed, Dragon's blood, and wet it with good draft ale.

FEVER.

The symptoms are redness of the eye, hot head, drooping, &c. Give a little Nitre in the water, and physic with Pul. Rhubarb.

CONSUMPTION.

The researches of M. Flourens, a distinguished French physiologist, who has investigated the subject of disorders produced in fowls by cold with great care and success, produces the following important results : 1st. That in these creatures cold exercises a constant and determined action on the lungs. 2d. That this action is more sudden and more serious in proportion, as the creature is of tender age. 3d. That when cold does not produce a pulmonary inflammation acute and speedily fatal it produces chronic inflammation, which in fact is pulmonary Phthisis. 4th. That warmth uniformly prevents the access of pulmonary Phthisis, and as uniformly suspends its progress when this has commenced, and somtimes even stops it entirely, and effects a complete cure. 5th. That this disease, at whatever stage it may have arrived, is never contagious. The chickens affected were with healthy chickens, and roosted at night in the same baskets without inconvenience."

The symptoms of consumption are unmistakable, attended with cold, hoarseness, sneezing, &c. They should be sheltered and well housed, and sometimes wrapped up in warm flannel ; keep them near the fire until they liven up.

LIMED LEGS.

This disease is a species of Tetter, and the appearance of the legs is as though the fowl had been walking through wet lime. This whiteish appearance increases until the scales of the leg will raise up like great oblong warts ; the legs will enlarge and get very rough to the feeling, and it will extend above the leg. In this locality of the leg the skin will look inflamed, the flesh fall away, and the skin be very flabby. If this disease is taken in time it can be very easily cured, and if the treatment is persisted in it will cure very bad cases. We have cured many with the following

Treatment:—Take sweet oil and spirits of turpentine, equal parts, shake well before using, and every second or third day give the parts affected a good greasing ; and do not let any part escape that is the least affected with the disease.

THE CHICKEN POX.

This disease is frequent with fowls. It comes sometimes without any apparent cause, and will affect a number of fowls at the same time. It is frequently the result of fighting, when the head of the fowl has been considerably pecked and no attention paid.

Symptoms:—It will make its appearance by little minute specks scattered over the head and throat of the fowl ; these specks will enlarge and spread until the head is covered and the eyes closed with the effects of the disorder. It is a disease easily told by persons in any way familiar with fowls.

Treatment:—Physic the fowl with Pulverized Rhubarb and grease the parts affected once a day, with equal parts of sweet oil and spirits of turpentine ; grease the head and throat regardless of the eyes ; it will not hurt them in the least. When the scabs form, each day before applying the mixture, take a stick made for the purpose and scrape carefully all the scabs off. If it bleeds no matter, and as soon as you get all the scabs scraped off, then grease the head and throat all over.—This process you will repeat every day until well. Stuff the fowl once a day with bread and milk, warm with plenty of pepper in it. The fowl should be fed in this way to prevent his getting weak and poor. The fowl cannot see, and has little desire to eat, hence the necessity of forcing soft food down with the above treatment.

MOULTING.

Moulting or shedding of coat is of annual occurrence, and though not properly a disease frequently requires treatment, as though it were one. After the third year fowls moult later every succeeding one, so that it is frequently as late as January when the old fowls come into feather. The time of moulting continues, according to the age, health and weather, from six weeks to three months. The symptoms are familiar, and consist in a loss of appetite, inactivity, moping, and loss of feathers.

Treatment.—Keep the fowls warm, feed well, and mix pulverized Ginger with their food ; give plenty of meat, let the diet be strong and nourishing ; change frequently to induce appetite for food.

LOSS OF FEATHER.

This is similar to moulting, only that the lost feathers are not supplied by new ones, and the bare skin is quite rough.—It is a constitutional as well as local affection.

Treatment.—Grease the part affected with lard mixed in sulphur and gun-powder, also apply sweet oil and turpentine, equal parts ; shake up before using. Either of these remedies will answer, or they may be used alternately. *Diet.*—Mix a little flower of sulphur and Cayenne pepper with their food. A good walk, grass and fresh water are indispensable.

EXTRACT FROM THE WORK OF S. M. SAUNDERS.

" Among the diseases of fowls, nothing is so fatal to the bird, or so vexatious to the fancier, as the Roup. Very close observation and experience have taught me the first premonitory symptom is a peculiar breathing. The fowl appears in perfect health for the time, but it will be seen that the skin hanging from the lower beak, and to which the wattle is attached, is inflated and emptied at every breath—such a bird should always be removed. The disease may be caused, first, by cold damp weather and easterly winds, when fowls of weakly habit and bad constitution will often sicken; but healthy, strong birds will not. Again, if by any accidental cause they are long without food and water, and then have an unlimited quantity of drink and whole corn given to them, they gorge themselves, and ill health is the consequence; but confinement is the chief cause, and above all being shut up in tainted coops. Nothing is so difficult as to keep healthy fowls in confinement in large cities; two days will often suffice to change the bright, bold cock into the spiritless, drooping, roupy fowl, carrying contagion wherever he goes.

But all roup does not come from cities; often in the spring of the year the cocks fight, and it is necessary to take one away; search is made for something to put him in, and a rabbit-hitch or open basket is found, wherein he is confined, and often irregularly supplied with food, till pity for his altered condition causes him to be let out; but he has become roupy, and the whole yard suffers. I dwell at length on this, because of all disorders it is the worst, and because, although a cure may seem to be effected, yet at moulting, or any time when out of condition, the fowl will be more or less affected with it again. One thing is here deserving of notice. The result of the attention paid to poultry of late years has been to improve the health and constitution of the birds. Roup is not nearly so common as it was, nor is it so difficult of cure. It went on unnoticed formerly, till it had become chronic. and it would not be difficult to name yards that have now a good reputation, but which, a few years since, never had a healthy fowl. It is now treated at the outset, if seen, but the improved management in most places renders it of rare occurrence. The cold which preceded it may often be cured by feeding twice a day with stale crust of bread soaked in strong ale ; there must be provided warm food and medicine. In my own case I generally give as medicine some tincture of Iron in water pans and some stimulants. The suspected fowl should be removed directly, and if there be plenty without it, and if it be not of any breed that makes its preservation a matter of moment, it should be killed. There is very little doubt of a cure if taken in the first stage. But, if the eyelids be swollen, the nostrils closed, the breathing difficult, and the discharge fetid and continual, it will be a long time before the bird is well. In this stage it may be termed the consumption of fowls, and with them, as in human benigs, most cases are beyond cure. However, I do not hesitate to say it is contagious in a high degree. Where fowls are wasting without any apparent disorder, a teasponful of cod-liver oil per day will often be found a most efficacious remedy. I will next mention a disease common to chickens at an early age—I mean the gapes. These are caused by numerous small worms in the throat. The best way I know of getting rid of them, is to take a hen's tail-feather, strip it to within an inch of the end, put it down the chicken's windpipe, twist it sharply round several times, and draw it quickly out ; the worms will be found entangled in the feathers. When this is not effectual in removing them, if the tip of the feather be dipped in turpentine, it will kill them, but it must be put down the windpipe, not the gullet.

I have always thought these are got from impure water, and I have been informed by a gentleman who inquires closely into those things, that having placed some of the worms taken from the throat of a chicken, and some from the bottom of a waterbutt, where rain-water had stood a long time, under a microscope, he found them identical. I have never met with gapes where fowls had running streams to drink at. Camphor is perhaps the best cure for gapes, and if some is constantly kept in the water they drink, they take it readily. This has been most successful.

There is also another description of gapes arising probably from internal fever; I have found meal mixed with milk and saltz a good remedy. They are sometimes caused by a hard substance at the tip of the tongue; in this case, remove it sharply with the thumbnail, and let it bleed freely. A gentleman mentioned this to me who had met with it in an old French writing on poultry.

Sometimes a fowl will droop suddenly, after being in perfect health ; if caught directly, it will be found it has eaten something that has hardened in the crop ; pour plenty of warm water down the throat, and loosen the food till it is soft, then give a tablespoonful of castor oil, or about as much Jalap as will lie on a ten-cent piece, mixed in butter ; make a pill of it and slide it into the crop ; the fowl will be well in the morning. Cayenne pepper or chalk, or both mixed with meal, are convenient and good remedies for scouring. When fowls are restless, dissatisfied, and continually scratching, it is often caused by lice ; these can be got rid of by supplying their houses or haunts with plenty of ashes, especially wood ashes, in which they may dust themselves, and the dust-bath is rendered more effectual by adding some sulphur to the dust. It must be borne in mind, all birds must have the bath; some use water, some dust ; but both from the same instinctive knowledge of its necessity. Where a shallow stream of water runs across a gravel road, it will be found full of small birds washing ; where a bank is dry, and well exposed to the sun, birds of all kinds will be found burying themselves in the dust. Sometimes fowls appear cramped, they have difficulty in standing upright, and rest on their knees ; in large young birds, especially cocks, this is merely the effect of weakness from fast growth, and the difficulty their long weak legs have in carrying their bodies. But if it lasts after they are getting age, then it it must be seen to. If their roosting-place has a wooden, stone, or brick floor, this is probably the cause; if this is not so, stimulating food, such as I have described for other diseases, must be given. The following tonic is highly recommended by Mr. John Douglas, of the Wolseley Aviaries, England, to prevent roup and gapes in chicks and old fowls:—"One pound of sulphate of iron, one pound of sulphuric acid dissolved in a jug with hot water, then let it stand twenty-four hours, and add one gallon of spring water; when fit for use, one teaspoonful to a pint of water given every other day to chicks and once a week to old fowls, will make roup and gapes entirely a stranger to your yard." This may be true if perfect cleanliness is maintained, and the fowls are in other respects well treated. *Canker* is cured by scraping the yellow substance out the mouth, then take your thumb and rub it well with dry table salt; if it bleeds no matter;—give it a good rubbing in this way once a day until well.

EXTRACTS FROM THE WORK OF DR. BENNETT.

While we cannot give Dr. John C. Bennett credit for judgment on the subject of game fowls, we nevertheless accord to him more credit than any other that we are acquainted with for his ably written articles upon the symptoms and causes of disease in fowls. His book should be in the hands of every fancier or breeder of fowls:—

" Poultry, like other animals, are liable to numerous diseases, some of them malignant, and many of them fatal. In our climate, however, the number of important disorders is small, and they usually yield to judicious treatment. That little attention has been bestowed on this subject, may arise from the fact that, in an economical point of view, the value of an individual fowl is comparatively insignificant; and, while the ailments of other domesticated animals generally claim a prompt and efficient care, the unhappy inhabitants of the poultry yard are too often relieved of their sufferings in the most summary way. But there are reasons which will justify a more careful regard to this matter, besides the humanity of adding to the comfort of these useful creatures; and the attempt to cure, in cases of disease, will often be rewarded by rendering their flesh more palatable, and the eggs more wholesome. Most of the diseases to which poultry is subject are the result of errors in diet or management, and should have been prevented, or may be removed by a change, and adoption of a suitable regimen. When an individual is attacked, it ought to be forthwith removed, to prevent the contamination of the rest of the flock. Nature, who proves a guardian to fowls in health, will nurse them in their weakness, and act as a most efficient physician to the sick. We can do no more than co-operate with her; and the aim of all medical treatment should be to follow the indications which nature holds out, and assist in the effort which she constantly makes for the restoration of health. Before treating in detail the maladies of greatest consequence, it is desirable to present a brief view of so much of the anatomical structure of fowls as will be necessary to the comprehension of disease and its management.

The digestive function in poultry is partly mechanical and partly chemical. In its several stages it differs widely from that of some quadrupeds who feed on similar food. In these, grains are frequently swallowed without being crushed by the teeth, and as their stomachs have not the power of digesting solid grain, it is voided whole. In fowls, on the other hand, the grain is all swallowed whole, and it is digested in the stomach. From this fact, the opinion has been derived of the necessity of giving stones and gravel to fowls, in order to enable them to grind the food which they take. But this is a vulgar error; for, though there are advantages derived from furnishing facilities to a flock to pick among gravel, it is by no means necessary to a perfect and regular digestion. The digestive organs of fowls consist of the gullet and crop, the gizzard, stomach, liver, and intestines. The gullet, or æophagus, runs down the neck towards the right side, swelling out in front of the chest, into a membraneous bag, which is called the crop or craw. The crop is somewhat analogous to the paunch in the ox or sheep. It receives the gullet into its upper part, and proceeds downwards, about the middle of the bag, in such a manner that the crop is in some measure aside from the regular communication between the upper and lower opening of the gullet. Its office is to receive the food when first swallowed, and to macerate it, and dissolve it by means of liquor, which is separated by the glands, which may be observed covering its surface. The food, after passing the crop, goes through the remaining part of the gullet, shaped like a funnel, of smaller dimensions. This is similar to the second stomach in some quadrupeds, and is furnished with a large number of glands. These glands may be called gastric glands; they are placed near each other, and are hollow. Their office is to secrete a solvent or digestive fluid, and to discharge it through a small opening into the cavity.

When this fluid has diluted and digested the food sufficiently, it is prepared to pass into the gizzard.

The gizzard is the last stomach, and is composed of a body of very firm and dense muscles, and lined with a thick, gristly membrane. Towards the cavity of the stomach, this lining forms folds and depressions, which on the opposite surfaces are adapted to each other.

The gizzard is comparatively small and narrow, and has its outlet near its entrance. It is calculated, in every respect, for producing very powerful trituration, and is adapted to answer the purposes which are subserved by grinding teeth in other animals. In consequence of the dark, gristly structure of the gizzard, it possesses little sensibility, and it is not uncommon for fowls to eat even when dying, while in the case of other animals, in such a state, all food becomes loathsome.

The outlet of the gizzard discharges the digested food in the form of paste, having a grayish color, into the chyle-gut, which is the first of the intestines. This is situated on the right side, depending into the belly, and joined at each end to the liver.— The liver prepares bile from the blood conducted to it by the veins, and by means of a duct carries the bile from the gallbladder into the chyle-gut, in a downward direction, to be mixed with the digested food. This peculiarity is different from other animals. Another fluid, brought from the pancreas to the chyle-gut, completes the apparatus for digestion.

The food now proceeds on to the small intestines. The surface of these is lined with the mouths of numerous absorbents, which perpetually open to take up the aliment prepared in the stomach and chyle-gut. The refuse is passed to the rectum, to be discharged from the body. Fowls are also furnished with kidneys, for removing superfluous fluid from the blood. The kidneys lie in a hollow beside the back-bone, and the urine is carried from there in a blueish-colored canal into the vent-gut, or rectum. It here mixes, and is discharged with the dung.—Fowls have no bladder, and it is, therefore, a criterion of health when the excrement is moist. The diseases affecting the organs now described will be considered in their order.

I. DISEASES OF THE DIGESTIVE ORGANS.

1ST. THE PIP, OR GAPES.

This is the most common disorder of poultry and all domestic birds. It is especially the disease of young fowls, and is most prevalent in the hottest months. It is not only troublesome, but frequently fatal. There is a great diversity of opinion respecting its cause and its nature.

Dr. Beehstein considers it a catarrhal inflammation, which produces a thickening of the membrane which lines the nostrils and the mouth, and particularly the tongue. M. Buchoz, however, is of opinion that it is caused by want of water, or by bad water. Others describe the disease as commencing in the form of a vesicle on the tip of the tongue, which occasions a thickened state of the skin, by the absorption of its contents. A writer in the *Farmer's Cabinet* says positively, that the gapes in chickens is occasioned by worms in the windpipe ; and this opinion is corroborated by the editor of the *American Farmer.* A writer of authority also remarks :—"On the dissection of chickens dying with this disorder, it will be found that the windpipe contains numerous small red worms, about the size of a small cambric needle ; on the first glance, they would be likely to be mistaken for blood-vessels." It is supposed by some that these worms continue to grow, until by their enlargement, the windpipe is so filled up that the chicken is suffocated.

Symptoms.—The common symptoms of this malady are the thickened state of the membrane of the tongue, particularly towards the tip. The breathing is impeded, and the beak is frequently held open, as if gasping for breath. The beak becomes yellow at its base, and the feathers on the head appear ruffled and disordered. The tongue is very dry. The appetite is not always impaired ; but yet the fowl cannot eat,—probably on account of the difficulty which the act involves, and sits in a corner, to pine in solitude.

Remedy.—Most writers recommend the immediate removal of the thickened membrane. This is said to be best done by scraping it off with the nail or with a needle ; but it seems to be attended with a degree of cruelty. Richardson say the same effects may be produced by anointing the part with butter or fresh cream. If necessary, the scab may be pricked with a needle. He also recommends a pill, composed of equal parts of scraped garlic and horse-raddish, with as much cayenne pepper as will out-weigh a grain of wheat, to be mixed with fresh butter, and given every morning—the fowl to be kept warm.

If the disease is in an advanced state, which is shown by the chicken holding up his head and gaping, for want of breath, it should be thrown on its back, and while the neck is held straight, the bill should be opened, and a quill should be inserted into the windpipe, with a little turpentine. This being turned round, will loosen and destroy a number of small red worms, some of which will be drawn up by the feather, and others will be coughed up by the chicken. The operation should be repeated the following day, if the gaping continues. If it ceases, the cure is effected. There can be little doubt that this troublesome disease is caused by inattention to cleanliness in the habits and lodgings of fowls. An intelligent and lucid writer in the *Southern Planter*, says, "The worms in the lungs of chickens are produced by the inhalation of the eggs of the hen-lice. The minute eggs are deposited in the feathers and down of the hen, and the chickens being hovered over by the hen, the eggs are drawn into the cells of the lungs, at each inspiration, which hatch and produce the worms which smother the chickens." W. C. F. Morton of New Windsor, also says: "There is one fact connected with this disease—that it is only old hen-roosts that are subject to it; and I am of opinion that when it prevails, if the chicken houses and coops were kept clean, and frequently whitewashed with thin whitewash, with plenty of salt or brine mixed with it, and those chickens that take the disease operated on and cured,—or, if they should die, have them burned up, or so destroyed that the eggs of the worms would not hatch out,—that the disease would be eradicated. With my first brood of chickens, there was not one escaped the gapes. But all that have been hatched since, I had the chicken-house and coops well whitewashed, inside and out, with thin whitewash, with plenty of brine in it, and kept clean, have been exempt from the disease, with occasionally an exception of one or two chickens out of a brood."

Mr. Benjamin Anderson, in the *Southern Planter*, states that some of his neighbors have entirely prevented this disease, by mixing a small quantity of spirits of turpentine with the food of their fowls.

"From five to ten drops, to a pint of meal, to be made into dough, are the proportions used," and Major Chandler, in the *Tennessee Agriculturalist*, gives the following recipe, as an infallable preventive:—"keep iron standing in vinegar, and put a little of the liquid in the food every few days; chickens so fed are free from gapes." It is the opinion of Garret Bergen that

Diseases.

this malady is prevented simply by "scanting them in their food;" and he pertinently asks, "Who ever heard of chickens, which were not confined with the hen, but both suffered to run at large and collect all their own food, to be troubled with this disease."

2ND. INDIGESTION.

Cases of indigestion among fowls are common, and deserve attention according to the causes from which they proceed.— A change of food will often produce crop-sickness, as it is called, when the fowl takes but little food, and suddenly loses flesh.— Such disease is of little consequence, and shortly disappears.— When it requires attention at all, all the symptoms will be removed by giving their diet in a warm state. Sometimes, however, a fit of indigestion thretens severe consequences, especially if long continued. Every effort should be made to ascertain the cause, and the remedy must be governed by the circumstances of the case.

Mowbray mentions a hen manifesting all the symptoms of indigestion, in whose crop beans were found, which had obstructed it long enough to present marks of vegetation. An incision was made, the wound healed, and health was restored.— Generally, affections of this kind, as in the human species, proceed from over-feeding or want of exercise. The symptoms are heaviness, moping, keep away from the nest, and want of appetite.

Remedy.—Lessen the quantity of food, and oblige the fowl to exercise in an open walk. Give some powdered cayenne and gentian, mixed with the usual food. Iron-rust, mixed with soft food, or piffused in water, is an excellent tonic, and is indicated when this is atrophy or diminution of flesh. It may be combined with oats or grain. In England, it is said that milk warm, ale has a good effect when joined to the diet of diseased fowl.

COSTIVENESS.

The existence of this disorder will become apparent by observing the unsuccessful attempts of the fowl to relieve itself. It frequently proceeds from continued feeding of dry diet, without access to green vegetables. Indeed, without the use of these, or some such substitute, as mashed potatoes, costiveness is certain to ensue. The want of a sufficient supply of good water will also produce the disease, on account of that peculiar structure which has already been explained, by which fowls are unable to void their urine except in connection with the fœces of solid food, and through the same channel.

Remedy.—Soaked bread, with warm skimmed milk, is a mild remedial agent, and will usually suffice. Boiled carrots or cabbage, are more efficient. A meal of earth-worms is sometimes advisable, and hot potatoes mixed with bacon fat, are said to be excellent. Castor-Oil and browned butter will relieve the most obstinate cases, though a clyster of oil may be sometimes required, in addition, to effect a cure.

4TH, DIARRHŒA.

There are times when fowls dung more loosely than at others, especially when they have been fed on green or soft food; but this may occur without the presence of disease. But should this state deteriorate into a confirmed and continued laxity, immediate attention is required, to guard against fatal effects.— The causes of diarrhœa are dampness, undue acidity in the bowles, or the presence of irritating matter there.

The Symptoms are, lassitude and emaciation, and, in very severe cases, the voiding of calcareous matter, white, streaked with yellow. This resembles the yolk of a stale egg, and sticks to the feathers near the vent. It bacomes acrid, from the presence of ammonia, and causes inflammation, which extends speedily throughout the intestines.

Remedy.—This, of course, depends upon the cause. When

the disease is brought on by a diet of green or soft food, the food must be changed, and water given sparingly. When it arises from undue acidity, chalk mixed with meal is advantageous, but rice flour boluses are most to be depended on. Dr. Handel, of Mayence, in cases of chronic looseness, recommends water impregnated with iron-rust, with great confidence. Alum-water, of moderate strength, is also beneficial. In cases of bloody flux, boiled rice and milk, given warm, with a little magnesia or chalk, may be given with success.

II. DISEASES OF THE RESPIRATORY ORGANS.

Fowls are so constructed, in their respiratory system, that their method of breathing is somewhat peculiar. The principal organ used by them in breathing is the nostril, rather than the mouth. It will easily be observed, that their nostrils are comparatively large. They have an immediate communication with the windpipe. The windpipe is constructed with a series of firm cartilages, bound together by strong membranes. These are exceedingly elastic, and are able to resist considerable pressure; so that it is difficult to disturb the cylindrical form of this organ, or to impede the free ingress or egress of the air necessary to breathing. The windpipe reaches down to the chest, and is there divided into branches, which becomes constantly smaller, till they seem to be mere holes. These ramifications of the windpipe, together with numerous blood-vessels, constitute the substance of the lungs. The spaces between them are occupied with a delicate membrane, which unites them, and gives a regular appearance to the mass. The holes in which the branches of the windpipe terminate are apertures into large air-sacs, which communicate with the various parts of the body, and constitute, as it were, an auxiliary lung.— The whole mass of the lungs proper is encased with a membrane called the pleura, of great delicacy, which secretes a watery fluid, of great use in preventing any adhesion of the several parts.

1ST, OBSTRUCTIONS OF THE NOSTRIL.

When the nostrils, which we have seen are so important a portion of the breathing apparatus, are obstructed, disease supervenes. This is sometimes produced in consequence of wounds received in fighting. The comb, when lacerated, will plug up the nostril with a hard crust of great tenacity. Canker and ulceration of the nostril is not infrequent, and a catarrhal affection commonly precedes this annoying disorder. The symptoms are similar to those attending the pip; the bird gapes and pants for breath.

Remedy.—In cases of laceration, the parts should be washed with warm water or suds till the crust is loosened and removed. Canker or ulceration, if recent, may be rubbed with honey, to defend from the effects of the air; but if of long standing, Dickson recommends to touch with a red-hot wire, which will produce a scab, and thus facilitate a cure. When obstructions arise from catarrh, bathe the nostrils with warm milk and water, or annoint with sweet oil or fresh butter.

2D, ASTHMA.

This disease, common among fowls, seems to differ in characteristics sufficiently to authorize a distinction into two species. In one, it appears to be caused by an obstruction of the air-cells, by an accumulation of phlegm, which interferes with the exercise of their functions. The fowl labors for breath, in consequence of not being able to take in the usual quantity of air at an inspiration. The capacity of the lungs is thereby diminished, the lining membrane of the windpipe becomes thickened, and its minute branches are more or less affected. These effects may reasonably be attributed, as Richardson thinks, to the fact, that, as our poultry are originally natives of tropical climates, however well they may appear acclimated, they, nevertheless, require a more equable temperature than is afforded except by artificial means.

Diseases. 291

Another variety of Asthma is induced by fright, or over excitement. It is sometimes produced by chasing fowls to catch them, by seizing them suddenly, or by their fighting with each other. In these cases, a blood-vessel is often ruptured, and sometimes one or more of the air-cells. The symptoms are short breathing, opening of the beak often, and for a space together, heaving and panting of the chest; and in case of a rupture of a blood-vessel, a drop of blood appearing on the beak.

Remedy.—Confirmed Asthma is difficult to cure. For the disease in its incipient state, it is recommended that the fowl be kept warm, and be treated with repeated doses of hippo powder and sulphur mixed with butter, with the addition of a small quantity of cayenne pepper.

3D. ROUP.

This term is used very loosely, both in common speaking and among writers on poultry, to characterize disease. It is indifferently applied to describe maladies as dissimilar as obstruction of the rump gland, the pip, and catarrh. It should be confined, however, to a dangerous disorder, with symptoms sufficiently marked to identify it, which is caused mostly by cold and moisture, but often ascribed to improproper feeding, want of cleanliness and exercise. The roup affects fowls of all ages, and is either acute or chronic; sometimes commencing suddenly, on exposure; at others, gradually, as the consequence of neglected colds, or damp weather or lodging. Chronic roup bas been kown to extend through two years.

Symptoms.—The most prominent symptoms of roup are difficult and noisy breathing, gaping, terminating in a rattling in the throat. The head swells and is feverish. They eyes are swollen, and the eye-lids appear livid; the sight decays and sometimes total blindness ensues. There are discharges from the nostrils and the mouth, at first thin and limpid, afterwards thick, purulent and fetid. In this stage, which resembles the glanders in horses, the disease becomes infectious. As secondary symptoms, it may be noticed that the appetite fails, except for drink, the crop feels hard, and the feathers are starving, ruffled, and without the gloss which appears in health. The fowl mopes by itself, and seems to suffer much pain.

Remedy.—When fowls are infected with roup, they ought to be kept on light food. When chronic, change of food and air is advisable. The common remedies, such as salt dissolved in water, are inefficacious. Richardson gives the following formula; powdered gentian and ginger, each one part; epsom saltz, one and a half parts, and flour of sulphur, one half part, to be made up with butter, and given every morning. But for roup and all putrid affections, I confidently prescribe the following, and consider it the only true treatment. Take finely pulverized, fresh burnt charcoal, and new yeast, of each three parts; pulverized sulphur, two parts; flour one part; water, quantity sufficient; mix well, and make into boluses of the size of a hazelnut, and give one three times a day. Cleanliness is no less necessary than warmth, and it will sometimes be desirable to bathe the eyes and nostrils with warm milk and water, or suds, as convenient.

With regard to this disease, Mr. Giles says:—"My method with the roup, or swelled head, which, by the way, is caused by a cold, is as follows: As soon as discovered, if in warm weather, remove the infected ones to some well ventilated apartment, or yard; if in winter, to some warm place; then give a desert spoonful of castor-oil; wash their heads with warm castile soap-suds, and let them remain until next morning fasting. Scald for them Indian meal, adding two and a half ounces of epsom saltz for ten hens, or in proportion for a lesser or larger number; give it warm, and repeat the dose in a day or two, if they do not recover." Mr. Giles is excellent authority, having had "more than thirty years' practice among the feathered tribes," and being now the owner of one of the most extensive collections of pure blooded fowls in this or any other country.

4TH. CONSUMPTION.

We should be apt to imagine from the warm clothing of feathers with which fowls are provided, that they would be exempt from colds and consumption. But all the symptoms of cold, such as hoarseness, sneezing, &c., are readily observed. That they should be susceptible to such influences appears reasonable, when the peculiar structure already adverted to is remembered. The air taken into the lungs of fowls is not stopped there, but by means of air-cells reaches every part of the body—pervading the interior of the bones. Their great susceptibility, also, is connected with the fact that they are originally tropical animals. They are also affected, more or less, by the circumstances in which they are placed, spending a large part of their existence in coops and under shelter, so that they are more liable to be affected by exposure.

Remedy.—Shelter and housing, and sometimes the indulgence of the fireside. Temperature alone is the dominant principle, to which attention ought to be paid.

III. DISEASES OF THE CIRCULATION.

The heart in fowls, as in man and quadrupeds, consists of two ventricles for throwing the blood into the arteries—one to be distributed to the lungs, and the other through the rest of the body, and two auricles, for receiving the returned blood. The blood itself is composed of a yellowish substance, called serum, and a red-colored mass, or crassumentum. The blood of fowls is liable to several diseases, the chief of which may be described as fever and inflammation.

IST. FEVER.

The most decided sort of fever to which fowls are subjected occurs at the period of hatching. At this time the animal heat is so increased that it is perceptible to the touch. A state of fever may also be observed when fowls are about to lay.

This is generally a small consequence when the birds are otherwise healthy, but is of moment if any other disorder is present; as in such case the original disorder will be aggravated. Fighting frequently occasions fever also, and sometimes proves fatal.

Symptoms.—An increased circulation of the blood, excessive heat, and restlessness.

Remedy.—Light food and change of air, and, if necessary, aperient medicine, such as castor-oil, with a little burnt butter. In a case of highly inflammatory fever in a chicken, supposed to have been caused by sudden hot weather in May, so that it burned the hand like hot water, a dose of nitre in milk and water, at night, produces so great a change that the chicken was cool and brisk in the morning. The dose was repeated and brought on a cold fever fit, like ague, which, however, changed to an intermittent, and the chicken completely recovered.— Such symptoms are probably rare, at least in this climate. In the country it is common to stop the hatching fever by turning the hen rapidly round, in order to produce giddiness, which effects a reduction in the velocity of the blood. The fever produced by the excitement of fighting may be abated by plunging the fowl in cold water. In this case, the patient must be immediately dried and housed.

2D, INFLAMMATION.

Inflammation may be described, for all practical purposes, as consisting in increased arterial action of the parts immediately surrounding points of stagnation, and it may occur indifferently in the external or internal parts. Inflammation of the lungs has been already considered, and various parts of the fowl are liable to similar affections, but most of these are of small consequence. The most serious is an inflammation of the eyes.— When this occurs small abscesses are found on the coma, which are filled with a white-colored pus. In an aggravated form, the whole of the eye becomes inflamed, the eye-lids swell to a great extent, and a coagulable albuminous matter, like the white of an egg, accumulates beneath the swelling. This affection sometimes results in blindness, and is sometimes fatal.

This disorder is originated by the vapors arising from close confinement, when over-care is exercised to shield the fowls from the effects of cold ; and it is produced likewise by exposure, and particularly to moist cold.

Treatment and Remedy.—Like other cases of inflammatory attacks, relief is to be sought in a suitable temperature being maintained where fowls are kept. A little aperient medicine will be beneficial, and applications of warm suds, made from castile soap, in case of abscess, or great swelling of the inflamed part.

3D. RHEUMATISM.

M. Flourens states a case of acute rheumatism and sciatica as occurring among fowls under his own observation. Dickson says that he has seen rheumatic affections among his fowls " even at midsummer, after much wet, and more than once as a consequence of plunging them in water for the hatching fever." After much exposure, especially in long-continued damp and rainy weather, this disease is very likely to exhibit itself.

The symptoms are, a stiffness of the limbs, and manifest pain in the attempt to move about, which, also renders the gait unsteady.

Remedy.—Warmth and shelter, with a cooling and opening diet.

4TH, GOUT.

This disorder is almost confined to old fowls, and therefore the opportunity afforded for observing it but seldom occurs.—

It will not always repay the necessary trouble to attempt a cure. The symptoms are somewhat like those of rheumatism, but a swelling of the joints is the most marked characteristic.

Remedy.—Sulphur, mixed with scalded bran or soaked bread. Pellets of colchicum are also recommended.

IV. DISEASES OF THE BRAIN.

The structure of the brain in fowls is very peculiar. There are two distinct parts—one unmarked by convolutions; and the other, which may be called the cerebellum, is distinguished by cross parallel streaks. In several other respects, there is an important difference between the brain of fowls and that of quadrupeds or men.

1ST. APOPLEXY.

The principal disorder to which the brain is subjected, among fowls, is what most resembles apoplexy. Some writers have spoken of this disease under other names, as Dr. Bechstein, who calls it epilepsy, and Mr. Clater, who chooses to designate it as the megrims. The causes are alleged to be, improper food, and general neglect or improper treatment. M. Flourens, who has devoted considerable attention to the subject, says that there are two degrees of this disease, which he denominates.— Deep-seated apoplexy is characterized by complete disorder of moment; while superficial apoplexy is manifested only by deficient muscular energy, and instability in walking. The deep-seated apoplexy is accompanied with the other; but, as this is the precursor of the former, it ought to be carefully attended to, in order to prevent the more serious attack. In sudden attacks, the fowl falls instantly, rolls on the back, struggles for a short time convulsively, and appears stupid and giddy. The fit often recurs at short intervals, and each one is more violent than the other.

M. Flourens had brought to him a young fowl, whose gait indicated that of a tipsy animal so much that the peasants called it the tipsy hen. Whether standing, walking, or running, it reeled and staggered, and apparently without control of its motions. It would go backward when it attempted to go forward, and *vice versa*. It often fell, from the bending of the legs beneath the body; and, on attempting to fly to the perch, it fell and rolled on the ground, without the power to recover its legs, or to find its balance. M. Flourens examined the brain, and found the bone of the skull to be covered with black, carous points; on penetrating the dura-mater, clear water exuded. The cerebellum was yellow, with streaks like rust, and in the centre was a mass of purulent, coagulated matter, contained in a cavity by itself, the sides of which were thin and smooth.

Remedy.—The old method of treating this disease is the result of ignorance of its cause and nature; and the hitherto popular recipe of castor-oil and syrup of ginger is to be avoided as useless, or worse. The application of leeches to the nape of the neck alone promises a successful cure. The diet should be light, and the quantity of food small. The diseased fowl should be confined in a dark coop.

2ND. MELANCHOLY AND MOPING.

Under these terms, such symptoms as want of appetite, drooping, and other effects of indigestion, are mentioned as indicating a separate disease. It is reasonable, however, to refer these characteristics to a disordered state of the nervous system. Such remedies as have already been mentioned, for costiveness, &c., should be attended to; and if any symptoms of greater gravity appear, such treatment as belongs to nervous affections will be indicated.

V. DISEASES OF THE SKIN.

1ST. MOULTING.

Moulting is a natural process of annual occurrence; and,

though it can scarcely be called a disease, yet it is necessary to treat it as if it were such, from the effects produced by it. It not unfrequently happens that young fowls do not pass the season of moulting safely, but sicken and die. Chickens of the later broods are most liable to bad effects, because the season of moulting comes to them so late, when the weather is most unfavorable. The summer moult is usually gradual, but few feathers falling at a time, and these being at once replaced. On the contrary, when the moult happens in autumn, the feathers fall faster, and are not so speedily replaced. The consequence is, that the fowl is in a degree naked, and suffers from the necessary exposure.

It is the remark of Dr. Beehstein, that in a state of nature, moulting occurs to wild birds precisely when their food is most plenty; hence, nature points out that the fowl should, during that period, be furnished with an extra supply of food. After the third year, it has been observed that fowls begin to moult later every succeeding year, so that it is frequently as late as January before the older fowls come into full feather; and, the weather being then cold, they are not in a laying state till the end of March, or later. The time of moulting continues, according to the age and health of the fowls, and also with reference to mild or cold weather, from six weeks to three months. "I think I have observed," says Dickson, "in some instances of late hatching, that the process is favorable to moulting."

Symptoms.—A falling off in appetite, moping, and inactivity; the feathers starving and falling off, till the naked skin appears.

Remedy.—In diseased moulting, M. Chomel advises to add sugar to the water which the fowls drink, and to give corn and hempseed. They should be kept warm, and occasionally be treated to doses of cayenne pepper.

2ND. LOSS OF FEATHERS.

This disease, which is common to confined fowls, is by no means to be confounded with the natural process of moulting.

In the annual healthy moult, the fall of the feathers is occasioned by the protrusion of new feathers from the skin. In the diseased state, which we now consider, where the feathers fall, no new ones come to replace them, but the fowl is left bald and naked. A sort of roughness appears also on the skin.

The *Symptoms* are like those just described in the previous article, and are easily distinguishable.

Remedy.—This affection is probably constitutional rather than local. External remedies, therefore, may not always be sufficient. Stimulants, applied externally, will serve to assist the operation of what medicine may be given. Sulphur may be thus applied, mixed with lard. Sulphur and cayenne, in the proportion of one quarter each, mixed with fresh butter, is good to be given internally, and will act as a powerful alterative.— The diet should be changed, and cleanliness and fresh air are indispensable.

VI. EXTERNAL DISORDERS.

1st, DISEASE OF THE RUMP GLANDS.

Mowbray speaks of an obstruction of the gland of the rump in fowls, under the name of Imposthume, and strangely enough denominates the disease as Roup. Concerning the functions of these glands, erroneous ideas have very generally prevailed; and the common notion has been, that its use was to secrete an oily matter, which was applied by the fowl to the purpose of making their feathery coating water-tight. M. Reaumur, has effectually exploded this fancy, by showing exclusively the perfect impractibility of producing a secretion of sufficient quantity to answer this end, and, in confirmation of this opinion, it is only necessary to mention, that while, in case of the Runkin fowl, there is no perceptible difference in the feathers so far as shedding water is concerned, they are deprived of any such gland. But this gland frequently becomes diseased, and in consequence of obstruction, it is inflamed and swollen, and occasions great pain and uneasiness. In severe cases, the whole rump is affected, and the consequences may be serious. This affection should be treated as a bile; when it becomes hard and ripe, let the pus or matter out by a slight incision. Reaumur advises that the outlet or duct of the gland should be cleared from obstructions by means of a tent (roll of linen) introduced into the orifice.

2ND, FRACTURES AND DISLOCATIONS.

In most cases, when severe fractures occur to the limbs of fowls, unless they are very valuable, undoubtedly the best course to pursue, in mercy to the birds, is to kill them at once.

But when it is deemed worth while to preserve them, splints may be used, when practicable. Great cleanliness must be observed, the diet should be reduced, and every precaution taken aganst the inflammation which is sure to supervene. When it is established, cooling lotions, such as warm milk and water, may be applied.

3RD, WOUNDS AND SORES.

Fowls are exposed to wounds from many sources. In their frequent encounters with each other, severe wounds often occur.

The poultry-house is beseiged by enemies at night, and despite of all precaution, rats and weasels, and other animals, will assault the occupants of the roost, or nest, to their damage.

These wounds, if not attended to, often degenerate into painful and dangerous ulcers. When such injuries occur, cleanliness is the first step to cure. The wound should be cleared from all foreign matter, washed with tepid milk water, and excluded as far as possible from the air. The fowl should be removed from its companions, who in such cases seldom or ever show sympathy, but, on the contrary, are always ready to assault the invalid, and aggravate the injury. Should the wound

Diseases. 301

not readily heal, and ulcerate, it may be bathed with alum-water, The ointment of creosote is said to be effectual, even when the ulcer exhibits a fungous character, or proud flesh is present. Richardson says that ulcers may be kept clean if dressed with a little lard, or washed with a weak solution of sugar of lead. If they are indolent, they may be touched with bluestone.

SCRAPS OF THE AUTHOR'S FIRST DOINGS IN COCK-FIGHTING.

FROM FIRST OR POCKET EDITION OF "GAME FOWLS."

In Westmoreland county, Penn., in 1819, there was a main of game fowls fought at Salem, on the first and second days of the Christmas holiday; between Barker & Drum, of the Salt Works, on the one side, and Capt. Samuel Cooper, (a brother) of Pittsburg, Judge Cook and Dr. Stowey, (renowned for discovering the cure of hydrophobia,) on the other. The fight was for the best three in five, staking $600. Judge Cook went to Fayette county to select the fowls, and I, though a boy of sixteen years, accompanied him. I was astonished to find that every farmer in that section raised games and no other. We went to the tavern of a man named Gad, the introducer of Games in that section; he had almost every description then known to the country. The Judges elected a snow-white, seven pounds, a red muff, seven pounds four ounces, and a red of seven pounds, besides several others to contend for the odd fights. These heavy weights were got to match the Barker fowls, all of which were large. In selecting the odd cocks, I espied a pretty black red, with large black eyes, and the most singular comb I ever witnessed. It was crown-shape, standing high, the indentations deep and quite regular. It was with considerable difficulty, and only by stratagem that I caught him. When I caught him he quacked very loud; at which the Judge cried, "John, put that chicken down, he is a "Dung-hill." The Judge had a notion (prevalent by the way, but in some cases erroneous, that if a fowl quacked he could not be game.) But I determined to hold on to him, and insisted that he was a game, despite the quack. The owner laughed at our dispute, averred that I was right, and ended by giving him to me. The Judge, unsatisfied, asked the man what breed he was. He replied that he did not know, but gave his history as well as he could, and in substance as follows:—Two years prior there was a man moving from the Eastern States to Ohio, and stopped at the hotel of our friend. Behind his wagon was attached a coop, containing one cock and four hens. He fancied it, and tried to trade with the Yankee, then to purchase, but all to no purpose.

At night he had the fowl stolen and put up in the mountains at a sugar camp. The rightful owner was much distressed at his loss, and offered ten dollars reward for its recovery. Then the Yankee, having failed to recover his cock, renewed his journey; the hotel keeper put four hens with the cock at the sugar camp, in the house usually kept for shelter while manufacturing maple sugar. Every thing was nicely arranged, and a stream of water ran close by. Here he left them to breed and roam through the woods at will; as a consequence they became very wild, and would fly away or hide at the sight of man. This account appeared to satisfy the Judge, and the fact that the cock was raised in a wild state, in some measure accounted for his eccentric quacking. Three days afterward this cock was cooped for the battle, by which time he was by far the tamest we had. I attended to the feeding and training, by the directions of Judge Cook, and of course I had an opinion, as to which were the best fighters, and I considered my own the greatest of them all. I named him Prince Charles, owing to the crown-like comb he had. When the time came for battle, the then most celebrated heeler in the United States was to heel and pit our fowls. The majority of our side felt sure of success, but I was acquainted with the Barker breed, being clerk of the adjoining salt works, and had daily opportunities of seeing and knowing them. I told my brother that Barker's chickens could not be whipped, but that he could easily whip the Drum Cocks. But he thought, by the superior heeling of Mr. Rigdon, they would win. When Christmas came on, the fight commenced, the Barker crowd winning the three first fights, and pocketted the stakes. After the regular main, then commenced the odd fights. I had not bet a cent yet, but when my Prince Charles came into the pit I bet my whole pile, consisting of three dollars, and a new silver watch worth twenty-five dollars, against an equivalent. My fowl bounced upon his opponent, seized him, and never loosed his hold until he had killed him. I won. The next cock on our side was the Marksman. This was another favorite of mine, and I again bet all, this time comprising six dollars and two silver watches. I won this fight in like manner. I bet on five cocks in all, on our side, and won every fight. When the second day's fight was over, our party were beaten; my brother lost five hundred dollars and a fox-hunting mare, and the Judge and Stowey had not a cent left. Rigdon was proud of my victory and judgment, and afterwards taught me the art of gafting; I already knew how to feed, Cook's method being the same as Rigdon's, the latter being a cried-down heeler when he lived in Washington. Thus trained in the art of cocking, I commenced with Prince Charles, and challenged Greensburg, fighting for ten dollars, a silver watch and a barrel of whisky. I won, and the same winter fought my Prince Charles five battles, always winning, with good piles. I then loaned him to Judge Cook to breed from, and the fame of the breed spread far and wide.— The Barker men had a grudge at the breed, and wished to divest them of some of their laurels. They therefore obtained a Barker cock within weight. They challenged me to fight for one hundred dollars worth of salt, worth then three dollars per barrel. I took them up, and the stakes were thirty-four barrels of salt each. The fight was to take place in two weeks, at Good's tavern. The Judge put him in the best order, and I first tried him against a dung-hill, in a blacksmith shop. The Prince soon compelled his opponent to hide behind a plough-shear, when in an attempt to strike him the Prince struck the shear, and broke the leader of his right leg, causing the toes to draw up like a clenched fist, so tightly that they could not be straightened. Here was a dilemma. He could only stand on the one leg, and this was the day for fighting! However, we finally concluded to take the Prince to the battle ground, and show his condition. We thought the opposite parties would let us off, but in this were mistaken. They said that we crippled the fowl purposely; that we knew we could not fight a Barker cock. The Judge said he had no hand or share in the bet, and plead my cause, yet still they insisted. The thought struck me that their cock was much heavier than mine; we weighed, and found their fowl two ounces heavier. Here was a just plea, but they were still stubborn. Drum, for whom these men worked, was the stake-holder, and told me he would have to give up the salt if I did not fight. I became indignant at this, and told them they would have to kill the Prince first. The Judge heeled and pitted mine, and when set down in the pit he stood on one foot, and held the other to his body. The Barker cock came picking up gravel, taking a circle around until he came directly behind the Prince, who wheeled like lightning and commenced a vigorous assault. Such striking and billing and tumbling I never saw before nor since. In about two minutes the Barker cock was cut down, and when pitted again he could not rise. The Prince hobbled at him, mounted and literally picked him to death. I jumped up, boy-like, and cried, "Drum, I guess you'll give me the salt now!" He replied, "Yes, Cooper, you deserve the salt and shall have it." Judge Cook kept the Prince until he died, and then buried him, and over his grave placed the following epitaph:—

"Here lies the Prince of all Game Fowls."

His breed I have kept until the present day, and it was with it that I kept the great Tartars from going into decay. The progeny of the Prince were from a pure American Wild Sugar Camp hen.

www.ingramcontent.com/pod-product-compliance
Lightning Source LLC
Chambersburg PA
CBHW030748250426
43672CB00028B/1319